THE GNU MAKE BOOK

THE GNU
MAKE BOOK

by John Graham-Cumming

**no starch
press**

San Francisco

Printed on demand in USA

ISBN-10: 1-59327-649-4
ISBN-13: 978-1-59327-649-2

Publisher: William Pollock
Production Editor: Alison Law
Cover Illustration: Josh Ellingson
Interior Design: Octopod Studios
Developmental Editors: Greg Poulos and Leslie Shen
Technical Reviewer: Paul Smith
Copyeditor: Anne Marie Walker
Compositor: Susan Glinert Stevens
Proofreader: James Fraleigh
Indexer: Nancy Guenther

For information on distribution, translations, or bulk sales, please contact No Starch Press, Inc. directly:

No Starch Press, Inc.
245 8th Street, San Francisco, CA 94103
phone: 415.863.9900; info@nostarch.com
www.nostarch.com

Library of Congress Cataloging-in-Publication Data:

Graham-Cumming, John.
  The GNU make book / by John Graham-Cumming. -- 1st edition.
      pages cm
  Includes index.
  Summary: "Covers GNU Make basics through advanced topics, including: user-defined functions,
macros, and path handling; creating makefile assertions and debugging makefiles; parallelization;
automatic dependency generation, rebuilding targets, and non-recursive Make; and using the GNU Make
Standard Library"-- Provided by publisher.
  ISBN 978-1-59327-649-2 -- ISBN 1-59327-649-4
  1. GNU Emacs. 2. Text editors (Computer programs) 3. Make (Computer file) I. Title.
  QA76.76.T49G725 2015
  005.13--dc23

                                                2015007254

About the Author

John Graham-Cumming is a longtime GNU make expert. He wrote the acclaimed machine learning–based POPFile email filter and successfully petitioned the British government to apologize for its treatment of Alan Turing. He holds a doctorate in computer security from Oxford University and works at CloudFlare.

About the Technical Reviewer

Paul Smith has been the Free Software Foundation's GNU make project maintainer since 1996. He's been using and contributing to free software since the 1980s and to GNU/Linux since 1993. Professionally, he writes networking and database system software. Personally, he enjoys biking and scuba diving with his wife and kids.

BRIEF CONTENTS

CONTENTS IN DETAIL

4
PITFALLS AND PROBLEMS

PREFACE

I can no longer remember when I first encountered a make program, but I imagine that, as with many programmers, I was trying to build someone else's software. And like many programmers, I was probably surprised and seduced by the simplicity of make's syntax without realizing the hidden depths and power of this universal program.

After many years of working with a variety of real makefiles, blogging about my findings, and answering GNU make questions from my blog readers, I gained real-world insights and a deep appreciation for GNU make. Many of these insights came from founding a company called Electric Cloud, where one of my projects was to completely replicate the functionality of GNU make. To do so, I absorbed the GNU make manual; wrote countless test makefiles to ensure that my "GNU make," written in C++, worked like the real program; and spent hours testing my version against enormous real-world makefiles supplied by our customers.

From my experiences with GNU make came my desire to write a book to share tips, warnings, solutions, and further possibilities, big and small, that would help programmers get the most out of this sometimes difficult but ultimately indispensable program. The core make syntax results in makefiles that are terse and understandable (at least small parts are) but can be difficult to maintain. On the bright side, make provides just enough functionality for software builds without including too many extra features. Many make replacements have found niches but have failed to displace GNU make (and other similar make programs).

I hope this book will be a practical source of help for those of you who wrangle makefiles daily or for anyone who has wondered, "Now, how do I do *that* using make?" If you're new to GNU make, I recommend that you start with Chapter 1 and work your way through the book. Otherwise, feel free to skip around. In any case, I hope you will find ideas to help you spend less time debugging makefiles and more time running fast builds.

NOTE *Because GNU make is sensitive about different types of whitespace, whenever a tab character is needed I've used → for clarity.*

I'd particularly like to thank the following people who encouraged me in my makefile hacking and GNU make programming: Mike Maciag, Eric Melski, Usman Muzaffar (who pops up in Chapter 4), John Ousterhout, and the maintainer of GNU make, Paul Smith. Finally, I'm very grateful to the team at No Starch Press who jumped at the idea of publishing a book about GNU make when I emailed them out of the blue; they have been a great team to work with.

1

THE BASICS REVISITED

This chapter covers material that might be considered basic GNU make knowledge but covers it to highlight commonly misunderstood functionality and clarify some confusing parts of GNU make. It also covers the differences between GNU make versions 3.79.1, 3.81, 3.82, and 4.0. If you're working with a version prior to 3.79.1, you should probably upgrade.

This chapter is in no way a replacement for the official GNU make manual (Free Software Foundation, 2004). I highly recommend owning a copy of it. You can also find the manual at *http://www.gnu.org/make/manual.*

Getting Environment Variables into GNU make

Any variable set in the environment when GNU make is started will be available as a GNU make variable inside the makefile. For example, consider the following simple makefile:

```
$(info $(FOO))
```

If FOO is set in the environment to foo when GNU make is run, this makefile will output foo, thus verifying that FOO was indeed set to foo inside the makefile. You can discover where FOO got that value by using GNU make's $(origin) function. Try adding to the makefile as follows (the new part is in bold):

```
$(info $(FOO) $(origin FOO))
```

If a variable FOO is defined in the environment and automatically imported into GNU make, $(origin FOO) will have the value environment. When you run the makefile, it should give the output foo environment.

A variable imported from the environment can be overridden inside the makefile. Simply set its value:

```
FOO=bar
$(info $(FOO) $(origin FOO))
```

This gives the output bar file. Notice how the value of $(origin FOO) has changed from environment to file, indicating that the variable got its value inside a makefile.

It's possible to prevent a definition in a makefile from overriding the environment by specifying the -e (or --environment-overrides) option on the command line of GNU make. Running the preceding makefile with FOO set to foo in the environment and the -e command line option gives the output foo environment override. Notice here that FOO has the value from the environment (foo) and that the output of $(origin FOO) has changed to environment override to inform us that the variable came from the environment, even though it was redefined in the makefile. The word override appears only if a variable definition was actually overridden; the $(origin) function simply returns environment (no override) if the variable being tested was defined in the environment, but there was no attempt to redefine it in the makefile.

If all you care about is whether the variable got its value from the environment, then using $(firstword $(origin VAR)) is always guaranteed to return the string environment if the variable VAR got its value from the environment, regardless of whether -e is specified or not.

Suppose you absolutely want to guarantee that the variable FOO gets its value inside the makefile, not from the environment. You can do this with the override directive:

```
override FOO=bar
$(info $(FOO) $(origin FOO))
```

This will output bar override regardless of the value of FOO in the environment or whether you specify the -e command line option. Note that $(origin) tells you this is an override by returning override.

The other way to get around -e and set the value of a variable is by setting it on the GNU make command line. For example, revert your makefile to the following:

```
FOO=bar
$(info $(FOO) $(origin FOO))
```

Running FOO=foo make -e FOO=fooey on the command line will output fooey command line. Here $(origin FOO) returned command line. Now try adding the override command back into the makefile:

```
override FOO=bar
$(info $(FOO) $(origin FOO))
```

If you run that same command on the command line (FOO=foo make -e FOO=fooey), now it outputs bar override.

Confused? A simple rule exists to help you keep it all straight: the override directive beats the command line, which beats environment overrides (the -e option), which beats variables defined in a makefile, which beats the original environment. Alternatively, you can always use $(origin) to find out what's going on.

Setting Variables from Outside the Makefile

It's common to have options in a makefile that can be set on the command line when you start a build. For example, you might want to change the type of build being performed or specify a target architecture outside the makefile.

Perhaps the most common use case is a debug option to specify whether the build should create debuggable or release code. A simple way to handle this is with a makefile variable called BUILD_DEBUG, which is set to yes in the makefile and overridden on the command line when building the release version. For example, the makefile might have the line BUILD_DEBUG := yes somewhere near the start. The BUILD_DEBUG variable would then be used elsewhere in the makefile to decide how to set compiler debug options. Because BUILD_DEBUG is set to yes in the makefile, the default would be to do debug builds. Then, at release time, this default can be overridden from the command line:

```
$ make BUILD_DEBUG=no
```

Close to release time it might be tempting to set BUILD_DEBUG to no in the shell's startup script (for example, in .cshrc or .bashrc) so that all builds are release rather than debug. Unfortunately, this doesn't work because of how GNU make inherits variables from the environment and how variables inside a makefile override the environment.

Consider this simple makefile that prints the value of BUILD_DEBUG, which has been set to yes at the start of the makefile:

```
BUILD_DEBUG := yes
.PHONY: all
all: ; @echo BUILD_DEBUG is $(BUILD_DEBUG)
```

NOTE   *In this example, the commands associated with the all target have been placed on the same line as the target name by using a semicolon. The alternative would be:*

```
BUILD_DEBUG := yes
.PHONY: all
all:
→ @echo BUILD_DEBUG is $(BUILD_DEBUG)
```

But that requires a tab to start the commands. When the commands fit on a single line, it's clearer to use the semicolon format available in GNU make.

Now try running the makefile three times: once with no options, once setting BUILD_DEBUG on GNU make's command line, and once with BUILD_DEBUG set in the environment:

```
$ make
BUILD_DEBUG is yes
$ make BUILD_DEBUG=no
BUILD_DEBUG is no
$ export BUILD_DEBUG=no
$ make
BUILD_DEBUG is yes
```

The last line shows that variables defined inside a makefile override values in the environment. But note that if BUILD_DEBUG had not been defined at all in the makefile, it would have been inherited from the environment and imported into the makefile automatically.

The problem with definitions in a makefile overriding imported environment variables can be *solved* with a GNU make hammer: the -e switch, which makes the environment take precedence. But that affects *every* variable.

```
$ export BUILD_DEBUG=no
$ make
BUILD_DEBUG is yes
$ make -e
BUILD_DEBUG is no
$ make -e BUILD_DEBUG=maybe
BUILD_DEBUG is maybe
```

The rule to remember is this: *command line beats makefile beats environment.* A variable defined on the command line takes precedence over the same variable defined in a makefile, which will take precedence over the same variable defined in the environment.

It's possible to have a BUILD_DEBUG variable that is set by default to yes and can be overridden *either* on the command line or in the environment. GNU make provides two ways to achieve this, both of which rely on checking to see if the variable is already defined.

Here's one way. Replace the setting of BUILD_DEBUG in the original makefile with this:

```
ifndef BUILD_DEBUG
BUILD_DEBUG := yes
endif
```

Now if BUILD_DEBUG has not already been set (that's what ndef means: *not defined*), it will be set to yes; otherwise, it is left unchanged. Because typing ifndef SOME_VARIABLE and endif is a bit unwieldy, GNU make provides a shorthand for this pattern in the form of the ?= operator:

```
BUILD_DEBUG ?= yes
.PHONY: all
all: ; @echo BUILD_DEBUG is $(BUILD_DEBUG)
```

The ?= operator tells GNU make to set BUILD_DEBUG to yes unless it is already defined, in which case leave it alone. Rerunning the test yields:

```
$ make
BUILD_DEBUG is yes
$ make BUILD_DEBUG=no
BUILD_DEBUG is no
$ export BUILD_DEBUG=no
$ make
BUILD_DEBUG is no
```

This technique provides the ultimate flexibility. A default setting in the makefile can be overridden in the environment and by a temporary override on the command line:

```
$ export BUILD_DEBUG=no
$ make BUILD_DEBUG=aardvark
BUILD_DEBUG is aardvark
```

NOTE *There's actually a subtle difference between ifndef and ?= in how they handle variables that are defined but set to an empty string. Whereas ifndef means if not empty even if defined, the ?= operator treats an empty, defined variable as defined. This difference is discussed in more detail in Chapter 4.*

The Environment Used by Commands

The environment GNU make uses when it runs commands (such as commands in any rules it executes) is the environment GNU make started with, plus any variables *exported* in the makefile—as well as a few variables GNU make adds itself.

Consider this simple makefile:

```
FOO=bar

all: ; @echo FOO is $$FOO
```

First, notice the double $ sign: it's an escaped $ and means that the command passed to the shell by GNU make is echo FOO is $FOO. You can use a double $ to get a single $ into the shell.

If you run this makefile with FOO not defined in the environment, you'll see the output FOO is. The value of FOO is not set because the makefile did not specifically export FOO into the environment used by GNU make to run commands. So when the shell runs the echo command for the all rule, FOO is not defined. If FOO had been set to foo in the environment before GNU make was run, you would see the output FOO is bar. This is because FOO was already present in the environment GNU make started with and then picked up the value bar inside the makefile.

```
$ export FOO=foo
$ make
FOO is bar
```

If you're not sure whether FOO is in the environment but want to ensure that it makes its way into the environment used for commands, use the export directive. For example, you can ensure that FOO appears in the environment of subprocesses by modifying the makefile, like so:

```
export FOO=bar

all: ; @echo FOO is $$FOO
```

Alternatively, you can just put export FOO on a line by itself. In both cases FOO will be exported into the environment of the commands run for the all rule.

You can remove a variable from the environment with unexport. To ensure that FOO is excluded from the subprocess environment, whether or not it was set in the parent environment, run the following:

```
FOO=bar
unexport FOO

all: ; @echo FOO is $$FOO
```

You'll see the output FOO is.

You might be wondering what happens if you export and unexport a variable. The answer is that the last directive wins.

The export directive can also be used with target-specific variables to modify the environment just for a particular rule. For example:

```
export FOO=bar

all: export FOO=just for all

all: ; @echo FOO is $$FOO
```

The makefile sets FOO to just for all for the all rule and bar for any other rule.

Note that you can't remove FOO from the environment of a specific rule with a target-specific unexport. If you write all: unexport FOO, you'll get an error.

GNU make also adds a number of variables to the subprocess environment—specifically, MAKEFLAGS, MFLAGS, and MAKELEVEL. The MAKEFLAGS and MFLAGS variables contain the flags specified on the command line: MAKEFLAGS contains the flags formatted for GNU make's internal use and MFLAGS is only there for historical reasons. Never use MAKEFLAGS in a recipe. If you really need to, you can set MFLAGS. The MAKELEVEL variable contains the depth of recursive make calls, via $(MAKE), starting at zero. For more detail on those variables, see the GNU make manual.

You can also ensure that every makefile variable gets exported, either by writing export on a line on its own or by specifying .EXPORT_ALL_VARIABLES:. But these shotgun approaches are probably a bad idea, because they fill the subprocess environment with useless—and perhaps harmful—variables.

The $(shell) Environment

You might expect that the environment used by a call to $(shell) would be the same as that used in the execution of a rule's commands. In fact, it's not. The environment used by $(shell) is exactly the same as the environment when GNU make was started, with nothing added or removed. You can verify this with the following makefile that gets the value of FOO from within a $(shell) call and a rule:

```
export FOO=bar

$(info $(shell printenv | grep FOO))

all: ; @printenv | grep FOO
```

That outputs:

```
$ export FOO=foo
$ make
FOO=foo
FOO=bar
```

No matter what you do, $(shell) gets the parent environment.

This is a bug in GNU make (bug #10593—see *http://savannah.gnu.org/bugs/?10593* for details). Part of the reason this hasn't been fixed is that the obvious solution—just using the rule environment in $(shell)—has a rather nasty consequence. Consider this makefile:

```
export FOO=$(shell echo fooey)
all: ; @echo FOO is $$FOO
```

What's the value of FOO in the rule for all? To get the value of FOO in the environment for all, the $(shell) has to be expanded, which requires getting the value of FOO—which requires expanding the $(shell) call, and so on, *ad infinitum*.

In the face of this problem, GNU make's developers opted for the easy way out: they just haven't fixed the bug.

Given that this bug isn't going away for the moment, a workaround is necessary. Luckily, most decent shells have a way to set an environment variable inline. So the first makefile in this section can be changed to:

```
export FOO=bar

$(info $(shell FOO=$(FOO) printenv | grep FOO))

all: ; @printenv | grep FOO
```

This obtains the desired result:

```
$ make
FOO=bar
FOO=bar
```

It works by setting the value of FOO within the shell used by the $(shell) function, using the FOO=$(FOO) syntax. Because the argument to $(shell) gets expanded before execution, that becomes FOO=bar, taking its value from the value of FOO set in the makefile.

The technique works fine if just one extra variable is needed in the environment. But if many are needed, it can be a bit problematic, because setting multiple shell variables on a single command line becomes messy.

A more comprehensive solution is to write a replacement for the $(shell) command that *does* export variables. Here's a function, env_shell, which does just that:

```
env_file = /tmp/env
env_shell = $(shell rm -f $(env_file))$(foreach V,$1,$(shell echo export
$V=$($V) >> $(env_file)))$(shell echo '$2' >> $(env_file))$(shell /bin/bash -e
$(env_file))
```

Before I explain how this works, here's how to use it in the previous makefile. All you need to do is to change $(shell) to $(call env_shell). The first argument of env_shell is the list of variables that you need to add to the environment, whereas the second argument is the command to be executed. Here's the updated makefile with FOO exported:

```
export FOO=bar

$(info $(call env_shell,FOO,printenv | grep FOO))

all: ; @printenv | grep FOO
```

When you run this you'll see the output:

```
$ make
FOO=bar
FOO=bar
```

Now back to how env_shell works. First, it creates a shell script that adds all the variables from its first argument to the environment; then, it executes the command from its second argument. By default the shell script is stored in the file named in the env_file variable (which was set to */tmp/env* earlier).

/tmp/env ends up containing

```
export FOO=bar
printenv | grep FOO
```

We can break down the call to env_shell into four parts:

- It deletes */tmp/env* with $(shell rm -f $(env_file)).
- It adds lines containing the definition of each of the variables named in the first argument ($1) with the loop $(foreach V,$1,$(shell echo export $V=$($V) >> $(env_file))).
- It appends the actual command to execute, which is in the second argument ($2), with $(shell echo '$2' >> $(env_file)).
- It runs */tmp/env* with a call to shell using the -e option: $(shell /bin/bash -e $(env_file)).

It's not a perfect solution; it would be nice if GNU make just figured out what should be in the environment. But it's a workable solution until GNU make's coders fix the bug.

Target-Specific and Pattern-Specific Variables

Every GNU make user is familiar with GNU make variables. And all GNU make users know that variables essentially have global scope. Once they are defined in a makefile, they can be used anywhere in the makefile. But how many GNU make users are familiar with GNU make's locally scoped target-specific and pattern-specific variables? This section introduces target- and pattern-specific variables, and shows how they can be used to selectively alter options within a build based on the name of a target or targets being built.

Target-Specific Variables

Listing 1-1 shows a simple example makefile that illustrates the difference between global and local scope in GNU make:

```
.PHONY: all foo bar baz

❶ VAR = global scope

all: foo bar
all: ; @echo In $@ VAR is $(VAR)

foo: ; @echo In $@ VAR is $(VAR)

❷ bar: VAR = local scope
bar: baz
bar: ; @echo In $@ VAR is $(VAR)

baz: ; @echo In $@ VAR is $(VAR)
```

Listing 1-1: An example makefile with four phony targets

This makefile has four targets: all, foo, bar, and baz. All four targets are phony; because we're interested only in illustrating global and local scope for now, this makefile doesn't actually make any files.

The all target requires that foo and bar be built, whereas bar depends on baz. The commands for each target do the same thing—they print the value of variable VAR using a shell echo.

The VAR variable is initially defined at ❶ to have the value global scope. That's the value VAR will have anywhere in the makefile—unless, of course, that value is overridden using a target- or pattern-specific variable.

To illustrate local scope, VAR is redefined to local scope at ❷ for the rule that creates bar. A target-specific variable definition is exactly like a normal variable definition: it uses the same =, :=, +=, and ?= operators, but it is preceded by the name of the target (and its colon) for which the variable should be defined.

If you run GNU make on this makefile, you'll get the output shown in Listing 1-2.

```
$ make
In foo VAR is global scope
In baz VAR is local scope
In bar VAR is local scope
In all VAR is global scope
```

Listing 1-2: Output from Listing 1-1 showing globally and locally scoped variables

You can clearly see that GNU make follows its standard depth-first, left-to-right search pattern. First it builds foo, because it's the first prerequisite of all. Then it builds baz, which is a prerequisite of bar, the second prerequisite of all. Then it builds bar and, finally, all.

Sure enough, within the rule for bar the value of VAR is local scope. And because there's no local definition of VAR in either all or foo, VAR has the value global scope in those rules.

But what about baz? The makefile output shows that the value of VAR in baz is local scope, yet there was no explicit target-specific definition of VAR for baz. This is because baz is a prerequisite of bar and so has the same locally scoped variables as bar.

Target-specific variables apply not just to a target, but also to all that target's prerequisites, as well as all *their* prerequisites, and so on. A target-specific variable's scope is the entire tree of targets, starting from the target for which the variable was defined.

Note that because all, foo, bar, and baz have exactly the same recipe, it's possible to write them all on a single line, as shown here:

```
all foo bar baz: ; @echo In $@ VAR is $(VAR)
```

But in this section, I've avoided having multiple targets because this sometimes causes confusion (many GNU make users think that this line represents a single rule that would run once for all, foo, bar, and baz, but it is actually four separate rules).

Pattern-Specific Variables

Pattern-specific variables work in a manner similar to target-specific variables. But instead of being defined for a target, they are defined for a pattern and are applied to all targets that match that pattern. The following example is similar to Listing 1-1 but has been modified to include a pattern-specific variable:

```
.PHONY: all foo bar baz

VAR = global scope

all: foo bar
all: ; @echo In $@ VAR is $(VAR)

foo: ; @echo In $@ VAR is $(VAR)

bar: VAR = local scope
bar: baz
bar: ; @echo In $@ VAR is $(VAR)

baz: ; @echo In $@ VAR is $(VAR)

❶ f%: VAR = starts with f
```

The last line ❶ sets VAR to the value starts with f for any target beginning with f and followed by anything else (that's the % wildcard). (It is also possible to use multiple targets to accomplish this. But don't worry about that for now.)

Now if you run make, you get the following output:

```
$ make
In foo VAR is starts with f
In baz VAR is local scope
In bar VAR is local scope
In all VAR is global scope
```

This is the same as in Listing 1-2, except that in the rule for foo the value of VAR has been set to starts with f by the pattern-specific definition.

It's worth noting that this is unrelated to GNU make pattern rules. You can use the pattern-specific variable definition to change the value of a variable in a normal rule. You can also use it with a pattern rule.

For example, imagine that a makefile uses the built-in %.o: %.c pattern rule:

```
%.o: %.c
#   commands to execute (built-in):
→ $(COMPILE.c) $(OUTPUT_OPTION) $<
```

It would be possible to set a variable on every .o file that rule builds using a pattern-specific variable. Here's how to add the -g option to CFLAGS for every .o file:

```
%.o: CFLAGS += -g
```

It's not uncommon in a project to have a standard rule for compiling files and to need a slightly different version of that rule for a specific file, or set of files, that otherwise use the same command. For example, here's a makefile that builds all the .c files in two subdirectories (lib1 and lib2) using a pattern rule:

```
lib1_SRCS := $(wildcard lib1/*.c)
lib2_SRCS := $(wildcard lib2/*.c)

lib1_OBJS := $(lib1_SRCS:.c=.o)
lib2_OBJS := $(lib2_SRCS:.c=.o)

.PHONY: all
all: $(lib1_OBJS) $(lib2_OBJS)
```

❶ %.o: %.c ; @$(COMPILE.C) -o $@ $<

First, the makefile gets the list of all .c files in *lib1/* into the variable lib1_SRCS, and the C files in *lib2/* into lib2_SRCS. Then it converts these to lists of object files using a substitution reference that changes .c to .o and stores the results in `lib1_OBJS` and `lib2_OBJS`. The pattern rule in the last line ❶ uses the GNU make built-in variable `COMPILE.C` to run a compiler that compiles a .c file into a .o file. The makefile builds all the objects in `lib1_OBJS` and `lib2_OBJS` because they are prerequisites of `all`. Both `lib1_OBJS` and `lib2_OBJS` contain a list of .o files corresponding to .c files. When GNU make searches for the .o files (the prerequisites of `all`), it finds that they are missing but that it can use the `%.o: %.c` rule to build then.

This works fine if all the .c files have the same compilation options. But now suppose that the .c file *lib1/special.c* requires the `-Wcomment` option to prevent the compiler from warning about an oddly written comment. Obviously, it would be possible to change the value of `CPPFLAGS` globally by adding the line `CPPFLAGS += -Wcomment` to the makefile. But this change would affect *every* compilation, which is probably not what you want.

Fortunately, you can use a target-specific variable to just alter the value of `CPPFLAGS` for that single file, like so:

```
lib1/special.o: CPPFLAGS += -Wcomment
```

The line alters the value of `CPPFLAGS` just for the creation of *lib1/special.o*.

Now suppose that an entire subdirectory requires a special `CPPFLAGS` option to maximize optimization for speed (the `-fast` option to gcc, for example). Here, a pattern-specific variable definition is ideal:

```
lib1/%.o: CPPFLAGS += -fast
```

This does the trick. Any .o files that are built in *lib1/* will be built using the `-fast` command line option.

Version Checking

Because GNU make is regularly updated and new features are added all the time, it's important to know the version of GNU make that's running or whether a specific GNU make feature is available. You can do this in two ways: either look at the `MAKE_VERSION` variable or look in the `.FEATURES` variable (added in GNU make 3.81). It's also possible to check for specific features, like $(eval).

MAKE_VERSION

The `MAKE_VERSION` variable contains the version number of GNU make that's processing the makefile where `MAKE_VERSION` is referenced. Here's an example makefile that prints the version of GNU make and stops:

```
.PHONY: all
all: ; @echo $(MAKE_VERSION)
```

And here's the output generated when GNU make 3.80 parses this makefile:

```
$ make
3.80
```

What if you want to determine that version 3.80 or later of GNU make is handling your makefile? If you assume the version number is always in the form X.YY.Z or X.YY, the following code fragment will set the ok variable to non-empty if the version mentioned in need is equal to or less than the running version of GNU make.

```
need := 3.80
ok := $(filter $(need),$(firstword $(sort $(MAKE_VERSION) $(need)))))
```

If ok is not blank, the required version of GNU make or later is being used; if it's blank, the version is too old. The code fragment works by creating a space-separated list of the running version of GNU make in MAKE_VERSION and the required version (from need), and sorting that list. Suppose the running version is 3.81. Then $(sort $(MAKE_VERSION) $(need)) will be 3.80 3.81. The $(firstword) of that is 3.80, so the $(filter) call will keep 3.80. Thus, ok will be non-empty.

Now suppose the running version is 3.79.1. Then $(sort $(MAKE_VERSION) $(need)) will be 3.79.1 3.80, and $(firstword) will return 3.79.1. The $(filter) call will remove 3.79.1 and thus ok will be empty.

NOTE   *This fragment won't work correctly with versions of GNU make starting at 10.01, because it assumes a single-digit major version number. Fortunately, that's a long way off!*

.FEATURES

GNU make 3.81 introduced the .FEATURES default variable, which contains a list of supported features. In GNU make 3.81, seven features are listed and supported in .FEATURES:

archives   Archive (ar) files using the archive(member) syntax

check-symlink   The -L and --check-symlink-times flags

else-if   Else branches in the non-nested form else if X

jobserver   Building in parallel using the job server

order-only   order-only prerequisite support

second-expansion   Double expansion of prerequisite lists

target-specific   Target-specific and pattern-specific variables

GNU make 3.82 adds and supports the following:

oneshell   The .ONESHELL special target

shortest-stem   Using the shortest stem option when choosing between pattern rules that match a target

undefine   The undefine directive

And GNU make 4.0 adds the following:

guile   If GNU make was built with GNU Guile support, this will be present and the $(guile) function will be supported.

load   The ability to load dynamic objects to enhance the capabilities of GNU make is supported.

output-sync   The -O (and --output-sync) command line options are supported.

You can find more details on these and many other features in "Recent GNU make Versions: 3.81, 3.82, and 4.0" on page 29.

To check if a specific feature is available, you can use the following is_feature function: it returns T if the requested feature is supported or an empty string if the feature is missing:

```
is_feature = $(if $(filter $1,$(.FEATURES)),T)
```

For example, the following makefile uses is_feature to echo whether the archives feature is available:

```
.PHONY: all
all: ; @echo archives are $(if $(call is_feature,archives),,not )available
```

And here's the output using GNU make 3.81:

```
$ make
archives are available
```

If you want to check whether the .FEATURES variable is even supported, either use MAKE_VERSION as described in "MAKE_VERSION" on page 13 or simply expand .FEATURES and see whether it's empty. The following makefile fragment does just this, setting has_features to T (for true) if the .FEATURES variable is present and contains any features:

```
has_features := $(if $(filter default,$(origin .FEATURES)),$(if $(.FEATURES),T))
```

The fragment first uses $(origin) to check that the .FEATURES variable is a default variable; this way, has_features is not fooled if someone has defined .FEATURES in the makefile. If it is a default variable, the second $(if) checks whether or not .FEATURES is blank.

Detecting $(eval)

The $(eval) function is a powerful GNU make feature that was added in version 3.80. The argument to $(eval) is expanded and then parsed as if it were part of the makefile, allowing you to modify the makefile at runtime.

If you use $(eval), it is important to check that the feature is available in the version of GNU make reading your makefile. You could use MAKE_VERSION as described earlier to check for version 3.80. Alternatively, you could use the following fragment of code that sets eval_available to T only if $(eval) is implemented:

```
$(eval eval_available := T)
```

If $(eval) is not available, GNU make will look for a variable called eval eval_available := T and try to get its value. This variable doesn't exist, of course, so eval_available will be set to the empty string.

You can use eval_available with ifneq to generate a fatal error if $(eval) isn't implemented.

```
ifneq ($(eval_available),T)
$(error This makefile only works with a Make program that supports $$(eval))
endif
```

The eval_available function is especially useful if you can't check MAKE_VERSION—if, for example, your makefile is being run using a non-GNU make tool, such as clearmake or emake.

Using Boolean Values

Both GNU make's $(if) function and ifdef construct treat the empty string and undefined variables as false, and anything else as true. But they differ subtly in how they evaluate their arguments.

The $(if) function—that is, $(if X,*if-part*,*else-part*)—expands *if-part* if X is not empty and *else-part* otherwise. When using $(if), the condition is expanded and the value *after expansion* is tested for emptiness. The following code fragment reports that it took the *else-part* branch:

```
EMPTY =
VAR = $(EMPTY)
$(if $(VAR),$(info if-part),$(info else-part))
```

Whereas the next fragment follows the *if-part* branch, because HAS_A_VALUE has a non-empty value.

```
HAS_A_VALUE = I'm not empty
$(if $(HAS_A_VALUE),$(info if-part),$(info else-part))
```

The `ifdef` construct works slightly differently: its argument is the *name* of a variable and is not expanded:

```
ifdef VAR
if-part...
else
else-part...
endif
```

The preceding example executes *if-part* if the variable VAR is non-empty and *else-part* if VAR is empty or undefined.

Undefined Variables in Conditionals

Because GNU make treats an undefined variable as simply empty, `ifdef` should really be called `ifempty`—especially because it treats a defined-but-empty variable as undefined. For example, the following fragment reports that VAR is undefined:

```
VAR =
ifdef VAR
$(info VAR is defined)
else
$(info VAR is undefined)
endif
```

In an actual makefile, this might not have been the intended result. You can ask for warnings of undefined variables with the `--warn-undefined-variables` command line option.

One further nuance of `ifdef` is that it does not expand the variable VAR. It simply looks to see if it has been defined to a non-empty value. The following code reports that VAR is defined even though its value, when completely expanded, is an empty string:

```
EMPTY =
VAR = $(EMPTY)
ifdef VAR
$(info VAR is defined)
else
$(info VAR is not defined)
endif
```

GNU make 3.81 introduced yet another wrinkle to `ifdef`: its argument is expanded so that the name of the variable being tested can be computed. This has no effect on conditionals, such as `ifdef VAR`, but allows you to write

```
VAR_NAME = VAR
VAR = some value
ifdef $(VAR_NAME)
$(info VAR is defined)
```

```
else
$(info VAR is not defined)
endif
```

This is exactly the same as:

```
VAR = some value
ifdef VAR
$(info VAR is defined)
else
$(info VAR is not defined)
endif
```

In both cases VAR is examined to see whether it is empty, exactly as described earlier, and in both output VAR is defined.

Consistent Truth Values

GNU make treats any non-empty string as true. But if you work with truth values and $(if) a lot, it can be helpful to use just one consistent value for true. The following make-truth function turns any non-empty string into the value T:

```
make-truth = $(if $1,T)
```

Notice how we can drop the else part of the $(if), because it's empty. Throughout this book I'll drop arguments that aren't necessary rather than polluting makefiles with extraneous trailing commas. But there's nothing to stop you from writing $(if $1,T,) if it makes you more comfortable.

All of the following calls to make-truth return T:

```
❶ $(call make-truth, )
$(call make-truth,true)
$(call make-truth,a b c)
```

Even ❶ returns T, because arguments to functions called using $(call) do not have any modifications made to them before being placed in $1, $2, and so on—not even the removal of leading or trailing space. So the second argument is a string with a single space in it, not the empty string.

All the following return an empty string (for false):

```
❷ $(call make-truth,)
EMPTY =
$(call make-truth,$(EMPTY))
VAR = $(EMPTY)
$(call make-truth,$(VAR))
```

Look carefully at the difference between ❶ and ❷: whitespace in GNU make can be very significant!

Logical Operations Using Boolean Values

GNU make had no built-in logical operators until version 3.81, when $(or) and $(and) were added. However, it's easy to create user-defined functions that operate on Boolean values. These functions often use GNU make's $(if) function to make decisions. $(if) treats any non-empty string as 'true' and an empty string as 'false'.

User-Defined Logical Operators

Let's create a user-defined version of the simplest logical operator, or. If either parameter is true (that is, a non-empty string), the result should also be a non-empty string. We can achieve this by just concatenating the arguments:

```
or = $1$2
```

You can use the make-truth function in "Consistent Truth Values" on page 18 to clean up the result of the or so that it's either T for true or an empty string for false:

```
or = $(call make-truth,$1$2)
```

Or for a more compact version you just can write:

```
or = $(if $1$2,T).
```

All the following return T:

```
$(call or, , )
$(call or,T,)
$(call or, ,)
$(call or,hello,goodbye my friend)
```

The only way to return false from or is to pass in two empty arguments:

```
EMPTY=
$(call or,$(EMPTY),)
```

Defining and is a little more complex, requiring two calls to $(if):

```
and = $(if $1,$(if $2,T))
```

There's no need to wrap this in make-truth because it always returns T if its arguments are non-empty and the empty string if either argument is empty.

Defining not is just a single $(if):

```
not = $(if $1,,T)
```

With and, or, and not defined, you can quickly create other logical operators:

```
nand = $(call not,$(call and,$1,$2)) nor = $(call not,$(call or,$1,$2))
xor = $(call and,$(call or,$1,$2),$(call not,$(call and,$1,$2)))
```

These all also have simplified versions that just use $(if):

```
nand = $(if $1,$(if $2,,T),T)
nor = $(if $1$2,,T)
xor = $(if $1,$(if $2,,T),$(if $2,T))
```

As an exercise, try writing an xnor function!

Built-in Logical Operators (GNU make 3.81 and Later)

GNU make 3.81 and later has built-in and and or functions that are faster than the versions defined earlier, so it's preferable to use those whenever possible. You should test whether the and and or functions already exist and only define your own if they don't.

The easiest way to determine whether and and or are defined is to try using them:

```
have_native_and := $(and T,T)
have_native_or := $(or T,T)
```

These variables will be T only if built-in and and or functions are present. In versions of GNU make prior to 3.81 (or in GNU make-emulating programs like clearmake), have_native_and and have_native_or will be empty because GNU make will not find functions called and or or, nor will it find variables called and T, T, or or T, T!

You can examine the results of these calls using ifneq and define your own functions only if necessary, like so:

```
ifneq ($(have_native_and),T)
and = $(if $1,$(if $2,T))
endif
ifneq ($(have_native_or),T)
or = $(if $1$2,T)
endif

$(info This will be T: $(call and,T,T))
```

You may be concerned that you've written $(call and,...) and $(call or,...) everywhere, using call to invoke your own logic operators. Won't you need to change all these to $(and) and $(or)—removing call to use the built-in operator?

That is not necessary. GNU make allows any built-in function to be called with the call keyword, so both $(and...) and $(call and,...) invoke the built-in operator. The opposite, however, is *not* true: it's not possible to call the *user-defined* function foo by writing $(foo arg1,arg2). You must write $(call foo,arg1,arg2).

So defining your own and and or functions, and behaving gracefully in the presence of GNU make 3.81 or later, requires only the lines shown earlier to define and and or—no other changes are necessary.

Note that there's an important difference between the built-in functions and user-defined versions. The built-in versions will not evaluate both arguments if the first argument fully determines their truth value. For example, $(and $a,$b) doesn't need to look at the value of $b if $a is false; $(or $a,$b) doesn't need to look at the value of $b if $a is true.

If you need that behavior, you can't use the preceding user-defined versions because when you do a $(call) of a function, all the arguments are expanded. The alternative is to replace a $(call and,X,Y) with $(if X,$(if Y,T)) and $(call or,X,Y) with $(if X,T,$(if Y,T)).

Command Detection

Sometimes it can be useful for a makefile to quickly return an error message if a specific piece of software is missing from the build system. For example, if the makefile needs the program curl, it can be helpful to determine at parse time, when the makefile is loaded by make, if curl is present on the system rather than waiting until partway through a build to discover that it's not there.

The simplest way to find out if a command is available is to use the which command inside a $(shell) call. This returns an empty string if the command is not found and the path to the command if it is, which works well with make's *empty string means false, non-empty string means true* logic.

So, for example, the following sets HAVE_CURL to a non-empty string if curl is present:

```
HAVE_CURL := $(shell which curl)
```

Then you can use HAVE_CURL to stop the build and output an error if curl is missing:

```
ifndef HAVE_CURL
$(error curl is missing)
endif
```

The following assert-command-present function wraps this logic into a single handy function. Calling assert-command-present with the name of a command causes the build to immediately exit with an error if the command is missing. The following example uses `assert-command-present` to check for the presence of a curl and a command called curly:

```
assert-command-present = $(if $(shell which $1),,$(error '$1' missing and needed for this build))

$(call assert-command-present,curl)
$(call assert-command-present,curly)
```

Here's what happens if you run this code on a system that has curl but no curly:

```
$ make
Makefile:4: *** 'curly' missing and needed for this build.  Stop.
```

If a command is used only by certain build targets, it can be useful to only use `assert-command-present` for the relevant target. The following makefile will check for the existence of curly only if the `download` target will actually be used as part of the build:

```
all: ; @echo Do all...

download: export _check = $(call assert-command-present,curly)
download: ; @echo Download stuff...
```

The first line of the download target sets a target-specific variable called _check and exports it to the result of the call to `assert-command-present`. This causes the `$(call)` to happen only if `download` is actually used as part of the build, because the value of _check will get expanded when it is being prepared for insertion into the environment of the recipe. For example, `make all` will not check for the presence of curly:

```
$ make
Do all...
$ make download
Makefile:5: *** 'curly' missing and needed for this build.  Stop.
```

Note that this makefile does define a variable called _, which you could access as $(_) or even $_. Using the underscore as a name is one way to indicate that the variable is just a placeholder, and its value should be ignored.

Delayed Variable Assignment

GNU make offers two ways to define a variable: the simple := operator and the recursive = operator. The simple operator := evaluates its right side immediately and uses the resulting value to set the value of a variable. For example:

```
BAR = before
FOO := $(BAR) the rain
BAR = after
```

This snippet results in FOO having the value before the rain, because at the time FOO was set using :=, BAR had the value before.

In contrast,

```
BAR = before
FOO = $(BAR) the rain
BAR = after
```

This results in FOO having the value $(BAR) the rain, and $(FOO) evaluates to after the rain. That happens because = defines a recursive variable (one that can contain references to other variables using the $() or ${} syntax) whose value is determined every time the variable is used. In contrast, simple variables defined using := have a single fixed value determined at the time they were defined by expanding all the variable references straight away.

Simple variables have a distinct speed advantage because they are fixed strings and don't need to be expanded each time they are used. They can be tricky to use because it's common for makefile writers to assume that variables can be set in any order since recursively defined variables (those set with =) get their final value only when they are used. Nevertheless, simple variables are usually faster to access than recursive variables, and I err on the side of always using := if I can.

But what if you could have the best of both worlds? A variable that gets set only when it is first used but gets to set to a fixed value that doesn't change. This would be useful if the variable's value requires a lot of computation but needs to be computed only once at most, and perhaps not at all if the variable never gets used. It is possible to achieve this with the $(eval) function.

Consider the following definition:

```
SHALIST = $(shell find . -name '*.c' | xargs shasum)
```

The SHALIST variable will contain the name and SHA1 cryptographic hash of every .c file found in the current directory and all subdirectories. This could take a long time to evaluate. And defining SHALIST using = means that this expensive call occurs every time you use SHALIST. If you use it more than once, this could significantly slow down execution of the makefile.

On the other hand, if you define SHALIST using :=, the $(shell) would only be executed once—but it would happen every time the makefile is loaded. This might be inefficient if the value of SHALIST is not always needed, like when running make clean.

We want a way to define SHALIST so the $(shell) doesn't happen if SHALIST is never used and is called only once if SHALIST is. Here's how to do it:

```
SHALIST = $(eval SHALIST := $(shell find . -name '*.c' | xargs shasum))$(SHALIST)
```

If $(SHALIST) is ever evaluated, the $(eval SHALIST := $(shell find . -name '*.c' | xargs shasum)) part gets evaluated. Because := is being used here, it actually does the $(shell) and redefines SHALIST to be result of that call. GNU make then retrieves the value of $(SHALIST), which has just been set by the $(eval).

You can see what's happening by creating a small makefile that uses the $(value) function (which shows the definition of a variable without expanding it) to examine the value of SHALIST without evaluating it:

```
SHALIST = $(eval SHALIST := $(shell find . -name '*.c' | xargs
shasum))$(SHALIST)

$(info Before use SHALIST is: $(value SHALIST))
❶ $(info SHALIST is: $(SHALIST))
$(info After use SHALIST is:  $(value SHALIST))
```

Running that with a single foo.c file in the directory results in the following output:

```
$ make
Before use SHALIST is: $(eval SHALIST := $(shell find . -name '*.c' | xargs
shasum))$(SHALIST)
SHALIST is: 3405ad0433933b9b489756cb3484698ac57ce821   ./foo.c
After use SHALIST is:   3405ad0433933b9b489756cb3484698ac57ce821   ./foo.c
```

Clearly, SHALIST has changed value since the first time it was used at ❶.

Simple List Manipulation

In GNU make, lists elements are separated by spaces. For example, peter paul and mary is a list with four elements, as is C:\Documents And Settings\Local User. GNU make has a several built-in functions for manipulating lists:

$(firstword)   Gets the first word in a list.

$(words)   Counts the number of list elements.

$(word)   Extracts a word at a specific index (counting from 1).

$(wordlist)   Extracts a range of words from a list.

$(foreach)   Lets you iterate over a list.

Getting the first element of a list is trivial:

```
MY_LIST = a program for directed compilation
$(info The first word is $(firstword $(MY_LIST)))
```

That would output The first word is a.

You can get the last element by counting the number of words in the list, *N*, and then taking the *N*th word. Here's a lastword function that returns the last word in a list:

❶ ```
lastword = $(if $1,$(word $(words $1),$1))
MY_LIST = a program for directed compilation
$(info The last word is $(call lastword,$(MY_LIST)))
```

The $(if) at ❶ is necessary because if the list were empty, $(words $1) would be 0 and $(word 0,$1) would generate a fatal error. The preceding example outputs The last word is compilation.

*Versions 3.81 and later of GNU make have a built-in lastword function, which is quicker than the preceding implementation.*

Chopping the first word off a list is simply a matter of returning a sublist range from the second element to the end. GNU make's built-in $(wordlist *S*,*E*,*LIST*) function returns a range of list elements from *LIST*, starting with the element at index *S* and ending at index *E* (inclusive):

```
notfirst = $(wordlist 2,$(words $1),$1)
MY_LIST = a program for directed compilation
$(info $(call notfirst,$(MY_LIST)))
```

You don't have to worry about the empty list in the preceding example, because $(wordlist) doesn't complain if its second argument isn't a valid index. That example outputs program for directed compilation.

Chopping the last element off a list requires some more mental gymnastics, because there's no simple way to do arithmetic in make: it's not possible to just write $(wordlist 1,$(words $1)-1, $1). Instead, we can define a notlast function that adds a dummy element to the start of the list and chops off the last element by using the *original* list length as the end index for $(wordlist). Then, because we added a dummy element, we need to remember to chop that off by setting the start index for $(wordlist) at 2:

```
notlast = $(wordlist 2,$(words $1),dummy $1)
MY_LIST = a program for directed compilation
$(info $(call notlast,$(MY_LIST)))
```

And that outputs a program for directed.

User-Defined Functions

This section is about defining make functions within a makefile. In Chapter 5, you'll learn how to modify the source of GNU make to define even more complex functions using C. We've used plenty of user-defined functions in previous sections, but now we'll take a closer look.
```

The Basics

Here's a very simple make function that takes three arguments and makes a date with them by inserting slashes between the three arguments:

```
make_date = $1/$2/$3
```

To use make_date, you $(call) it like this:

```
today := $(call make_date,5,5,2014)
```

That results in today containing 5/5/2014.

The function uses the special variables $1, $2, and $3, which contain the arguments specified in the $(call). There's no maximum number of arguments, but if you use more than nine, you need parentheses—that is, you can't write $10 but instead must use $(10). If the function is called with missing arguments, the content of those variables will be undefined and treated as an empty string.

The special argument $0 contains the name of the function. In the preceding example, $0 is make_date.

Because functions are essentially variables that reference some special variables that are created and filled in automatically by GNU make for you (if you use the $(origin) function on any of the argument variables [$1, etc.], they are classed as automatic just like $@), you can use built-in GNU make functions to build up complex functions.

Here's a function that uses the $(subst) function to turn every / into a \ in a path:

```
unix_to_dos = $(subst /,\,$1)
```

Don't be worried about the use of / and \ in this code. GNU make does very little escaping, and a literal \ is most of the time an actual backslash character. You'll read more about how make handles escaping in Chapter 4.

Argument-Handling Gotchas

make starts processing a $(call) by splitting the argument list on commas to set the variables $1, $2, and so on. The arguments are then expanded so that these variables are completely expanded before they are ever referenced. It's as if make used := to set them. If expanding an argument has a side effect, such as calling $(shell), that side effect will always occur as soon as the $(call) is executed, even if the argument never gets used by the function being called.

One common problem is that the splitting of arguments can go wrong if an argument contains a comma. For example, here's a simple function that swaps its two arguments:

```
swap = $2 $1
```

If you do $(call swap,first,argument,second), make doesn't have any way of knowing whether the first argument was meant to be first,argument or just first. It will assume the latter and ends up returning argument first instead of second first,argument.

You have two ways around this. First, you could simply hide the first argument inside a variable. Because make doesn't expand the arguments until after splitting, a comma inside a variable will not cause any confusion:

```
FIRST := first,argument
SWAPPED := $(call swap,$(FIRST),second)
```

The other approach is to create a simple variable that contains just a comma and use that instead:

```
c := ,
SWAPPED := $(call swap,first$cargument,second)
```

Or even call that , variable and use it (with parentheses):

```
, := ,
SWAPPED := $(call swap,first$(,)argument,second)
```

As we'll see in Chapter 4, giving variables clever names like , can be useful but also error prone.

Calling Built-in Functions

It's possible to use the $(call) syntax with make's built-in functions. For example, you could call $(info) like this:

```
$(call info,message)
```

This means that you can pass any function name as an argument to a user-defined function and $(call) it without needing to know whether it's built in; therefore, it lets you create functions that act on functions. For example, you can create the classic map function from functional programming, which applies a function to every member of a list and returns the resulting list:

```
map = $(foreach a,$2,$(call $1,$a))
```

The first argument is the function to call, and the second is the list to iterate over. Here's an example use of map—iterating over a list of variable names and printing out the defined value and the expanded value of each variable:

```
print_variable = $(info $1 ($(value $1) -> $($1)) )

print_variables = $(call map,print_variable,$1)
```

```
VAR1 = foo
VAR2 = $(VAR1)
VAR3 = $(VAR2) $(VAR1)

$(call print_variables,VAR1 VAR2 VAR3)
```

The print_variable function takes the name of a variable as its first and only argument, and returns a string consisting of the name of the variable, its definition, and its value. The print_variables function simply applies print_variable to a list of variables using map. Here's the output of the make-file snippet:

```
$ make
VAR1 (foo -> foo) VAR2 ($(VAR1) -> foo) VAR3 ($(VAR2) $(VAR1) -> foo foo)
```

Functions in make can also be recursive: it's possible for a function to $(call) itself. The following is a recursive implementation of the reduce function from functional programming, which takes two arguments: a function that will be called by reduce and a list to process.

```
reduce = $(if $(strip $2),$(call reduce,$1,$(wordlist 2,$(words $2),$2), \
$(call $1,$(firstword $2),$3)),$3)
```

The first argument (the function) is repeatedly called with two arguments: the next element of the list is reduce's second argument and the result of the previous call to the function.

To see this in action, here's a uniq function that removes duplicates from a list:

```
check_uniq = $(if $(filter $1,$2),$2,$2 $1)
uniq = $(call reduce,check_uniq,$1)
$(info $(call uniq,c b a a c c b a c b a))
```

The output here is c b a. This works because reduce will call check_uniq with each member of the input list, building up a new list from the result of check_uniq. The check_uniq function just determines whether an element is present in the given list (using the built-in function filter) and, if not present, returns the list with the element appended.

To see that in action, here's a modified version that uses $(info) to output the arguments sent to check_uniq on each invocation:

```
check_uniq = $(info check_uniq ($1) ($2))$(if $(filter $1,$2),$2,$2 $1)
uniq = $(call reduce,check_uniq,$1)
$(info $(call uniq,c b a a c c b a c b a))
```

And here's the output:

```
$ make
check_uniq (c) ()
check_uniq (b) ( c)
```

```
check_uniq (a) ( c b)
check_uniq (a) ( c b a)
check_uniq (c) ( c b a)
check_uniq (c) ( c b a)
check_uniq (b) ( c b a)
check_uniq (a) ( c b a)
check_uniq (c) ( c b a)
check_uniq (b) ( c b a)
check_uniq (a) ( c b a)
 c b a
```

If you don't need to preserve order, then using the built-in $(sort) function will be faster than this user-defined function since it also removes duplicates.

Recent GNU make Versions: 3.81, 3.82, and 4.0

GNU make changes slowly, and new releases (both major and minor) become available only every few years. Because of this slow release cycle, it's common to come across older versions of GNU make and useful to know the differences between them. This section assumes that the oldest common version in use is 3.79.1 (which was released on June 23, 2000) and highlights major changes in releases 3.81, 3.82, and 4.0.

What's New in GNU make 3.81

GNU make 3.81 was released on April 1, 2006, three and a half years after the last version (GNU make 3.80), and it was packed with goodies: support for OS/2, a new command line option, new built-in variables, new conditionals, and new functions. For a complete list of changes, see the *NEWS* file in the GNU make 3.81 source code distribution.

.SECONDEXPANSION

One frustrating problem users of GNU make run into is that the automatic variables are valid and assigned only when a rule's commands are run; they are not valid as part of the rule definition. For example, it's not possible to write foo: $@.c to mean that foo should be made from foo.c, even though $@ will have the value foo when that rule's commands are executed. That's frustrating, because it would be nice to not have to repeat yourself like this:

```
foo: foo.c
```

Before version 3.81, GNU make supported using $$@ (note the two $ signs) in the prerequisite list of a rule (this syntax comes from SysV make). For example, it was possible to say foo: $$@.c, and it was equivalent to foo: foo.c. That is, $$@ had the value that $@ has in the rule's commands. To get that functionality in GNU make 3.81 and later, you must define .SECONDEXPANSION in the makefile. As a bonus, GNU make supports all the standard automatic variables in the rule definition (although note that automatic variables like

$$ will always be blank because they cannot be computed when the makefile is being parsed). This happens because GNU make will expand the prerequisite list of a rule twice: once when it reads the makefile and once again when searching for what to make.

You can use second expansion for more than just automatic variables. User-defined variables can also be *second expanded*, and they'll end up getting the last value to which they were defined in the makefile. For example, you can do the following:

```
.SECONDEXPANSION:

FOO = foo

all: $$(FOO)
all: ; @echo Making $@ from $?

bar: ; @echo Making $@

FOO = bar
```

This gives the following output:

```
$ make
Making bar
Making all from bar
```

When the makefile was read, all: $$(FOO) was expanded to all: $(FOO). Later, when figuring out how to build all, $(FOO) was expanded to bar—that is, the value FOO had when makefile parsing ended. Note that if you enable .SECONDEXPANSION and have filenames with $s in them, the $s will need to be escaped by writing $$.

else

Another feature introduced in GNU make 3.81 was support for non-nested else branches by having the conditional on the same line as the else. For example, it's possible to write:

```
ifdef FOO
$(info FOO defined)
else ifdef BAR
$(info BAR defined)
else
$(info BAR not defined)
endif
```

That syntax will be familiar to anyone who has used a language that supports else if, elseif, or elsif. This is GNU make's way of having else and if on the same line.

Previously, the code would have looked like this:

```
ifdef FOO
$(info FOO defined)
else
ifdef BAR
$(info BAR defined)
else
$(info BAR not defined)
endif
endif
```

That's a lot messier and much harder to read than the version with non-nested else branches.

The -L Command Line Option

The command line option -L (and its long equivalent, --check-symlink-times) causes make to consider the modification time of the symlink and the modification time of the file pointed to by the symlink as GNU make decides which files need to be remade. Whichever is more recent is taken as the modification time. This can be useful if a build uses symlinks to point to different versions of source files because changing the symlink will change the modification time and force a rebuild.

.INCLUDE_DIRS

The .INCLUDE_DIRS variable contains the list of directories that make will search when looking for makefiles that are included using the include directive. This variable is set by the standard list of directories built into GNU make and can be modified by the -I command line option. Although it's possible to change the value of .INCLUDE_DIRS in the actual makefile with = or :=, this has no effect on how GNU make searches for makefiles.

For example, running make -I /usr/foo on Linux with the following makefile outputs /usr/foo /usr/local/include /usr/local/include /usr/include:

```
$(info $(.INCLUDE_DIRS))
all: ; @true
```

.FEATURES

The .FEATURES variable expands to a list of features that GNU make supports and can be used to determine if a specific feature is available. With GNU make 3.81 on Linux, the list of .FEATURES is target-specific order-only second-expansion else-if archives jobserver check-symlink. This means that GNU make 3.81 supports target- and pattern-specific variables, has order-only prerequisites, supports second-expansion (.SECONDEXPANSION), supports else if non-nested conditionals, supports ar files, supports parallel making using the job server, and supports the new -L command line option for checking symlinks.

To test whether a specific feature is available, you can use $(filter). For example:

```
has-order-only := $(filter order-only,$(.FEATURES))
```

This line sets has-order-only to true if the version of make running has order-only prerequisite support. This isn't backward compatible, though; for example, .FEATURES would expand to an empty list in GNU make 3.80, indicating that target-specific variables are not available even though they are. A backward compatible check would first need to determine whether .FEATURES is present by seeing if it is non-blank.

.DEFAULT_GOAL

Normally, if no goal is specified on the command line, make will build the first target it sees in the first makefile it parses. It's possible to override this behavior by setting the .DEFAULT_GOAL variable anywhere in a makefile. For example, the following makefile will build all when run with no goal on the command line, despite the fact that the first target encountered is called fail:

```
fail: ; $(error wrong)
.DEFAULT_GOAL = all
all: ; $(info right)
```

The .DEFAULT_GOAL variable can also be read to get the current default goal; if set to blank (.DEFAULT_GOAL :=), make will automatically pick the next target it encounters as the default goal.

MAKE_RESTARTS

The MAKE_RESTARTS variable is the count of the number of times that make has restarted while performing makefile *remaking*. GNU make has a special feature that allows makefiles to be rebuilt by make. This remaking happens automatically when any makefile is included with include, as well as to the makefile make first started with, and any set with the -f command line option. make searches to see if there's a rule to rebuild any of the makefiles. If it finds one, the makefile is rebuilt just like any other file make is capable of building, and GNU make restarts.

If GNU make has not restarted, MAKE_RESTARTS is blank, not 0.

New Functions

GNU make 3.81 also introduced a variety of built-in functions:

$(info text)   This function is like the existing $(warning) function, but it prints the expanded *text* argument to STDOUT without reporting the makefile and line number. For example, the following makefile generates the output Hello, World!:

```
$(info Hello, World!)
all: ; @true
```

$(lastword LIST)   This function returns the last word of a GNU make list. Previously this was possible by writing $(word $(words *LIST*),*LIST*), but $(lastword) is more efficient. If you are using the GNU Make Standard Library (GMSL), there's a function called last, which is the same as $(lastword). If you are using GNU make 3.81 and GMSL 1.0.6 or later, last automatically uses the built-in lastword for speed.

$(flavor VAR)   This function returns the flavor of a variable (either recursive for recursively expanded or simple for simply expanded). For example, the following makefile prints that REC is recursive and SIM is simple:

```
REC = foo
SIM := foo
$(info REC is $(flavor REC))
$(info SIM is $(flavor SIM))

all: ; @true
```

$(or arg1 arg2 ...) and $(and) $(or) returns a non-blank string if any of its arguments is non-blank, whereas $(and) returns a non-blank string if and only if all of its arguments are non-blank. If you are using the GMSL, and and or functions are part of the library. If you are using GNU make 3.81 and GMSL 1.0.6 or later, the new built-in functions are *not* overridden with the GMSL versions, which means that makefiles that use GMSL are fully backward- and forward-compatible with GNU make 3.81.

$(abspath DIR)   This function returns the absolute path of DIR relative to the directory that GNU make was started in (taking into account any -C command line options). The path has all . and .. elements resolved and duplicate slashes removed. Note that GNU make does not check whether the path *exists*; it just resolves the path elements to make an absolute path. For example, the following makefile prints /home/jgc/bar on my machine when it's placed in */home/jgc*:

```
$(info $(abspath foo/./..///////bar))

all: ; @true
```

$(realpath DIR)   This function returns the same result as $(abspath DIR) except that any symbolic links are resolved. For example, if bar is symlinked to over-here, the following makefile would return /home/jgc/over-here if read from */home/jgc*:

```
$(info $(realpath ../jgc/./bar))

all: ; @true
```

What's New in GNU make 3.82

GNU make 3.82 was released four years after 3.81 and introduced a number of new features—as well as several backward incompatibilities.

Backward Incompatibilities

The *NEWS* file for GNU make 3.82 starts with seven backward-incompatibility warnings. Here's a quick overview:

- In GNU make, the shell that executes a rule's commands is invoked with the -c command line option, which tells the shell to read the command to be executed from the first non-parameter argument to the shell. For example, when the following small rule is executed, make actually executes execve("/bin/sh", ["/bin/sh", "-c", "echo \"hello\""], ...). To run the echo "hello", make uses the shell /bin/sh and adds the -c command line option to it.

```
all: ; @echo "hello"
```

   But the POSIX standard for make was changed in 2008 to require that -e must be specified on the shell command line. The default behavior of GNU make 3.82 and later is to not pass -e unless the .POSIX special target is specified. Anyone using this target in a makefile needs to watch out for this change.

- The $? automatic variable includes the name of all prerequisites to a target that caused a rebuild, *even if they do not exist*. Previously, any prerequisites that did not exist were not placed into $?.

- The $(wildcard) function had always returned a sorted list of files, but this was never actually documented. This behavior changed in GNU make 3.82 so that any makefile relying on a sorted list from $(wildcard) needs to wrap it in a call to $(sort); for example, do $(sort $(wildcard *.c)) to get a sorted list of .c files.

- It used to be possible to write a rule that mixed pattern targets and explicit targets, like this:

```
myfile.out %.out: ; @echo Do stuff with $@
```

   This had been undocumented and was completely removed in GNU make 3.81, because it was never intended to work. It now results in an error message.

- It's no longer possible to have a prerequisite that contains an = sign, even when escaped with \. For example, the following no longer works:

```
all: odd\=name

odd%: ; @echo Make $@
```

If you need an equal sign in a target or prerequisite name, first define a variable that expands to =, like so:

```
eq := =

all: odd$(eq)name
odd%: ; @echo Make $@
```

- Variable names can't contain whitespace in GNU make 3.82. It was previously possible to do this:

```
has space := variable with space in name
$(info $(has space))
```

If you need a variable with a space in its name, first define another variable that contains just a space and use it as follows. But watch out; this sort of thing can be dangerous and hard to debug.

```
sp :=
sp +=
has$(sp)space := variable with space in name

$(info $(has space))
```

- The order in which pattern rules and pattern-specific variables are applied used to be in the order in which they were found in the makefile. This changed in GNU make 3.82: they are now applied in 'shortest stem' order. For example, the following makefile shows how different pattern rules are used with GNU make 3.81 and 3.82.

```
all: output.o

out%.o: ; @echo Using out%.o rule
outp%.o: ; @echo Using outp%.o rule
```

The *stem* is the part of the pattern that is matched by the %. In GNU make 3.81 and earlier, the out%.o rule matches because it is defined first:

```
$ make-3.81
Using out%.o rule
```

In GNU make 3.82 and later, the outp%.o rule is used because the stem is shorter:

```
$ make-3.82
Using outp%.o rule
```

Similar behavior occurs with pattern-specific variables.

New Command Line Option: --eval

The new --eval command line option causes make to run its argument through $(eval) before parsing makefiles. For example, if you have this makefile and run make --eval=FOO=bar, you'll see the output FOO has value bar.

```
all: ; @echo FOO has value $(FOO)
```

This is because before the makefile is parsed, the line FOO=bar is treated as if it were the first line in the makefile and it sets FOO to bar.

New Special Variables: .RECIPEPREFIX and .SHELLFLAGS

GNU make 3.82 introduced two new special variables:

.RECIPEPREFIX   GNU make uses a TAB character as significant whitespace to start the commands in a rule. You can change this with the .RECIPEPREFIX variable. (If .RECIPEPREFIX is an empty string, then TAB is used). For example:

```
.RECIPEPREFIX = >

all:
> @echo Making all
```

Also, .RECIPEPREFIX can be changed over and over again in a makefile as needed.

.SHELLFLAGS   This variable contains the parameters sent to the shell when a rule's commands are run. By default it is -c (or -ec if .POSIX: is specified in the makefile). It can be read or changed if a different shell is being used.

The .ONESHELL Target

When a rule's commands are executed, each line is sent to the shell as a separate shell invocation. With GNU make 3.82, a new special target called .ONESHELL changes this behavior. If .ONESHELL: is set in the makefile, a single shell invocation is used for all the lines in a rule. For example:

```
all:
→ @cd /tmp
→ @pwd
```

This does not output /tmp (unless make was started in /tmp) because each line is executed in a separate shell. But with the .ONESHELL special target, both lines are executed in the same shell and pwd will output /tmp.

```
.ONESHELL:
all:
→ @cd /tmp
→ @pwd
```

Changing Variables with the private and undefine Keywords

A target-specific variable is normally defined for a target and all its pre-requisites. But if the target-specific variable is prefixed with the keyword private, it is defined only for that target, *not* its prerequisites.

In the following makefile, DEBUG is only set to 1 for the foo.o target because it is marked as private:

```
DEBUG=0

foo.o: private DEBUG=1
foo.o: foo.c
→ @echo DEBUG is $(DEBUG) for $@

foo.c: foo.in
→ @echo DEBUG is $(DEBUG) for $@
```

Another new keyword in GNU make 3.82 is undefine, which makes it possible to undefine a variable:

```
SPECIAL_FLAGS := xyz
$(info SPECIAL_FLAGS $(SPECIAL_FLAGS))
undefine SPECIAL_FLAGS
$(info SPECIAL_FLAGS $(SPECIAL_FLAGS))
```

You can detect the difference between an empty variable and an undefined variable using the $(flavor) function. For example, the following outputs simple and then undefined:

```
EMPTY :=
$(info $(flavor EMPTY))
undefine EMPTY
$(info $(flavor EMPTY))
```

In versions of GNU make prior to 3.82, the define directive (which is used to define a multiline variable) would always create a recursively defined variable. For example, COMMANDS here would be a recursive variable, getting expanded at each use:

```
FILE = foo.c

define COMMANDS
wc -l $(FILE)
shasum $(FILE)
endef
```

In GNU 3.82 it's possible to add an optional =, :=, or += after the variable name in a define statement. The default behavior is for the new variable to be recursively expanded each time; this is the same as adding an =. Adding a := creates a simple variable, expanding the body of the define at definition time. And adding += appends multiple lines to an existing variable.

The following makefile creates a simple variable called COMMANDS and then adds lines to it:

```
FILE = foo.c

define COMMANDS :=
wc -l $(FILE)
shasum $(FILE)
endef

define COMMANDS +=

wc -c $(FILE)
endef

$(info $(COMMANDS))
```

❶

Notice the extra blank line at ❶. It's necessary for the wc -c $(FILE) to appear on a new line after the shasum $(FILE). Without it the wc -c $(FILE) would get appended to shasum $(FILE) without a newline.

What's New in GNU make 4.0

The release of GNU make 4.0 introduced two major features: integration with the GNU Guile language and an experimental option to dynamically load objects to expand make's functionality at runtime. In addition, new command line options are especially helpful for debugging.

GNU Guile

The biggest change in GNU make 4.0 is the new $(guile) function, whose argument is code written in the GNU Guile language. The code is executed and its return value is converted to a string, which gets returned by the $(guile) function.

The ability to drop into another language adds enormous functionality to GNU make. The following is a simple example of using Guile to check whether a file exists:

```
$(if $(guile (access? "foo.c" R_OK)),$(info foo.c exists))
```

Using GNU Guile inside GNU make is covered in further detail in Chapter 5.

Loading Dynamic Objects

We don't use the load operator in this book to define functions in C, but defining functions in C and loading dynamic objects are explained in Chapter 5.

Syncing Output with --output-sync

If you use recursive make or use the job server to run rules in parallel, the output produced by make can be very hard to read because output from different rules and sub-makes gets intermingled.

Consider the following (slightly contrived) makefile:

```
all: one two three four

one two:
→ @echo $@ line start
→ @sleep 0.1s
→ @echo $@ line middle
→ @echo $@ line finish

three four:
→ @echo $@ line start
→ @sleep 0.2s
→ @echo $@ line middle
→ @echo $@ line finish
```

This makefile contains four targets: one, two, three, and four. The targets will be built in parallel if you use the -j option. Two calls to sleep have been added to simulate commands that get executed for different lengths of time.

When run with the -j4 option, which runs four jobs in parallel, the output might look like this:

```
$ make -j4
one line start
three line start
four line start
two line start
one line middle
two line middle
one line finish
two line finish
four line middle
three line middle
three line finish
four line finish
```

The output lines for each rule are mixed together, making it very hard to decipher which output goes with which rule. Specifying -Otarget (or --output-sync=target) causes make to keep track of which output is associated with which target and flush the output only when the rule is complete. Now the complete output for each target is clearly readable:

```
$ make -j4 -Otarget
two line start
two line middle
```

```
two line finish
one line start
one line middle
one line finish
four line start
four line middle
four line finish
three line start
three line middle
three line finish
```

Specifying --output-sync=recurse handles recursive sub-makes—that is, rules that invoke $(MAKE)—by buffering the entire output of the rule *including* the sub-make and outputting it all in one go. This prevents sub-make output from getting mixed together but can lead to long pauses in output from make.

The --trace Command Line Option

You can use the new --trace option to trace the execution of rules in a makefile. When specified on the make command line, the commands for each rule that is executed are printed along with information about where the rule is defined and why it was executed.

For example, this simple makefile has four targets:

```
all: part-one part-two

part-one: part-three
→ @echo Make $@

part-two:
→ @echo Make $@

part-three:
→ @echo Make $@
```

Run it with --trace:

```
$ make --trace
makefile:10: target 'part-three' does not exist
echo Make part-three
Make part-three
makefile:4: update target 'part-one' due to: part-three
echo Make part-one
Make part-one
makefile:7: target 'part-two' does not exist
echo Make part-two
Make part-two
```

This shows you why each rule was run, where it is in the makefile, and what commands were executed.

New Assignment Operators: != and ::=

You can use the != operator to execute a shell command and set a variable to the output of the command in a similar manner to $(shell). For example, the following line uses != to get the current date and time into a variable:

```
CURRENTLY != date
```

An important subtlety with != is that the resulting variable is recursive, so its value is expanded each time the variable is used. If the command executed (that is, the RHS of the !=) returns a $, it will be interpreted by make as a variable reference and expanded. For this reason it's safer to use a $(shell) with := instead of !=. (This was added for compatibility with BSD make and might also be added to POSIX.)

The ::= operator is exactly like := and was added for POSIX compatibility.

The $(file) Function

You can use the new $(file) function to create or append to a file. The following makefile uses $(file) to create a file and append to it each time a rule is executed. It creates a log of the makefile's execution:

```
LOG = make.log

$(file > $(LOG),Start)

all: part-one part-two

part-one: part-three
→ @$(file >> $(LOG),$@)
→ @echo Make $@

part-two:
→ @$(file >> $(LOG),$@)
→ @echo Make $@

part-three:
→ @$(file >> $(LOG),$@)
→ @echo Make $@
```

The first $(file) creates the log file using the > operator, and subsequent calls to $(file) use >> to append to the log:

```
$ make
Make part-three
Make part-one
Make part-two
$ cat make.log
Start
part-three
part-one
part-two
```

It's easy to see that the $(file) function is a useful addition to GNU make.

What's New in GNU make 4.1

The most recent version of GNU make (at the time of this writing) is 4.1. Released on October 5, 2014, it contains two useful changes and a large number of bug fixes and small improvements.

New variables MAKE_TERMOUT and MAKE_TERMERR have been introduced. These Boolean values are set to true (that is, they are not empty) if make believes that stdout and stderr (respectively) are being sent to the console.

The $(file) function has been modified so that it's possible to open a file without writing anything to it. If no text argument is present, the file is simply opened and closed again; you can use that to create an empty file with $(file > $(MY_FILE)).

2

MAKEFILE DEBUGGING

This chapter covers techniques that can be useful when debugging makefiles. The lack of built-in debugging tools, and the complexities of following variables in make, can make it very challenging to understand why a particular target was (or more often was not) built.

The first recipe in this chapter shows the single most useful line that you can add to a makefile; it's the equivalent of a print statement inserted into code for debugging.

Printing the Value of a Makefile Variable

If you've ever looked in a makefile, you'll realize that makefile variables (often just called variables) form the backbone of any make process. Variables often define which files will be compiled, what command line parameters to pass to compilers, and even where to find the compiler. And if you've ever tried to debug a makefile, you know that the number one question you ask yourself is, "What is the value of variable X?"

GNU make doesn't have a built-in debugger, nor does it provide the sort of interactivity you'd get from a scripting language like Perl or Python. So how do you figure out the value of a variable?

Take a look at the simple makefile shown in Listing 2-1, which just sets various variables:

```
X=$(YS) hate $(ZS)
Y=dog
YS=$(Y)$(S)
Z=cat
ZS=$(Z)$(S)
S=s


all:
```

Listing 2-1: A simple makefile that sets various variables

What is the value of X?

The small size and simplicity of this makefile make it feasible to trace through all the variable assignments, but even then it takes some work to conclude that X is dogs hate cats. In a multi-thousand-line makefile, one that fully utilizes the power of GNU make's variables and functions, figuring out the value of a variable can be laborious indeed. Fortunately, here's a little make recipe that does all the work for you:

```
print-%: ; @echo $* = $($*)
```

Now you can find the value of variable X with the following command:

```
$ make print-X
```

Because an explicit rule for the print-X target doesn't exist, make looks for a pattern rule, finds print-% (the % acts as a wildcard), and runs the associated command. The command uses $*, a special variable that contains the value matched by the % in the rule, to print the name of the variable, and then does $($*) to get its value. This is a very useful technique in makefiles because it allows the name of a variable to be computed. In this case, the name of the variable to be printed comes from another variable, $*.

Here's how this rule can be used to print the values of variables defined in the makefile in Listing 2-1:

```
$ make print-X
X = dogs hate cats
$ make print-YS
YS = dogs
$ make print-S
S = s
```

Sometimes it's useful to know *how* a variable was defined. make has the $origin function, which returns a string containing the *type* of a variable—that is, whether it was defined in a makefile, on the command line, or in the environment. Modifying print-% to print out origin information as well is easy:

```
print-%: ; @echo $* = '$($*)' from $(origin $*)
```

Now we see that YS is defined in the makefile:

```
$ make print-YS
YS = 'dogs' from file
```

If we override the value of YS on the command line, we'll see:

```
$ make print-YS YS=fleas
YS = 'fleas' from command line
```

Because YS was set on the make command line, its $(origin) is now command line and no longer file.

Dumping Every Makefile Variable

The previous section showed you how to print the value of a single makefile variable using a special rule. But what if you want to print every variable defined in a makefile?

Fortunately, GNU make 3.80 introduced a couple of new features that make it feasible to print the value of all the variables defined in a makefile using a single rule.

Consider Listing 2-1 again. It sets five variables: X, Y, Z, S, YS, and ZS. Adding the following lines to the example creates a target called printvars that will dump all the variables defined in the makefile, as shown in Listing 2-2.

```
.PHONY: printvars
printvars:
→ @$(foreach V,$(sort $(.VARIABLES)),               \
→ $(if $(filter-out environ% default automatic,    \
→ $(origin $V)),$(info $V=$($V) ($(value $V)))))
```

Listing 2-2: A target to print all variables

Before we look closely at how this works, try it out on your own, as shown in Listing 2-3.

```
$ make printvars
MAKEFILE_LIST= Makefile helper.mak ( Makefile helper.mak)
MAKEFLAGS= ()
S=s (s)
SHELL=/bin/sh (/bin/sh)
```

```
X=dogs hate cats ($(YS) hate $(ZS))
Y=dog (dog)
YS=dogs ($(Y)$(S))
Z=cat (cat)
ZS=cats ($(Z)$(S))
```

Listing 2-3: All the variables from Listing 2-1 dumped by printvars

Notice how make has thrown in three extra variables that weren't explicitly defined—MAKEFILE_LIST, MAKEFLAGS, and SHELL—but the rest are all defined in the makefile. Each line shows the name of the variable, its fully substituted value, and the way in which it was defined.

It's a lot easier to understand the long complex line used to print the variables when it's reformatted like this:

```
$(foreach V,$(sort $(.VARIABLES)),
  $(if
❶    $(filter-out environment% default automatic,$(origin $V)),
      $(info $V=$($V) ($(value $V)))
  )
)
```

The .VARIABLES variable is a new feature in GNU make 3.80: its value is a list of the names of all the variables defined in the makefile. First, the code sorts it into order: $(sort $(.VARIABLES)). Then it goes through the sorted list, variable name by variable name, and sets V to each name in turn: $(foreach V,$(sort (.VARIABLES)),...).

For each variable name, the loop decides whether to print or ignore the variable depending on how it was defined. If it's a built-in variable, like $@ or $(CC), or came from the environment, it shouldn't get printed. This decision is made by the predicate at ❶. It first figures out how the variable referenced by $V was defined by calling $(origin $V). This call returns a string describing how the variable was defined: environment for environment variables, file for variables defined in a makefile, and default for things the make defines. The $(filter-out) statement says if the result of $(origin) matches any of the patterns environment%, default, or automatic (automatic is returned by $(origin) for make's automatic variable like $@, $<, and so on), then return an empty string; otherwise, leave it alone. This means $(if)'s predicate will be true only if the variable was defined in the makefile or set on the command line.

If $(if)'s predicate is true, then $(info $V=$($V) ($(value $V))) outputs a message containing the name of the variable, its fully expanded value, and its defined value. The $(value) function is another new feature in GNU make 3.80; it outputs the value of a variable without expanding it. In Listing 2-3, $(YS) would return the value dogs, but $(value YS) would return (Y)(S). That is, $(value YS) shows us how YS is defined, not its final value. That's a very useful debugging feature.

Tracing Variable Values

As a makefile grows, it can become difficult to figure out where a variable is used. This is especially true because of GNU make's recursive variables: the use of a variable could be hidden deep inside some other variable declaration in the makefile. This recipe shows how to trace individual variables as they are used.

For this example, we'll use the makefile in Listing 2-4 (the lines have been numbered for later reference purposes).

```
1 X=$(YS) hate $(ZS)
2 Y=dog
3 YS=$(Y)$(S)
4 Z=cat
5 ZS=$(Z)$(S)
6 S=s
7
8 all: $(YS) $(ZS)
9 all: ; @echo $(X)
10
11 $(YS): ; @echo $(Y) $(Y)
12 $(ZS): ; @echo $(Z) $(Z)
```

Listing 2-4: Example makefile for tracing

When run, this makefile prints:

```
dog dog
cat cat
dogs hate cats
```

As you can see in Listing 2-4, the makefile contains a number of recursively defined variables and uses them in rule definitions and commands.

Tracing Variable Use

If you trace through Listing 2-4, you'll see that the variable $(Y) is used on lines 8, 9, and 11, and twice on line 12. It's amazing how often variables are used! The reason is that make gets the value of a recursively expanded variable (such as YS in Listing 2-4) only when it is needed (that is, when the variable is used and hence expanded), and recursively expanded variables are frequently deeply nested.

It's annoying enough to trace a variable through the simple makefile in Listing 2-4, but doing so for a real makefile would be practically impossible. Fortunately, it's possible to get make to do the work for you with the following code, which you should add to the start of the makefile to be traced (it'll only get used when explicitly called):

```
ifdef TRACE
.PHONY: _trace _value
_trace: ; @$(MAKE) --no-print-directory TRACE= \
```

```
      $(TRACE)='$$(warning TRACE $(TRACE))$(shell $(MAKE) TRACE=$(TRACE) _value)'
_value: ; @echo '$(value $(TRACE))'
endif
```

Before we dive into how it works, here's an example of using it to trace the value of Y in our example makefile. To use the tracer, tell make to run the trace target by setting the TRACE variable to the name of the variable you want to trace. Tracing the variable Y looks like this:

```
$ make TRACE=Y
Makefile:8: TRACE Y
Makefile:11: TRACE Y
Makefile:12: TRACE Y
Makefile:12: TRACE Y
dog dog
cat cat
Makefile:9: TRACE Y
dogs hate cats
```

From the TRACE output you can see Y being used first on line 8 in the definition of the all target, which references Y via the $(YS); then on line 11 the definition of the cats target, which also uses $(YS); then twice on line 12 with the two direct references to $(Y); and finally on line 9 via $(X), which references $(YS), which references $(Y).

Likewise, we can use the tracer to find out where $(S) is used:

```
$ make TRACE=S
Makefile:8: TRACE S
Makefile:8: TRACE S
Makefile:11: TRACE S
Makefile:12: TRACE S
dog dog
cat cat
Makefile:9: TRACE S
Makefile:9: TRACE S
dogs hate cats
```

The output shows that S is first used twice on line 8 (the all target used XS and YS, which both use S). Then S appears again on line 4 (because YS is used) and line 12 (because XS is used). Finally, S is used twice on line 9, when X is echoed as X is used by XS and YS, which both use S.

How the Variable Tracer Works

GNU make has a special $(warning) function that outputs a warning message to STDERR and returns the empty string. At a high level, our tracer code changes the value of the variable to be traced to include a $(warning) message. Every time the variable is expanded, the warning is printed, and whenever make outputs a warning message, it prints the name of the makefile in use and the line number.

For example, say the definition of Y is changed from

```
Y=dog
```

to

```
Y=$(warning TRACE Y)dog
```

Then, whenever $(Y) is expanded, a warning would be generated, and $(Y) would have the value dog. And because $(warning) doesn't return any value, the value of Y is unaffected.

To add this $(warning) call, the tracer code first obtains the unexpanded value of the variable to be traced, then prepends it with an appropriate $(warning), and finally runs the desired make with the specially modified value of the variable being examined. It uses the $(value) function, which as you saw in Listing 2-2 enables you to get the unexpanded value of a variable.

Here's how the tracer works in detail. If TRACE is defined, make will process the block of tracer definitions. In that case, because _trace is the first target encountered, it will be the rule that runs by default. The _trace rule contains a single, complex command:

```
@$(MAKE) --no-print-directory TRACE= \
        $(TRACE)='$$(warning TRACE $(TRACE))$(shell $(MAKE) TRACE=$(TRACE) _value)'
```

On the right side of the command is a $(shell) invocation that reruns the makefile with a different goal. If we are tracing YS, for example, this $(shell) runs the command:

```
make TRACE=YS _value
```

This will run the _value rule, which is defined like so:

```
_value: ; @echo '$(value $(TRACE))'
```

Because TRACE has been set to YS, this rule simply echoes the definition of YS, which is the literal string (Y)(S). So that's what $(shell) ends up evaluating to.

That $(shell) call is in fact inside a command line variable definition (usually called a *command line override*):

```
$(TRACE)='$$(warning TRACE $(TRACE))$(shell $(MAKE)TRACE=$(TRACE) _value)'
```

This adds the $(warning) needed to output the TRACE X messages. Notice how the name of the variable being defined is a computed value: its name is contained in $(TRACE). When tracing YS, this definition turns into:

```
YS='$(warning TRACE YS)$(Y)$(S)'
```

The single quotes are used to prevent the shell from seeing the $ sign. The double $ is used to prevent make from seeing the $. In either case a variable expansion would occur (either in make or by the shell), and we want to delay any variable expansion until YS is actually used.

Finally, the _trace rule recursively runs make:

```
make TRACE= YS='$(warning TRACE YS)$(Y)$(S)'
```

The value of TRACE is reset to the empty string, because this recursive invocation of make should run the real rules rather than the tracer rules. Also, it overrides the value of YS. Recall that variables defined on the command line override definitions in the makefile: even though YS is defined in the makefile, the warning-enabled, command line definition is the one that's used. Now, every time YS is expanded, a warning is printed.

Note that this technique doesn't work for a variable that is target specific. make allows you to define a variable as specific to a target in the manner shown in Listing 2-5:

```
all: FOO=foo
all: a
all: ; @echo $(FOO)

a: ; @echo $(FOO)
```

Listing 2-5: Defining a target-specific variable

The variable FOO will have the value foo in the rule that builds all and in any prerequisites of all. The makefile in Listing 2-5 will print foo twice, because FOO is defined in both the all and a rules. The tracer is unable to obtain the value of FOO and would in fact cause this makefile to behave incorrectly.

The tracer works by redefining the variable being traced as described earlier. Because this happens outside a rule definition, the tracer has no way of obtaining the value of a variable that is target specific. For example, in Listing 2-5, FOO is defined only when running the all or a rules. The tracer has no way of obtaining its value. Using the tracer on that makefile to trace FOO results in the wrong behavior:

```
$ make TRACE=FOO
Makefile:10: TRACE FOO
Makefile:8: TRACE FOO
```

That should have output foo twice (once for the all rule and once for a), but the tracer has redefined FOO and messed up its value. Don't use this tracer for target-specific variables.

The $(warning) function sends its output to STDERR, which makes it possible to separate normal make output from the tracer. Simply redirect STDERR to a trace log file. Here's an example:

```
$ make TRACE=S 2> trace.log
dog dog
cat cat
dogs hate cats
```

This command will write normal make output to the command line while redirecting the trace output to *trace.log*.

Tracing Rule Execution

Until GNU make 4.0, there was no built-in way to trace the order of execution of makefile targets. GNU make 4.0 added the --trace option, which I cover in "GNU make 4.0 Tracing" on page 54, but if you need to use an earlier version of make, it's handy to have another way to trace a makefile. The techniques shown here work with GNU make 4.0 and earlier.

NOTE *If you've ever stared at a cryptic log output and asked yourself, "What rule caused that output?" or "Where's the output for the foo rule?" then this section is for you. And to be honest, who hasn't wondered what GNU make's log file output means?*

An Example

This section uses the following example makefile:

```
.PHONY: all
all: foo.o bar

bar: ; @touch $@
```

It builds two files: foo.o and bar. We'll assume that foo.c exists so that make's built-in rules create foo.o; whereas bar is a simple rule that just touches $@. If you run make for the first time with this makefile, you'd see the following output:

```
$ make
cc -c -o foo.o foo.c
```

This log output is rather cryptic. There's no sign of the rule for bar being run (because touch $@ was hidden using the @ modifier, which prevents the command from being printed). And there's no indication that it was the rule for foo.o that generated the cc compilation line. Nor is there any indication that the all rule was used.

You could, of course, use make -n (which just prints the commands to be run without actually executing them) to look at the work that GNU make would perform:

```
$ make -n
cc -c -o foo.o foo.c
touch bar
```

In this case it's practical, but in general make -n's output can be just as cryptic as a normal log file, and it doesn't provide any way of matching lines in the log with lines in the makefile.

The SHELL Hack

One simple way to enhance the output of GNU make is to redefine SHELL, which is a built-in variable that contains the name of the shell to use when make executes commands. Most shells have an -x option that causes them to print each command they are about to execute; therefore, if you modify SHELL in a makefile by appending -x, it will cause every command to be printed as the makefile is run.

Here's the example makefile modified using GNU make's += operator to append -x to SHELL:

```
SHELL += -x

.PHONY: all
all: foo.o bar

bar: ; @touch $@
```

In some shells this may not work (the shell may expect a single word of options). In GNU make 4.0 and later, a variable called .SHELLFLAGS contains the flags for the shell and can be set to avoid this problem instead of altering SHELL.

Now the makefile output reveals that touch bar was generated by the rule for bar:

```
$ make
cc -c -o foo.o foo.c
+ cc -c -o foo.o foo.c
+ touch bar
```

The SHELL technique has one disadvantage: it slows make down. If SHELL is left untouched, make will often avoid using the shell altogether if it knows it can execute the command directly—for simple operations like compilation and linking, for example. But once SHELL is redefined in a makefile, make will always use the shell, thus slowing it down.

Of course, that doesn't make this a bad debugging trick: getting additional information for a brief slowdown is a very small price to pay. But redefining SHELL doesn't help track the relationship between the lines in a log file and the makefile. Fortunately, this is possible to do with an even smarter redefinition of SHELL.

An Even Smarter SHELL Hack

If SHELL has been redefined, make will expand its value before it runs each line of each rule. This means that if the expansion of SHELL were to output information, it would be possible to print information before each rule runs.

As you saw in "Tracing Variable Values" on page 47, the $(warning) function helpfully outputs a string of your choosing, along with the name of the makefile and the line number at which the $(warning) was written. By adding a $(warning) call to SHELL, it's possible to print detailed information every time SHELL gets expanded. The following code snippet does just this:

```
OLD_SHELL := $(SHELL)
SHELL = $(warning Building $@)$(OLD_SHELL)

.PHONY: all
all: foo.o bar

bar: ; @touch $@
```

The first line captures the normal value of SHELL in a variable called OLD_SHELL. Notice the use of := to get SHELL's final value, not its definition. The second line defines SHELL to include the old shell value and a $(warning) that will print the name of the target being built.

Running GNU make now produces very useful information:

```
$ make
make: Building foo.o
cc -c -o foo.o foo.c
Makefile:7: Building bar
```

The first line of output is produced when the built-in pattern rule to build foo.o is about to be executed. Because no makefile or line number information gets printed, we know that a built-in rule was used here. Then you see the actual output of the built-in rule (the cc command). This is followed by another piece of output from the $(warning), stating that bar is about to be built using the rule in the makefile at line 7.

We used $@ in the $(warning) statement that we added to SHELL, but there's nothing stopping us from using other automatic variables. For example, in Listing 2-6, we use $<, which holds the first prerequisite from which the target is being built, and $?, which holds the list of prerequisites that are newer than the target and tells us why the target is being built.

```
OLD_SHELL := $(SHELL)
SHELL = $(warning Building $@$(if $<, (from $<))$(if $?, ($? newer)))$(OLD_SHELL)

.PHONY: all
```

```
all: foo.o bar

bar: ; touch $@
```

Listing 2-6: Using the SHELL hack

Here SHELL has been redefined to output three pieces of information: the name of the target being built ($@), the name of the first prerequisite ($<, which is wrapped in a $(if) so that nothing is printed if there is no prerequisite), and the names of any newer prerequisites ($?).

Deleting foo.o and running make on this makefile now shows that foo.o was built from foo.c because foo.c was newer than foo.o (because it was missing):

```
$ make
make: Building foo.o (from foo.c) (foo.c newer)
cc -c -o foo.o foo.c
Makefile:7: Building bar
```

There's nothing to stop us from combining this $(warning) trick with -x to get output showing which rules ran and what commands were executed, as shown in Listing 2-7.

```
OLD_SHELL := $(SHELL)
SHELL = $(warning Building $@$(if $<, (from $<))$(if $?, ($? newer)))$(OLD_SHELL) -x

.PHONY: all
all: foo.o bar

bar: ; @touch $@
```

Listing 2-7: Combining the $(warning) trick with -x

Here's the full output of the makefile in Listing 2-7.

```
$ make
make: Building foo.o (from foo.c) (foo.c newer)
cc -c -o foo.o foo.c
+ cc -c -o foo.o foo.c
Makefile:7: Building bar
+ touch bar
```

This assumes that foo.c was newer than foo.o (or foo.o was missing) when make was run.

GNU make 4.0 Tracing

GNU make 4.0 added a --trace command line option that you can use to trace rule execution. It provides output similar to that of Listing 2-7. Here's what happens when Listing 2-6, minus the SHELL modifications, is traced using GNU make 4.0:

```
$ make --trace
<builtin>: update target 'foo.o' due to: foo.c
cc    -c -o foo.o foo.c
Makefile:4: target 'bar' does not exist
touch bar
```

When called with the --trace option, GNU make 4.0 overrides the @ modifier (used in the earlier example to suppress touch bar) in the same way that the -n and --just-print flags do.

Makefile Assertions

Most programming languages have assertions: statements that do nothing if the value they assert is true but cause a fatal error if not. They're commonly used as a runtime debugging aid to catch very odd situations. A typical assert in C might look like assert(foo != bar) and would result in a fatal error if foo and bar are the same.

Unfortunately, GNU make does not have any form of built-in assertions. But they are easy to create from existing functions, and there are even convenient assertion functions defined in the GNU Make Standard Library (GMSL).

The GMSL project (which is covered in Chapter 6) provides two assertion functions: assert and assert_exists.

assert

The assert function will output a fatal error if its first argument is false. As with make's $(if) function, GMSL treats any non-empty string as true and an empty string as false. Thus, if assert's argument is an empty string, the assertion will cause a fatal error; the second argument to assert will be printed as part of the error. For example, this makefile breaks immediately because $(FOO) and $(BAR) are the same:

```
include gmsl

FOO := foo
BAR := foo

$(call assert,$(call sne,$(FOO),$(BAR)),FOO and BAR should not be equal)
```

Because assert is not a built-in function—it's user defined in the GMSL makefile—we must use $(call).

We get the message:

```
Makefile:5: *** GNU Make Standard Library: Assertion failure: FOO and BAR should
not be equal. Stop.
```

The assertion uses another GMSL function, sne, which compares two strings and returns true if they are not equal or false otherwise.

Because true simply means *not an empty string*, it's easy to assert that a variable be defined:

```
include gmsl

$(call assert,$(FOO),FOO is not defined)
```

You can use this assertion, for example, to check that a user has set all necessary command line variables; if FOO is required for the makefile to run properly but the user forgot to set it on the command line, the assertion will cause an error.

You can even use assertions to enforce that certain command line flags are not used. Here's an example that prevents the user from setting -i, the ignore errors flag:

```
include gmsl

$(foreach o,$(MAKEFLAGS),$(call assert,$(call sne,-i,$o),You can't use the -i option))

ifneq ($(patsubst -%,-,$(firstword $(MAKEFLAGS))),-)
$(call assert,$(call sne,$(patsubst i%,i,$(patsubst %i,i,$(firstword \
$(MAKEFLAGS)))),i),You can't use the -i option)
endif
```

This example is more complex than the previous two because make can store the -i flag in MAKEFLAGS in two ways: as a flag in the familiar form -i or as a block of single characters in the first word of MAKEFLAGS. That is, setting the command line flags -i -k results in MAKEFLAGS having the value ki. So the first assert in the loop looks for -i, and the second assert searches for i in the first word of MAKEFLAGS.

assert_exists

Because the success of a build relies on having all necessary files present, the GMSL provides an assertion specifically designed to warn if a file is missing. The assert_exists function has a single argument: the name of the file that must exist. For example, to check that the file *foo.txt* exists before any commands are run by the makefile, you can add an assertion at the start:

```
include gmsl

$(call assert_exists,foo.txt)
```

If the file does not exist, the build stops:

```
Makefile:3: *** GNU Make Standard Library: Assertion failure: file 'foo.txt'
missing. Stop.
```

The assertion stopped the build and the line on which the assertion is found in the makefile—in this case, 3—is shown.

assert_target_directory

A common problem in building real-world makefiles is that you must construct directory hierarchies during or before the build. You can ensure that every directory exists before each rule runs by creating a special assert_target_directory variable, as shown in Listing 2-8.

```
include gmsl

assert_target_directory = $(call assert,$(wildcard $(dir $@)),Target directory $(dir $@) missing)

foo/all: ; @$(call assert_target_directory)echo $@
```

Listing 2-8: Creating an assert_target_directory variable

By inserting $(call assert_target_directory) at the start of each rule or pattern rule's recipe, make automatically checks that the directory in which the target is to be written exists. For example, if *foo/* does not exist, the makefile in Listing 2-8 results in the following error:

```
Makefile:6: *** GNU Make Standard Library: Assertion failure: Target directory foo/ missing. Stop.
```

The error gives the name of the makefile and the line number at which the problem occurred, making it trivial to find the problem.

For a final trick, it's possible to use a two-line modification to cause the makefile to check every rule for a missing directory. Instead of adding $(call assert_target_directory) to every rule, just redefine the SHELL variable to include $(call assert_target_directory). This does slow performance but can be useful in tracking down a missing directory somewhere deep in nested makefiles:

```
include gmsl

assert_target_directory = $(call assert,$(wildcard $(dir $@)),Target directory $(dir $@) missing)

OLD_SHELL := $(SHELL)
SHELL = $(call assert_target_directory)$(OLD_SHELL)

foo/all: ; @echo $@
```

make expands the value of SHELL and hence performs a call to assert_target_directory for every rule that is run. This simple change means that every rule checks that the target directory exists.

The new value of SHELL consists of a call to assert_target_directory, which always returns an empty string, followed by the old value of SHELL, which had been stored in OLD_SHELL. Note how OLD_SHELL is defined using := so that SHELL doesn't refer to itself—OLD_SHELL contains the value of SHELL at runtime and can be safely used to redefine SHELL. If OLD_SHELL were defined using =, make would fail to run because of a circular reference: SHELL would refer to OLD_SHELL, which in turn would refer to SHELL, and so on.

The assert_target_directory function works by calling the built-in $(wildcard) function with the name of the directory where the current target being built should be written. The $(wildcard) function simply checks to see whether the directory exists and returns the name of the directory if so or the empty string if the directory is missing. The target is defined by the automatic variable $@, and the directory portion is extracted with $(dir).

An Interactive GNU make Debugger

Despite GNU make's popularity, debugging facilities are few and far between. GNU make has a -d option that outputs extensive (but not necessarily useful) debugging information about a build, and a -p option that prints GNU make's internal database of rules and variables. This section shows how to build an interactive debugger for GNU make using only GNU make's internal functions and the shell read command.

The debugger has breakpoints, dumps information about the rule at which a breakpoint is hit, and allows interactive querying of variable values and definitions.

The Debugger in Action

Before you see how the debugger works, let's look at how to use it. The debugger and these examples all assume that you are using GNU make 3.80 or later. Listing 2-9 shows an example makefile that builds all from the prerequisites foo and bar.

```
MYVAR1 = hello
MYVAR2 = $(MYVAR1) everyone
all: MYVAR3 = $(MYVAR2)
all: foo bar
→ $(__BREAKPOINT)
→ @echo Finally making $@
foo bar:
→ @echo Building $@
```

Listing 2-9: Setting a breakpoint using the __BREAKPOINT variable

To illustrate the use of the debugger, a breakpoint is set in the all rule by inserting a line at the start of the rule's recipe that consists of just the variable __BREAKPOINT. $(__BREAKPOINT) gets expanded when the rule runs, causing the debugger to break execution and prompt when the all rule is about to run, as shown in Listing 2-9.

Here's what happens when this makefile is executed with no existing files called all, foo, or bar:

```
$ make
Building foo
Building bar
Makefile:51: GNU Make Debugger Break
Makefile:51: - Building 'all' from 'foo bar'
Makefile:51: - First prerequisite is 'foo'
Makefile:51: - Prerequisites 'foo bar' are newer than 'all'
1>
```

First, you see the output from the execution of the rules for foo and bar (the Building foo and Building bar lines), and then there's a break into the debugger. The debugger break shows the line at which the break occurred and in which makefile. In this case, the breakpoint occurred at line 51 of the makefile. (It's line 51 because what's not shown in Listing 2-9 is all the actual GNU make variables that make the debugger work.)

The debugger also outputs information about the rule being built. Here you can see that all is built from foo and bar and that the first prerequisite is foo. That's important because it's the first prerequisite that is stored in GNU make's $< automatic variable. ($< is typically used as the source code filename for compilation.) The debugger also shows why the all rule ran: foo and bar are both newer than all (because they were both just built by their respective rules).

Finally, the debugger prompts 1> for a command. The debugger will accept 32 commands before automatically continuing execution of the makefile. The number 1 indicates that this is the first command; once 32> is reached, the debugger will continue automatically. The first thing to do is ask for help by typing h:

```
1> h
Makefile:51: c        continue
Makefile:51: q        quit
Makefile:51: v VAR    print value of $(VAR)
Makefile:51: o VAR    print origin of $(VAR)
Makefile:51: d VAR    print definition of $(VAR)
2>
```

The debugger provides two means of stopping debugging: typing c continues with normal execution of the makefile; typing q quits make. The three debugger commands v, o, and d allow the user to interrogate GNU make variables by asking for the value of a variable, its origin (where it was defined), or its definition. For example, the makefile in Listing 2-9 contains two variables—MYVAR1 and MYVAR2—and a variable that is specific to the all rule: MYVAR3. A first step is to ask the debugger for the values of each of these variables:

```
2> v MYVAR1
Makefile:55: MYVAR1 has value 'hello'
```

```
3> v MYVAR2
Makefile:55: MYVAR2 has value 'hello everyone'
4> v MYVAR3
Makefile:55: MYVAR3 has value 'hello everyone'
5>
```

If it wasn't clear how MYVAR3 got its value, you could ask the debugger for its definition:

```
5> d MYVAR3
Makefile:55: MYVAR3 is defined as '$(MYVAR2)'
6>
```

This shows that MYVAR3 is defined as $(MYVAR2). And so the obvious next step is to find out how MYVAR2 is defined (and also MYVAR1):

```
6> d MYVAR2
Makefile:55: MYVAR2 is defined as '$(MYVAR1) everyone'
7> d MYVAR1
Makefile:55: MYVAR1 is defined as 'hello'
8>
```

And if it wasn't clear where MYVAR1 got its value, the o command will show its origin:

```
8> o MYVAR1
Makefile:55: MYVAR1 came from file
9>
```

This means that MYVAR1 is defined in a makefile. In contrast:

```
$ make MYVAR1=Hello
1> v MYVAR1
Makefile:55: MYVAR1 has value 'Hello'
2> o MYVAR1
Makefile:55: MYVAR1 came from command line
3>
```

If the user has overridden the value of MYVAR1 on the command line (by running, say, make MYVAR1=Hello), the o command reflects that.

Breakpoints in Patterns

As well as setting breakpoints in normal rules, you can also set them in patterns. Every time that pattern rule is used, the breakpoint is hit. For example:

```
all: foo.x bar.x

%.x: FOO = foo
%.x: %.y
```

```
→ $(__BREAKPOINT)
→ @echo Building $@ from $<...

foo.y:
bar.y:
```

Here, all is built from foo.x and bar.x, which requires building them from foo.y and bar.y using the %.x: %.y rule. A breakpoint is inserted in the pattern rule, and the debugger breaks twice: once for foo.x and once for bar.x:

```
$ make
Makefile:66: GNU Make Debugger Break
Makefile:66: - Building 'foo.x' from 'foo.y'
Makefile:66: - First prerequisite is 'foo.y'
Makefile:66: - Prerequisites 'foo.y' are newer than 'foo.x'
1> c
Building foo.x from foo.y...
Makefile:66: GNU Make Debugger Break
Makefile:66: - Building 'bar.x' from 'bar.y'
Makefile:66: - First prerequisite is 'bar.y'
Makefile:66: - Prerequisites 'bar.y' are newer than 'bar.x'
1> c
Building bar.x from bar.y...
```

Even pattern-specific variables work:

```
$ make
Makefile:67: GNU Make Debugger Break
Makefile:67: - Building 'foo.x' from 'foo.y'
Makefile:67: - First prerequisite is 'foo.y'
Makefile:67: - Prerequisites 'foo.y' are newer than 'foo.x'
1> v FOO
Makefile:67: FOO has value 'foo'
2>
```

%.x has a pattern-specific variable FOO with the value foo; the debugger v command can access it during a breakpoint on the pattern rule.

Breakpoints in Makefiles

Additionally, you can simply insert a breakpoint in a makefile if needed. Parsing of makefiles will pause at the breakpoint so you can examine the current state of variables in the makefile. For example, with a breakpoint after each definition of FOO in this makefile, you can see its value change:

```
FOO = foo
$(__BREAKPOINT)
FOO = bar
$(__BREAKPOINT)
```

Here's a sample run:

```
$ make
Makefile:76: GNU Make Debugger Break
1> v FOO
Makefile:76: FOO has value 'foo'
2> c
Makefile:78: GNU Make Debugger Break
1> v FOO
Makefile:78: FOO has value 'bar'
2>
```

The two separate breakpoints are activated (one after each time FOO is set). Using the debugger's v command shows how the value of FOO changes at each breakpoint.

Debugger Internals

The debugger draws on functions defined in the GMSL (you can read more about the GMSL in Chapter 6). The first line of the debugger includes the GMSL functions:

```
include gmsl

__LOOP := 1 2 3 4 5 6 7 8 9 10 11 12 13 14 15 16 17 18 19 20 21 22 23 24 25 26 27 28 29 30 31 32
```

The debugger uses the __PROMPT variable to output the n> and read in a command followed by a single argument. __PROMPT uses the read shell command to get the command and argument into shell variables $CMD and $ARG and then returns a list of two elements: the first element is the command and the second is the argument. Expanding __PROMPT prompts for and returns a single command and argument pair:

```
__PROMPT = $(shell read -p "$(__HISTORY)> " CMD ARG ; echo $$CMD $$ARG)
```

You use the __BREAK variable to get and handle a single command. First, it stores the result of __PROMPT in __INPUT, and then it calls the __DEBUG function (which handles debugger commands) with two arguments: the command and its argument returned by __PROMPT in __INPUT.

```
__BREAK = $(eval __INPUT := $(__PROMPT))              \
          $(call __DEBUG,                             \
              $(word 1,$(__INPUT)),                   \
              $(word 2,$(__INPUT)))
```

The __DEBUG function handles the core of the debugger. __DEBUG takes a single character command in $1, its first argument, and an optional argument to the command in $2. $1 is stored in the variable __c and $2 in __a.

Then `__DEBUG` examines `__c` to see whether it is one of the supported debugger commands (c, q, v, d, o, or h); if not, a call to $(warning) will output an error message.

`__DEBUG` consists of a set of nested $(if) statements that use the GMSL seq function to determine if the `__c` is a valid debugger command. If it is, $(if)'s first argument is expanded; if not, the next $(if) is examined. For example, the v command (which outputs the value of a variable) is handled like this:

```
$(if $(call seq,$(__c),v),$(warning $(__a) has value '$($(__a))'), ... next if ... )
```

If the `__c` command is v, then $(warning) is used to output the value of the variable named by `__a` (the $($(__a)) outputs the value of the variable whose name is stored in `__a`).

When `__DEBUG` is done, it returns either $(true) or $(false) (the empty string). $(true) indicates that the debugger should stop prompting for commands and continue execution (the q command is handled by calling GNU make's $(error) function to cause a fatal error, which stops make):

```
__DEBUG = $(eval __c = $(strip $1))                           \
          $(eval __a = $(strip $2))                           \
          $(if $(call seq,$(__c),c),                          \
           $(true),                                           \
           $(if $(call seq,$(__c),q),                         \
            $(error Debugger terminated build),               \
            $(if $(call seq,$(__c),v),                        \
             $(warning $(__a) has value '$($(__a))'),         \
             $(if $(call seq,$(__c),d),                       \
        $(warning $(__a) is defined as '$(value $(__a))'),    \
              $(if $(call seq,$(__c),o),                      \
        $(warning $(__a) came from $(origin $(__a))),         \
               $(if $(call seq,$(__c),h),                     \
               $(warning c        continue)                   \
               $(warning q        quit)                       \
           $(warning v VAR    print value of $$(VAR))         \
           $(warning o VAR    print origin of $$(VAR))        \
        $(warning d VAR    print definition of $$(VAR)),      \
        $(warning Unknown command '$(__c)')))))))
```

Finally, we come to the definition of `__BREAKPOINT` (the breakpoint variable we used in Listing 2-9). It first outputs a banner containing information (you'll see what `__BANNER` does in a moment); then it loops asking for commands by calling `__BREAK`. The loop terminates either if it runs out of items in `__LOOP` (which is where the 32-command limit is defined) or if a call to `__BREAK` returns $(true):

```
__BREAKPOINT = $(__BANNER)                            \
               $(eval __TERMINATE := $(false))        \
               $(foreach __HISTORY,                   \
                  $(__LOOP),                          \
                  $(if $(__TERMINATE),,               \
                   $(eval __TERMINATE := $(__BREAK))))
```

__BANNER shows that the debugger has stopped at a breakpoint, and by examining GNU make automatic variables, it is able to give information about the current rule being built:

```
__BANNER = $(warning GNU Make Debugger Break)              \
          $(if $^,                                         \
              $(warning - Building '$@' from '$^'),        \
              $(warning - Building '$@'))                  \
        $(if $<,$(warning - First prerequisite is '$<')) \
          $(if $%,$(warning - Archive target is '$%')) \
          $(if $?,$(warning - Prerequisites '$?' are newer than '$@'))
```

Here's the complete debugger code:

```
__LOOP := 1 2 3 4 5 6 7 8 9 10 11 12 13 14 15 16 17 18 19 20 21 22 23 24 25 26 27 28 29 30 31 32

__PROMPT = $(shell read -p "$(__HISTORY)> " CMD ARG ; echo $$CMD $$ARG)

__DEBUG =  $(eval __c = $(strip $1))                      \
           $(eval __a = $(strip $2))                      \
           $(if $(call seq,$(__c),c),                     \
            $(true),                                      \
            $(if $(call seq,$(__c),q),                    \
             $(error Debugger terminated build),          \
             $(if $(call seq,$(__c),v),                   \
              $(warning $(__a) has value '$($(__a))'),  \
              $(if $(call seq,$(__c),d),                  \
     $(warning $(__a) is defined as '$(value $(__a))'), \
               $(if $(call seq,$(__c),o),                 \
     $(warning $(__a) came from $(origin $(__a))),      \
                $(if $(call seq,$(__c),h),                \
                 $(warning c        continue)             \
                 $(warning q        quit)                 \
                $(warning v VAR    print value of $$(VAR))  \
                $(warning o VAR    print origin of $$(VAR)) \
            $(warning d VAR    print definition of $$(VAR)), \
        $(warning Unknown command '$(__c)')))))))

__BREAK = $(eval __INPUT := $(__PROMPT))                  \
          $(call __DEBUG,                                 \
             $(word 1,$(__INPUT)),                        \
             $(word 2,$(__INPUT)))

__BANNER = $(warning GNU Make Debugger Break)             \
          $(if $^,                                        \
              $(warning - Building '$@' from '$^'),       \
              $(warning - Building '$@'))                 \
        $(if $<,$(warning - First prerequisite is '$<')) \
          $(if $%,$(warning - Archive target is '$%')) \
          $(if $?,$(warning - Prerequisites '$?' are newer than '$@'))
__BREAKPOINT = $(__BANNER)                                \
              $(eval __TERMINATE := $(false))             \
              $(foreach __HISTORY,                        \
```

```
$(__LOOP),                          \
$(if $(__TERMINATE),,               \
    $(eval __TERMINATE := $(__BREAK))))
```

For the most up-to-date version, visit the GNU make Debugger open source project at *http://gmd.sf.net/*.

Dynamic Breakpoints in the GNU make Debugger

The preceding section showed how to build a debugger for GNU make entirely in GNU make. But it had only static (hardcoded) breakpoints. This section shows you how to enhance the debugger by adding dynamic breakpoints. That makes it possible to set and remove breakpoints on the name of a file (in GNU make language, a *target*) that the makefile will build.

It's no longer necessary to insert the $(__BREAKPOINT) string in a makefile. Typing a simple set breakpoint command has the same effect. And another keystroke lists all breakpoints currently in effect.

This section shows the use of the new breakpoints and how they are coded. The new code is written entirely in GNU make's variable language and uses the GMSL set functions (detailed in Chapter 6) to maintain the list of current breakpoints.

Getting the breakpoints to activate requires a little GNU make magic, but first let's look at an example.

Dynamic Breakpoints in Action

Before you see how the debugger works, let's look at how to use it. The debugger and these examples all assume that you are using GNU make 3.80 or later.

Here's an example makefile that builds all from prerequisites foo and bar.

```
include gmd

MYVAR1 = hello
MYVAR2 = $(MYVAR1) everyone

all: MYVAR3 = $(MYVAR2)
all: foo bar
all: ; @echo Finally making $@
foo bar: ; @echo Building $@

$(__BREAKPOINT)
```

To illustrate the use of the debugger, a breakpoint is set in the makefile by inserting a line at the end of the makefile that consists of just the variable $(__BREAKPOINT). $(__BREAKPOINT) will get expanded when the makefile finishes being parsed, causing the debugger to break execution before any rules are run and prompt for input. (The debugger is included here with the include gmd command at the start. You can get the GMD files from the GMD website at *http://gmd.sf.net/*; it's all open source code.)

Here's what happens when this makefile is executed with no existing files called all, foo, or bar.

```
$ make
Makefile:11: GNU Make Debugger Break
1> h
Makefile:11: c:      continue
Makefile:11: q:      quit
Makefile:11: v VAR: print value of $(VAR)
Makefile:11: o VAR: print origin of $(VAR)
Makefile:11: d VAR: print definition of $(VAR)
Makefile:11: b TAR: set a breakpoint on target TAR
Makefile:11: r TAR: unset breakpoint on target TAR
Makefile:11: l:      list all target breakpoints
2>
```

The debugger immediately breaks and waits for input. The first thing to do is type h to see the help text and the three new commands: b (to set a breakpoint), r (to remove a breakpoint), and l (to list current breakpoints).

Then set two breakpoints in the makefile: one when foo gets built and one for all. (If you look back at "The Debugger in Action" on page 58, you'll see that you can also achieve this by modifying the makefile, but these new breakpoints can be set dynamically at runtime.)

After setting the breakpoints, use the l command to verify that they are set:

```
2> b foo
Makefile:11: Breakpoint set on `foo'
3> b all
Makefile:11: Breakpoint set on `all'
4> l
Makefile:11: Current target breakpoints: `all' `foo'
5>
```

Continuing execution by entering c causes the foo breakpoint to be hit immediately. foo is the first target that the makefile will build (followed by bar and finally all). The breakpoint indicates that the rule for foo is at line 9:

```
5> c
Makefile:9: GNU Make Debugger Break
Makefile:9: - Building 'foo'
1>
```

Continuing on, first the output (generated when bar is created) appears, and then the all breakpoint is hit.

```
1> c
Building foo
Building bar
Makefile:7: GNU Make Debugger Break
Makefile:7: - Building 'all' from 'foo bar'
Makefile:7: - First prerequisite is 'foo'
```

```
Makefile:7: - Prerequisites 'foo bar' are newer than 'all'
1>
```

The all breakpoint prints out much more information than foo because all has prerequisites.

The Easy Part

To add the breakpoint functions to the GNU make debugger, the debugger code that handles the keyboard was first altered to recognize the b, r, and l commands and call user-defined GNU make functions __BP_SET, __BP_UNSET, and __BP_LIST.

The targets for which breakpoints are defined are simply a GMSL set of target names. Initially, there are no breakpoints and so the set, called __BREAKPOINTS, is empty:

```
__BREAKPOINTS := $(empty_set)
```

Setting and removing breakpoints is a matter of calling the GMSL functions set_insert and set_remove to add or remove an element from __BREAKPOINTS:

```
__BP_SET = $(eval __BREAKPOINTS := $(call set_insert,$1,$(__BREAKPOINTS))) \
        $(warning Breakpoint set on `$1')

__BP_UNSET = $(if $(call set_is_member,$1,$(__BREAKPOINTS)),              \
        $(eval __BREAKPOINTS := $(call set_remove,$1,$(__BREAKPOINTS)))   \
        $(warning Breakpoint on `$1' removed),                           \
        $(warning Breakpoint on `$1' not found))
```

Both functions use the GNU make $(eval) function to change the value of __BREAKPOINTS. $(eval FOO) evaluates its argument FOO as if it were a piece of text during parsing of the makefile: this means that at runtime you can change variable values or define new rules.

__BP_UNSET used the GMSL function set_is_member to determine whether the breakpoint being removed was actually defined and output a helpful message in the case that the user tries to remove a nonexistent breakpoint (which may be caused by a typing error on their part).

Listing the current breakpoints is simply a matter of outputting the contents of the set stored in __BREAKPOINTS. Because that set is just a list with no duplicates, __BP_LIST feeds its value into the GNU make functions $(addprefix) and $(addsuffix) to put quotation marks around the target names:

```
__BP_LIST = $(if $(__BREAKPOINTS),                               \
            $(warning Current target breakpoints:            \
        $(addsuffix ',$(addprefix `,$(__BREAKPOINTS)))),  \
            $(warning No target breakpoints set))
```

__BP_LIST uses the GNU make $(if) function to choose between listing the breakpoints if there are any or saying No target breakpoints set if the `__BREAKPOINTS` set is empty. `$(if)` will evaluate its second argument if `$(__BREAKPOINTS)` is a non-empty string and evaluate its third argument if there are no breakpoints.

The Trick

To get GNU make to break into the debugger, it has to expand the `__BREAKPOINT` variable, which outputs information about the breakpoint and prompts for commands. But for that to happen, we need a way to check which breakpoints are defined every time a rule is about to run. If we can engineer that, then make can expand `$(__BREAKPOINT)` if necessary, causing make to stop at the breakpoint.

Fortunately, it's possible to cause make to expand `__BREAKPOINT` by modifying the built-in `SHELL` variable.

The `SHELL` variable is also expanded every time a command is about to run inside a rule. That makes it ideal for checking breakpoints. Here's the actual code in the GNU make debugger that uses `SHELL` for breakpoint handling:

```
__BP_OLD_SHELL := $(SHELL)
__BP_NEW_SHELL = $(if $(call seq,$(__BP_FLAG),$@),      \
                $(call $1,),                            \
                $(__BP_CHECK))$(__BP_OLD_SHELL)
SHELL = $(call __BP_NEW_SHELL,$1)
```

First, the real value of `SHELL` is stored in `__BP_OLD_SHELL` (note that the GNU make `:=` operator is used to capture the value, not the definition, of `SHELL`). Then `SHELL` is redefined to call the `__BP_NEW_SHELL` variable.

`__BP_NEW_SHELL` is where the interesting work is done. The last part of it is `$(__BP_OLD_SHELL)`, which is the value of the original `SHELL` variable. After all, once it's done checking breakpoints, GNU make needs to use the original shell to actually run commands. Before that there's a rather complex `$(if)`. Concentrate for a moment on the call to `$(__BP_CHECK)`. That's the variable that will actually check to see whether the breakpoint should be executed. It's defined like this:

```
__BP_CHECK = $(if $(call set_is_member,$@,            \
              $(__BREAKPOINTS)),                      \
              $(eval __BP_FLAG := $@)                 \
              $(eval __IGNORE := $(call SHELL,        \
                          __BREAKPOINT)))

__BP_FLAG :=
```

`__BP_CHECK` checks to see whether the current target being built (stored in the standard GNU make automatic variable `$@`) is present in the list of breakpoints. It does this using the GMSL function `set_is_member`. If the target is present, it does two things: it sets an internal variable called `__BP_FLAG` to be the target for which the breakpoint has activated and then proceeds to `$(call)` a variable and throw away the result by storing it in a variable called

__IGNORE. That's done so that __BP_CHECK's return value will always be empty; it's used, after all, in the definition of SHELL, which ultimately needs to be just the name of the shell to execute.

Experienced GNU make users will be scratching their heads wondering about the odd syntax $(call SHELL,__BREAKPOINT). That's where some GNU make rocket science comes in.

Rocket Science

Instead of writing $(call SHELL,__BREAKPOINT), it's tempting to write $(__BREAKPOINT) to get the breakpoint to activate. But that doesn't work.

Doing so would cause a fatal GNU make error. Follow the chain of variables up from __BP_CHECK, and it becomes clear that it's been expanded because SHELL was being expanded (because a rule was about to run). Follow into __BREAKPOINT, and there's a nasty surprise: a call to $(shell) (this can be seen in the GMD code on page 64 or in the preceding section), which will cause SHELL to be expanded.

Danger, Will Robinson! SHELL is defined in terms of SHELL, which causes GNU make to spot the recursion and give up. The $(call SHELL,__BREAKPOINT) syntax lets us play with fire. Any time a variable is $(call)ed in GNU make, the flag used to check for recursion is disabled. So doing $(call SHELL,__BREAKPOINT) means that the recursion flag on SHELL is turned off (avoiding the error) and the definition of SHELL calls __BP_NEW_SHELL with one argument. The argument is the word __BREAKPOINT. __BP_NEW_SHELL checks to see whether __BP_FLAG is set to the same value as $@ (which it does using the GMSL seq function) and then proceeds to $(call) its first argument (which is __BREAKPOINT); the breakpoint fires and the prompt appears.

It might seem that some horrible infinite recursion will occur when the $(shell) gets executed and SHELL is expanded again. Two things prevent that: __BP_FLAG is still the same as $@ (so __BP_CHECK is not called again), and this time SHELL has no argument (the value in $1 is empty), so the $(call $1,) does nothing and recursion stops.

An Introduction to remake

The remake project (*http://bashdb.sourceforge.net/remake/*) is a fork of GNU make that integrates a complete debugger created by modifying the GNU make source code. remake forked from GNU make 3.82 and is currently at version 3.82+dbg-0.9.

Just Print and Trace

To illustrate the operation of remake, let's use Listing 2-10, a sample makefile:

```
.PHONY: all
all: foo bar baz

foo: bar
→ @touch $@
```

```
bar:
→ @touch $@

baz: bam
→ @touch $@

bam:
→ @touch $@
```

Listing 2-10: A simple makefile to illustrate remake

Running the standard GNU make -n (or --just-print) option against this makefile produces the following output:

```
$ make -n
touch bar
touch foo
touch bam
touch baz
```

But remake provides a makefile and line number information for each rule. The information shows the target (the value of $@) and the commands to be run:

```
$ remake -n
##>>>>>>>>>>>>>>>>>>>>>>>>>>>>>>>>>>>>>>>>>>>>>>>>>>>>>>>
Makefile:8: bar
touch bar
##<<<<<<<<<<<<<<<<<<<<<<<<<<<<<<<<<<<<<<<<<<<<<<<<<<<<<<<
##>>>>>>>>>>>>>>>>>>>>>>>>>>>>>>>>>>>>>>>>>>>>>>>>>>>>>>>
Makefile:5: foo
touch foo
##<<<<<<<<<<<<<<<<<<<<<<<<<<<<<<<<<<<<<<<<<<<<<<<<<<<<<<<
##>>>>>>>>>>>>>>>>>>>>>>>>>>>>>>>>>>>>>>>>>>>>>>>>>>>>>>>
Makefile:14: bam
touch bam
##<<<<<<<<<<<<<<<<<<<<<<<<<<<<<<<<<<<<<<<<<<<<<<<<<<<<<<<
##>>>>>>>>>>>>>>>>>>>>>>>>>>>>>>>>>>>>>>>>>>>>>>>>>>>>>>>
Makefile:11: baz
touch baz
##<<<<<<<<<<<<<<<<<<<<<<<<<<<<<<<<<<<<<<<<<<<<<<<<<<<<<<<
```

Of course, you have to run any real makefile to understand its execution. remake provides a handy tracing option, -x, which runs the makefile while outputting information about why targets are being built and showing the commands executed and their output:

```
$ remake -x
Reading makefiles...
Updating goal targets....
Makefile:2  File `all' does not exist.
```

```
Makefile:4 File `foo' does not exist.
  Makefile:7        File `bar' does not exist.
  Makefile:7        Must remake target `bar'.
##>>>>>>>>>>>>>>>>>>>>>>>>>>>>>>>>>>>>>>>>>>>>>>>>>>>>>>
Makefile:8: bar
touch bar
##<<<<<<<<<<<<<<<<<<<<<<<<<<<<<<<<<<<<<<<<<<<<<<<<<<<<<<
+ touch bar
  Makefile:7        Successfully remade target file `bar'.
 Makefile:4 Must remake target `foo'.
##>>>>>>>>>>>>>>>>>>>>>>>>>>>>>>>>>>>>>>>>>>>>>>>>>>>>>>
Makefile:5: foo
touch foo
##<<<<<<<<<<<<<<<<<<<<<<<<<<<<<<<<<<<<<<<<<<<<<<<<<<<<<<
+ touch foo
 Makefile:4 Successfully remade target file `foo'.
  Makefile:10       File `baz' does not exist.
    Makefile:13       File `bam' does not exist.
    Makefile:13       Must remake target `bam'.
##>>>>>>>>>>>>>>>>>>>>>>>>>>>>>>>>>>>>>>>>>>>>>>>>>>>>>>
Makefile:14: bam
touch bam
##<<<<<<<<<<<<<<<<<<<<<<<<<<<<<<<<<<<<<<<<<<<<<<<<<<<<<<
+ touch bam
    Makefile:13       Successfully remade target file `bam'.
 Makefile:10 Must remake target `baz'.
##>>>>>>>>>>>>>>>>>>>>>>>>>>>>>>>>>>>>>>>>>>>>>>>>>>>>>>
Makefile:11: baz
touch baz
##<<<<<<<<<<<<<<<<<<<<<<<<<<<<<<<<<<<<<<<<<<<<<<<<<<<<<<
+ touch baz

Makefile:10 Successfully remade target file `baz'.
Makefile:2   Must remake target `all'. Is a phony target.
Makefile:2   Successfully remade target file `all'.
```

The trace option really comes into its own when an error occurs. Here's the output when a nonexistent option -z is added to the touch in the commands for target bar:

```
$ remake -x
Reading makefiles...
Updating goal targets....
Makefile:2   File `all' does not exist.
  Makefile:4 File `foo' does not exist.
    Makefile:7        File `bar' does not exist.
    Makefile:7        Must remake target `bar'.
##>>>>>>>>>>>>>>>>>>>>>>>>>>>>>>>>>>>>>>>>>>>>>>>>>>>>>>
Makefile:8: bar
touch -z bar
##<<<<<<<<<<<<<<<<<<<<<<<<<<<<<<<<<<<<<<<<<<<<<<<<<<<<<<
+ touch -z bar
touch: invalid option -- 'z'
Try `touch --help' for more information.
```

```
Makefile:8: *** [bar] Error 1

#0 bar at Makefile:8
#1 foo at Makefile:4
#2 all at Makefile:2
Command-line arguments:
    "-x"
```

Right at the bottom of that output is the call stack of targets that were dependent on bar building successfully, plus, of course, the error generated by touch, the actual command that was executed, and where to find it in the makefile.

Debugging

Because remake contains an interactive debugger, you can use it to debug the touch problem. Run remake with the -X option (uppercase X for the debugger; lowercase x for tracing), and the debugger breaks at the first target to be built:

```
$ remake -X
GNU Make 3.82+dbg0.9
Built for x86_64-unknown-linux-gnu
Copyright (C) 2010  Free Software Foundation, Inc.
License GPLv3+: GNU GPL version 3 or later <http://gnu.org/licenses/gpl.html>
This is free software: you are free to change and redistribute it.
There is NO WARRANTY, to the extent permitted by law.
Reading makefiles...
Updating makefiles....
Updating goal targets....
  Makefile:2     File `all' does not exist.
-> (Makefile:4)
foo: bar
remake<0>
```

So the first break is at line 2 of the makefile and shows that the first target is all (and the complete prerequisite list is shown). Entering h gives complete help information:

```
remake<0> h
  Command                  Short Name  Aliases
  ----------------------   ----------  ---------
  break [TARGET|LINENUM] [all|run|prereq|end]* (b)  L
  cd DIR                        (C)
  comment TEXT                  (#)
  continue [TARGET [all|run|prereq|end]*] (c)
  delete breakpoint numbers..   (d)
  down [AMOUNT]                 (D)
  edit                          (e)
  eval STRING                   (E)
  expand STRING                 (x)
  finish [AMOUNT]               (F)
```

```
frame N                             (f)
help [COMMAND]                      (h)  ?, ??
info [SUBCOMMAND]                   (i)
list [TARGET|LINE-NUMBER]          (l)
next [AMOUNT]                       (n)
print {VARIABLE [attrs...]}        (p)
pwd                                 (P)
quit [exit-status]                 (q)  exit, return
run [ARGS]                          (R)  restart
set OPTION {on|off|toggle}
set variable VARIABLE VALUE         (=)
setq VARIABLE VALUE                 (")
shell STRING                        (!)  !!
show [SUBCOMMAND]                   (S)
source FILENAME                     (<)
skip                                (k)
step [AMOUNT]                       (s)
target [TARGET-NAME] [info1 [info2...]] (t)
up [AMOUNT]                         (u)
where                               (T)  backtrace, bt
write [TARGET [FILENAME]]           (w)
```

Because the touch problem occurs later in the make execution (in the bar rule), just continue by single stepping with s:

```
remake<1> s
    Makefile:4   File `foo' does not exist.
-> (Makefile:7)
bar:
remake<2> s
      Makefile:7 File `bar' does not exist.
      Makefile:7 Must remake target `bar'.
Invoking recipe from Makefile:8 to update target `bar'.
##>>>>>>>>>>>>>>>>>>>>>>>>>>>>>>>>>>>>>>>>>>>>>>>>>>>>>
touch -z bar
##<<<<<<<<<<<<<<<<<<<<<<<<<<<<<<<<<<<<<<<<<<<<<<<<<<<<
++ (Makefile:7)
bar
remake<3> s
touch: invalid option -- 'z'
Try 'touch --help' for more information.
Makefile:7: *** [bar] Error 1

#0  bar at Makefile:7
#1  foo at Makefile:4
#2  all at Makefile:2

***Entering debugger because we encountered a fatal error.
** Exiting the debugger will exit make with exit code 1.
!! (Makefile:7)
bar
remake<4>
```

While in the debugger, you can fix the error in the makefile and then enter R to restart the build:

```
remake<4> R
Changing directory to /home/jgc and restarting...
GNU Make 3.82+dbg0.9
Built for x86_64-unknown-linux-gnu
Copyright (C) 2010  Free Software Foundation, Inc.
License GPLv3+: GNU GPL version 3 or later <http://gnu.org/licenses/gpl.html>
This is free software: you are free to change and redistribute it.
There is NO WARRANTY, to the extent permitted by law.
Reading makefiles...
Updating makefiles....
Updating goal targets....
  Makefile:2    File `all' does not exist.
-> (Makefile:4)
foo: bar
remake<0> c
```

Now things work correctly.

Targets, Macro Values, and Expansion

When stopped in the debugger, it's possible to interrogate information about targets in the makefile, such as variable values (expanded and unexpanded) and commands. For example, in Listing 2-10, when stopped at a breakpoint, you can find all the information remake has about the all target by using the target command:

```
$ remake -X
GNU Make 3.82+dbg0.9
Built for x86_64-unknown-linux-gnu
Copyright (C) 2010  Free Software Foundation, Inc.
License GPLv3+: GNU GPL version 3 or later <http://gnu.org/licenses/gpl.html>
This is free software: you are free to change and redistribute it.
There is NO WARRANTY, to the extent permitted by law.
Reading makefiles...
Updating makefiles....
Updating goal targets....
  /home/jgc/src/thirdparty/remake-3.82+dbg0.9/Makefile:2    File `all' does not exist.
-> (/home/jgc/src/thirdparty/remake-3.82+dbg0.9/Makefile:4)
foo: bar
remake<0> target all
all: foo bar baz
#  Phony target (prerequisite of .PHONY).
#  Implicit rule search has not been done.
#  Implicit/static pattern stem: `'
#  File does not exist.
#  File has not been updated.
#  Commands not yet started.
```

```
# automatic
# @ := all
# automatic
# % :=
# automatic
# * :=
# automatic
# + := foo bar baz
# automatic
# | :=
# automatic
# < := all
# automatic
# ^ := foo bar baz
# automatic
# ? :=
remake<1>
```

remake shows that all is a phony target and dumps information about the automatic variables that will be set for this rule. There's no restriction on asking about the current target:

```
remake<1> target foo
foo: bar
#  Implicit rule search has not been done.
#  Implicit/static pattern stem: `'
#  File does not exist.
#  File has not been updated.
#  Commands not yet started.
# automatic
# @ := foo
# automatic
# % :=
# automatic
# * :=
# automatic
# + := bar
# automatic
# | :=
# automatic
# < := bar
# automatic
# ^ := bar
# automatic
# ? :=
#  commands to execute (from `Makefile', line 5):
    @touch $@

remake<2>
```

Because target foo has commands, they are listed at the bottom (along with where to find them in which makefile). To see the expanded form of the commands, use the expand modifier of the target command:

```
remake<2> target foo expand
foo:
#  commands to execute (from `Makefile', line 5):
    @touch foo

remake<3>
```

To get information about a variable, we use the handy print and expand commands: print gives the definition of a variable, and expand gives its post-expansion value. Here's how to find out the definition of the built-in COMPILE.c variable (which contains the command used to compile .c files):

```
remake<4> print COMPILE.c
(origin default) COMPILE.c = $(CC) $(CFLAGS) $(CPPFLAGS) $(TARGET_ARCH) -c
```

To see the expanded value, expand it:

```
remake<7> expand COMPILE.c
(origin default) COMPILE.c := cc    -c
```

remake can also set variable values using set (which expands a string and sets the variable to that value) and setq (which sets the variable to a string without expansion). For example, changing CC from cc to gcc changes the C compiler make will use:

```
remake<7> expand COMPILE.c
(origin default) COMPILE.c := cc    -c
remake<8> print CC
(origin default) CC = cc
remake<9> setq CC gcc
Variable CC now has value 'gcc'
remake<10> print CC
(origin debugger) CC = gcc
remake<11> expand COMPILE.c
(origin default) COMPILE.c := gcc    -c
remake<12>
```

remake is a very useful tool to add to your make toolkit. You don't need to use it every day, but switching from make to remake when you have a knotty problem to solve is hassle-free if you are not using any features added in GNU make 4.0.

3

BUILDING AND REBUILDING

Knowing when and why targets are rebuilt
and recipes run is fundamental to using
GNU make. For simple makefiles, it's easy
to understand why a particular object file
was built, but for real-world makefiles, building and
rebuilding becomes complex. In addition, GNU make dependencies can be
limiting because files are updated when the modification time of a prerequisite is later than the target. And in most cases, only a single target is
updated by a single rule.

This chapter explains advanced techniques for handling dependencies
in GNU make, including rebuilding when the recipe of a target changes,
rebuilding when a checksum of a file changes, how best to implement recursive make, and how to build multiple targets in a single rule.

Rebuilding When CPPFLAGS Changes

This section shows you how to implement an important "missing feature"
of GNU make: the ability to rebuild targets when the commands for those

targets change. GNU make rebuilds a target when it is *out of date*; that is, it rebuilds when some of the prerequisites are newer than the target itself. But what if the target appears up-to-date when looking at file timestamps, but the actual commands to build the target have changed?

For example, what happens when a non-debug build is followed by a debug build (perhaps by running make followed by make DEBUG=1)? Unless the build has been structured so the names of targets depend on whether the build is debug or non-debug, nothing happens.

GNU make has no way of detecting that some targets ought to be rebuilt, because it doesn't take into account any change to the commands in recipes. If, for example, DEBUG=1 causes the flags passed to the compiler to change, the target should be rebuilt.

In this section you'll learn how to make that happen in a few lines of GNU make code.

An Example Makefile

The example makefile in Listing 3-1 is used throughout this section to demonstrate the *rebuilding when commands change* system. To make the operation of the system very clear, I've avoided using built-in GNU make rules, so this makefile isn't as simple as it could be:

```
all: foo.o bar.o

foo.o: foo.c
→ $(COMPILE.C) -DDEBUG=$(DEBUG) -o $@ $<

bar.o: bar.c
→ $(COMPILE.C) -o $@ $<
```

Listing 3-1: An example makefile for demonstrating the rebuilding when commands change system.

The makefile creates two .o files, foo.o and bar.o, by compiling corresponding .c files. The compilation is done using the built-in variable COMPILE.C (which will normally be the name of a suitable compiler for the system, followed by references to variables like CPPFLAGS and use of $@ and $< to compile the code into an object file).

A specific reference to $(DEBUG) is turned into a pre-processor variable called DEBUG using the compiler's -D option. The contents of foo.c and bar.c have been omitted because they are irrelevant.

Here's what happens when make is run with no command line options (which means that DEBUG is undefined):

```
$ make
g++  -c -DDEBUG= -o foo.o foo.c
g++  -c -o bar.o bar.c
```

Now `foo.o` and `bar.o` have been created, so typing `make` again does nothing:

```
$ make
make: Nothing to be done for `all'.
```

Typing `make DEBUG=1` also does nothing, even though the object file `foo.o` would likely be different if it were rebuilt with `DEBUG` defined (for example, it would likely contain extra debugging code controlled by #ifdefs that use the `DEBUG` variable in the source code):

```
$ make DEBUG=1
make: Nothing to be done for `all'.
```

The signature system in the next section will correct that problem and require very little work for the makefile maintainer.

Changing Our Example Makefile

To fix the problem in the preceding section, we'll use a helper makefile called `signature`. We'll look at how signature works in a moment; first let's look at how to modify the makefile in Listing 3-1 to use it:

```
include signature

all: foo.o bar.o

foo.o: foo.c
→ $(call do,$$(COMPILE.C) -DDEBUG=$$(DEBUG) -o $$@ $$<)

bar.o: bar.c
→ $(call do,$$(COMPILE.C) -o $$@ $$<)

-include foo.o.sig bar.o.sig
```

Three changes were made to the file: first, `include signature` was added at the start so the code that handles the updating of *signatures* is included. These signatures will capture the commands used to build files and be used to rebuild when the commands change.

Second, the commands in the two rules were wrapped with $(call do,...), and the $ signs for each command have been quoted with a second $.

Third, for each .o file being managed by signature, there's an include of a corresponding .sig file. The final line of the makefile includes foo.o.sig (for foo.o) and bar.o.sig (for bar.o). Notice that -include is used instead of just include in case the .sig file is missing (-include doesn't generate an error when one of the files to be included is not present).

Before you see how this works, here are some examples of it in operation:

```
$ make
g++  -c -DDEBUG= -o foo.o foo.c
g++  -c -o bar.o bar.c
$ make
make: Nothing to be done for `all'.
```

First, there's a clean build (with no .o files present) and then a rerun of make to see that there's nothing to do.

But setting DEBUG to 1 on the make command line now causes foo.o to rebuild:

```
$ make DEBUG=1
g++  -c -DDEBUG=1 -o foo.o foo.c
```

This happens because its *signature* (the actual commands to be run to build foo.o) has changed.

Of course, bar.o was not rebuilt because it was truly up-to-date (its object code was new and there were no command changes). Run make DEBUG=1 again, and it'll say there's nothing to be done:

```
$ make DEBUG=1
make: Nothing to be done for `all'.
$ make
g++  -c -DDEBUG= -o foo.o foo.c
```

But just typing make (going back to a non-debug build) rebuilds foo.o again because DEBUG is now undefined.

The signature system also works for variables within recursive variables. In GNU make, COMPILE.C actually expands CPPFLAGS to create the complete compiler command line. Here's what happens if CPPFLAGS is modified on the GNU make command line by adding a definition:

```
$ make CPPFLAGS+=-DFOO=foo
g++ -DFOO=foo -c -DDEBUG= -o foo.o foo.c
g++ -DFOO=foo -c -o bar.o bar.c
```

Both foo.o and bar.o were rebuilt because CPPFLAGS changed (and because CPPFLAGS was part of the commands used to build those two object files).

Of course, changing a variable that isn't referenced doesn't update anything. For example:

```
$ make
g++  -c -DDEBUG= -o foo.o foo.c
g++  -c -o bar.o bar.c
$ make SOMEVAR=42
make: Nothing to be done for `all'.
```

Here we're starting from a clean build and redefining SOMEVAR.

How Signature Works

To understand how signature works, first look inside a .sig file. The .sig files are automatically generated by rules in the signature makefile for each rule that uses the $(call do,...) form.

For example, here are the contents of the foo.o.sig file after the first clean build was run:

```
$(eval @ := foo.o)
$(eval % := )
$(eval < := foo.c)
$(eval ? := foo.o.force)
$(eval ^ := foo.c foo.o.force)
$(eval + := foo.c foo.o.force)
$(eval * := foo)

foo.o: foo.o.force

$(if $(call sne,$(COMPILE.C) -DDEBUG=$(DEBUG) -o $@ $<,\
g++  -c -DDEBUG= -o foo.o foo.c),$(shell touch foo.o.force))
```

The first seven lines capture the state of the automatic variables as defined when the foo.o rule is being processed. We need the values of these variables so we can compare the current commands for a rule (which likely use automatic variables) with the commands the last time the rule was run.

Next comes the line foo.o: foo.o.force. This states that foo.o must be rebuilt if foo.o.force is newer. It's this line that causes foo.o to get rebuilt when the commands change, and it's the next line that touches foo.o.force if the commands have changed.

The long $(if) statement uses the GMSL sne (string not equal) function to compare the current commands for foo.o (by expanding them) against their value the last time they were expanded. If the commands have changed, $(shell touch foo.o.force) is called.

Because the .sig files are processed when the makefile is being parsed (they are just makefiles, read using include), all the .force files will have been updated before any rules run. And so this small .sig file does all the work of forcing an object file to rebuild when commands change.

The .sig files are created by signature:

```
include gmsl

last_target :=

dump_var = \$$(eval $1 := $($1))

define new_rule
@echo "$(call map,dump_var,@ % < ? ^ + *)" > $S
@$(if $(wildcard $F),,touch $F)
@echo $@: $F >> $S
endef
```

```
define do
$(eval S := $@.sig)$(eval F := $@.force)$(eval C := $(strip $1))
$(if $(call sne,$@,$(last_target)),$(call new_rule),$(eval last_target := $@))
@echo "S(subst ",\",$(subst $$,\$$,$$(if $$(call sne,$(strip $1),$C),$C,$$(shell touch $F)))))" >> $S
$C
endef
```

signature includes the GMSL and then defines the important do variable used to wrap the commands in a rule. When do is called, it creates the appropriate .sig file containing the state of all the automatic variables.

The new_rule function called by do captures the automatic variables. It uses the GMSL map function to call another function (dump_var) for each of @ % < ? ^ + *. The new_rule function also ensures that the corresponding .force file has been created.

In addition, do writes out the complex $(if) statement that contains the unexpanded and expanded versions of the commands for the current rule. Then it actually runs the commands (that's the $C) at the end.

Limitations

The signature system has some limitations that could trap the unwary. First, if the commands in a rule contain any side effects—for example, if they call $(shell)—the system may misbehave if there was an assumption that the side effect happens only once.

Second, it's vital that signature is included before any of the .sig files.

Third, if the makefile is edited and the commands in a rule change, the signature system will not notice. If that happens, it's vital to regenerate the corresponding target so the .sig is updated.

Try adding the following line at the end of the definition of new_rule:

```
@echo $F: Makefile >> $S
```

You can make the signature system automatically rebuild when the makefile changes by having the makefile as a prerequisite to each of the makefile's targets. This line is the simplest way to achieve that.

Rebuilding When a File's Checksum Changes

Besides having GNU make rebuild targets when commands change, another common technique is to rebuild when the contents of a file change, not just the file's timestamp.

This usually comes up because the timestamps on generated code, or in code extracted from a source code control system, are older than related objects, so GNU make does not know to rebuild the object. This can happen even when the contents of the file are different from the last time the object was built.

A common scenario is that an engineer working on a build on their local machine rebuilds all objects and later gets the latest version of source files from source code control. Some older source control systems set the timestamp on the source files to the timestamp of the file when it was checked in to source control; in that case, newly built object files may have timestamps that are newer than the (potentially changed) source code.

In this section you'll learn a simple hack to get GNU make to do the right thing (rebuild) when the contents of a source file change.

An Example Makefile

The simple makefile in Listing 3-2 builds object file foo.o from foo.c and foo.h using the built-in rule to make a .o file from a .c:

```
.PHONY: all
all: foo.o

foo.o: foo.c foo.h
```

Listing 3-2: A simple makefile that builds foo.o from foo.c and foo.h

If either foo.c or foo.h are newer than foo.o, then foo.o will be rebuilt.

If foo.h were to change without updating its timestamp, GNU make would do nothing. For example, if foo.h were updated from source code control, this makefile might do the wrong thing.

To work around this problem, we need a way to force GNU make to consider the contents of the file, not its timestamp. Because GNU make can handle timestamps internally only, we need to hack the makefile so that file timestamps are related to file contents.

Digesting File Contents

An easy way to detect a change in a file is to use a message digest function, such as MD5, to generate a digest of the file. Because any change in the file will cause the digest to change, just examining the digest will be enough to detect a change in the file's contents.

To force GNU make to check the contents of each file, we'll associate a file with the extension .md5 with every source code file to be tested. Each .md5 file will contain the MD5 checksum of the corresponding source code file.

In Listing 3-2, source code files foo.c and foo.h will have associated .md5 files foo.c.md5 and foo.h.md5. To generate the MD5 checksum, we use the md5sum utility; it outputs a hexadecimal string containing the MD5 checksum of its input file.

If we arrange for the *timestamp* of the .md5 file to change when the *checksum* of the related file changes, GNU make can check the timestamp of the .md5 file in lieu of the actual source file.

In our example, GNU make would check the timestamp of foo.c.md5 and foo.h.md5 to determine whether foo.o needs to be rebuilt.

The Modified Makefile

Here's the completed makefile that checks the MD5 checksum of source files so that objects are rebuilt when the contents of those files (and hence their checksums) change:

```
to-md5 = $1 $(addsuffix .md5,$1)

.PHONY: all
all: foo.o

foo.o: $(call to-md5,foo.c foo.h)

%.md5: FORCE
→ @$(if $(filter-out $(shell cat $@ 2>/dev/null),$(shell md5sum $*)),md5sum $* > $@)

FORCE:
```

Notice first that the prerequisite list for foo.o has changed from foo.c foo.h to $(call to-md5,foo.c foo.h). The to-md5 function defined in the makefile adds the suffix .md5 to all the filenames in its argument.

So after expansion, the line reads:

```
foo.o: foo.c foo.h foo.c.md5 foo.h.md5.
```

This tells GNU make to rebuild foo.o if either of the .md5 files is newer, as well as if either foo.c or foo.h is newer.

To ensure that the .md5 files always contain the correct timestamp, they are always rebuilt. Each .md5 file is remade by the %.md5: FORCE rule. The use of the empty rule FORCE: means that the .md5 files are examined every time. Use of FORCE here is a little like using .PHONY: if there's no file called FORCE, GNU make will build it (there's no recipe so nothing happens) and then GNU make will consider FORCE to be newer than the %.md5 file and rebuild it. Because we can't do .PHONY: %.md5, we use this FORCE trick instead.

The commands for the %.md5: FORCE rule will only actually rebuild the .md5 file if it doesn't exist or if the checksum stored in the .md5 file is different from the corresponding file's checksum, which works as follows:

1. $(shell md5sum $*) checksums the file that matches the % part of %.md5. For example, when this rule is being used to generate the foo.h.md5 file, then % matches foo.h and foo.h is stored in $*.

2. $(shell cat $@ 2>/dev/null) gets the contents of the current .md5 file (or a blank if it doesn't exist; note how the 2>/dev/null means that errors are ignored). Then, the $(filter-out) compares the checksum retrieved from the .md5 file and the checksum generated by md5sum. If they are the same, the $(filter-out) is an empty string.

3. If the checksum has changed, the rule will actually run `md5sum $* > $@`, which will update the .md5 file's contents and timestamp. The stored checksum will be available for later use when running GNU make again, and the changed timestamp on the .md5 file will cause the related object file to be built.

The Hack in Action

To see how the hack updates an object file when one of its prerequisites changes checksum, let's create files foo.c and foo.h and run GNU make:

```
$ touch foo.c foo.h
$ ls
foo.c foo.h makefile
$ make
cc  -c -o foo.o foo.c
$ ls
foo.c foo.c.md5 foo.h foo.h.md5 foo.o makefile
```

GNU make generates the object file foo.o and two .md5 files, foo.c.md5 and foo.h.md5. Each .md5 file contains the checksum of the file:

```
$ cat foo.c.md5
d41d8cd98f00b204e9800998ecf8427e foo.c
```

First, we verify that everything is up-to-date and then verify that changing the timestamp on either foo.c or foo.h causes foo.o to be rebuilt:

```
$ make
make: Nothing to be done for `all'.
$ touch foo.c
$ make
cc  -c -o foo.o foo.c
$ make
make: Nothing to be done for `all'.
$ touch foo.h
$ make
cc  -c -o foo.o foo.c
```

To demonstrate that changing the contents of a source file will cause foo.o to be rebuilt, we can cheat by changing the contents of, say, foo.h and then touch foo.o to make foo.o newer than foo.h, which would normally mean that foo.o would not be built.

As a result, we know that foo.o is newer than foo.h but that foo.h's contents have changed since the last time foo.o was built:

```
$ make
make: Nothing to be done for `all'.
$ cat foo.h.md5
d41d8cd98f00b204e9800998ecf8427e foo.h
$ cat >> foo.h
```

```
// Add a comment
$ touch foo.o
$ make
cc  -c -o foo.o foo.c
$ cat foo.h.md5
65f8deea3518fcb38fd2371287729332 foo.h
```

You can see that foo.o was rebuilt, even though it was newer than all the related source files, and that foo.h.md5 has been updated with the new checksum of foo.h.

Improving the Code

We can make a couple of improvements to the code: the first is an optimization. When the checksum of a file has changed the rule to update, the .md5 file actually ends up running md5sum twice on the same file with the same result. That's a waste of time. If you are using GNU make 3.80 or later, it's possible to store the output of md5sum $* in a temporary variable called CHECKSUM and just use the variable:

```
%.md5: FORCE
→ @$(eval CHECKSUM := $(shell md5sum $*))$(if $(filter-out \
$(shell cat $@ 2>/dev/null),$(CHECKSUM)),echo $(CHECKSUM) > $@)
```

The second improvement is to make the checksum insensitive to changes in whitespace in a source file. After all, it would be a pity if two developers' differing opinions on the right amount of indentation caused object files to rebuild when nothing else had changed.

The md5sum utility does not have a way of ignoring whitespace, but it's easy enough to pass the source file through tr to strip whitespace before handing it to md5sum for checksumming. (However, note that removing all whitespace might not be a good idea, at least not for most languages.)

Automatic Dependency Generation

Any project larger than a simple example faces a dependency management problem. Dependencies must be generated and kept up to date as engineers modify the project. GNU make provides no tools for dealing with this. All GNU make provides is a mechanism for expressing the relationships between files with its familiar *target : prerequisite1 prerequisite2* ... syntax.

GNU make's dependency syntax is flawed because it is more than just a list of prerequisites: the first prerequisite has a special meaning. Anything to the right of the : is a prerequisite, but the first prerequisite where there's a recipe (that is, commands) is special: it's the prerequisite that is assigned to the automatic variable $< and is also frequently the prerequisite passed to the compiler (or other command) to generate the target.

The $< variable is also special in another way. Sometimes a target will have a recipe and other rules specifying prerequisites. For example, it's not uncommon to see something like this:

```
foo.o: foo.c
4 @compile -o $@ $<

foo.o: myheader.h string.h
```

The value of $< is set from the rule that has a recipe (it will be foo.c in this case).

Take a look at this:

```
foo.o: foo.c header.h system.h
→ @echo Compiling $@ from $<...
```

which outputs

```
$ make
Compiling foo.o from foo.c...
```

Here foo.o is built if foo.c, header.h, or system.h change, but the rule also states that foo.o is made from foo.c. Say our example were written like this:

```
foo.o: foo.c
foo.o: header.h system.h
→ @echo Compiling $@ from $<...
```

The output would be:

```
$ make
Compiling foo.o from header.h...
```

This is clearly wrong.

An Example Makefile

The biggest problem is generating all the rules expressing all the dependencies for a large project. The rest of this section uses the following contrived example makefile as a starting point:

```
.PHONY: all
all: foo.o bar.o baz.o

foo.o: foo.c foo.h common.h header.h
bar.o: bar.c bar.h common.h header.h ba.h
baz.o: baz.c baz.h common.h header.h ba.h
```

Three object files (foo.o, bar.o, and baz.o) are built from corresponding .c files (foo.c, bar.c, and baz.c). Each .o file has dependencies on various different header files, as shown in the last three lines of the makefile. The makefile uses GNU make's built-in rules to perform compilation using the system's compiler.

There's no mention here of the final executable being built. The reason is that this example focuses on dealing with dependencies between sources and objects; relationships between objects are usually easier to maintain by hand because there are fewer of them and the relationships are part of the product design.

makedepend and make depend

Because maintaining any real makefile by hand is impossible, many projects use the widely available makedepend program. makedepend reads C and C++ files, looks at the #include statements, opens the files that are included, and builds the dependency lines automatically. A basic way of incorporating makedepend in a project is a special depend target, as shown in Listing 3-3.

```
.PHONY: all
all: foo.o bar.o baz.o

SRCS = foo.c bar.c baz.c

DEPENDS = dependencies.d
.PHONY: depend
depend:
→ @makedepend -f - $(SRCS) > $(DEPENDS)

-include $(DEPENDS)
```

Listing 3-3: Using makedepend in your makefile

Executing make depend with this makefile causes the depend rule to execute, which runs makedepend on the sources (defined in the SRCS variable) and outputs the dependency lines to a file called dependencies.d (defined by the DEPENDS variable).

The makefile adds the dependencies in its final line by including the dependencies.d file. dependencies.d would look like this:

```
# DO NOT DELETE

foo.o: foo.h header.h common.h
bar.o: bar.h header.h common.h ba.h
baz.o: baz.h header.h common.h ba.h
```

Notice that makedepend doesn't try to define the relationship between an object file (like foo.o) and the source file it is made from (foo.c). In this case GNU make's standard rules will find the related .c file automatically.

Automating makedepend and Removing make depend

Two problems exist with the make depend style. Running make depend can be slow, because every source file must be searched, even if there are no changes. Also, it's a manual step: before every make the user will have to do make depend to ensure that the dependencies are correct. The solution to these problems is automation.

Listing 3-4 shows another version of the makefile from Listing 3-3:

```
.PHONY: all
all: foo.o bar.o baz.o

SRCS = foo.c bar.c baz.c

%.d : %.c
→ @makedepend -f - $< | sed 's,\($*\.o\)[ :]*,\1 $@ : ,g' > $@

-include $(SRCS:.c=.d)
```

Listing 3-4: Automatically running makedepend when needed

This version still uses makedepend to generate dependencies but automates the process and only runs makedepend for sources that have changed. It works by associating a .d file with each .c. For example, foo.o (built from foo.c) has a foo.d file that just contains the dependency line for foo.o.

Here are the contents of foo.d:

```
# DO NOT DELETE

foo.o foo.d : foo.h header.h common.h
```

Notice one addition: this line specifies when to rebuild foo.o, but also that foo.d should be rebuilt under the same conditions. If any of the sources associated with foo.o change, foo.d is rebuilt. foo.c isn't mentioned in this list because it's mentioned as part of the pattern rule for rebuilding a .d file (the %.d : %.c rule in the main makefile means that foo.d will be rebuilt if foo.c changes). foo.d was added to the dependency line created by makedepend using the sed magic shown in Listing 3-4.

The final line of the main makefile includes all the .d files: the $(SRCS:.c=.d) transforms the list of sources in the SRCS variable by changing the extension from .c to .d. The include also tells GNU make to check whether the .d files need rebuilding.

GNU make will check if there are rules to rebuild included makefiles (in this case the .d files), rebuild them if necessary (following the dependencies specified in the makefile), and then restart. This makefile remaking feature (*http://www.gnu.org/software/make/manual/html_node/Remaking-Makefiles.html*) means that simply typing make will do the right thing: it'll rebuild any dependency files that need rebuilding but only if the sources have changed. Then GNU make will perform the build, taking the new dependencies into account.

Making Deleted Files Disappear from Dependencies

Unfortunately, our makefile breaks with a fatal error if a source file is removed. If header.h is no longer needed, all references to it are removed from the .c files, the file is removed from disk, and running make produces the following error:

```
$ make
No rule to make target `header.h', needed by `foo.d'.
```

This happens because header.h is still mentioned in foo.d as a prerequisite of foo.d; hence, foo.d cannot be rebuilt. You can fix this by making the generation of foo.d smarter:

```
# DO NOT DELETE

foo.d : $(wildcard foo.h header.h common.h)
foo.o : foo.h header.h common.h
```

The new foo.d includes the dependencies for foo.o and foo.d separately. foo.d's dependencies are wrapped in a call to GNU make's $(wildcard) function.

And here's the updated makefile with a new invocation of makedepend followed by a sed line that creates the modified .d file:

```
.PHONY: all
all: foo.o bar.o baz.o

SRCS = foo.c bar.c baz.c

%.d : %.c
→ @makedepend -f - $< | sed 's,\($*\.o\)[ :]*\(.*\),$@ : $$\(wildcard \2\)\n\1 : \2,g' > $@

-include $(SRCS:.c=.d)
```

Removing a header file now doesn't break the make: when foo.d is parsed, the dependency line for foo.d is passed through $(wildcard). When there are no globbing symbols like * or ? in the filename, $(wildcard) acts as a simple existence filter, removing from the list any files that do not exist. So if header.h had been removed, the first line of foo.d would be equivalent to this:

```
foo.d : foo.h common.h
```

The make would work correctly. This example makefile now works when .c files are added (the user just updates SRCS and the new .d file is created automatically), when .c files are removed (the user updates SRCS and the old .d file is ignored), when headers are added (because that requires altering an existing .c or .h, the .d file will be regenerated), and when headers are removed (the $(wildcard) hides the deletion and the .d file is regenerated).

A possible optimization is to remove the need for GNU make to restart by merging the rule that makes the .d file into the rule that makes the .o:

```
.PHONY: all
all: foo.o bar.o baz.o

SRCS = foo.c bar.c baz.c

%.o : %.c
→ @makedepend -f - $< | sed 's,\($*\.o\)[ :]*\(.*\),$@ : $$\(wildcard \2\)\n\1 : \2,g' > $*.d
→ @$(COMPILE.c) -o $@ $<

-include $(SRCS:.c=.d)
```

Because the .d file is updated if and only if the .o file needs to be updated (both are updated when any of the sources for the .o change), it's possible to have the makedepend happen at the same time as the compilation.

This rule uses $*, another GNU make variable. $* is the part of the pattern %.c that matches the %. If this rule is building foo.o from foo.c, $* is just foo. $* creates the name of the .d file that makedepend writes to.

This version does not use GNU make's makefile remaking system. There are no rules for making .d files (they are made as a side effect of making the .o files), so GNU make doesn't have to restart. This provides the best combination of accuracy and speed.

In general, it's a bad idea to have a rule that makes multiple files because it's impossible for GNU make to find the rule that makes a file if it's created as a side effect of something else. In this case, that behavior is desired: we want to hide the creation of .d files from GNU make so it doesn't try to make them and then have to restart.

Tom Tromey proposed a similar idea without the $(wildcard) trick. You can find this and more information about building dependency files on GNU make maintainer Paul Smith's website at *http://make.mad-scientist.net/ papers/advanced-auto-dependency-generation/*.

Doing Away with makedepend

Additionally, it's possible to omit makedepend altogether if you are using GNU gcc, llvm, or clang, or a similar compiler.

An -MD option does the work of makedepend at the same time as the compilation:

```
.PHONY: all
all: foo.o bar.o baz.o

SRCS = foo.c bar.c baz.c

%.o : %.c
→ @$(COMPILE.c) -MD -o $@ $<
→ @sed -i 's,\($*\.o\)[ :]*\(.*\),$@ : $$\(wildcard \2\)\n\1 : \2,g' $*.d

-include $(SRCS:.c=.d)
```

For example, the compilation step for foo.o will create foo.d from foo.c. Then, sed is run on the foo.d to add the extra line for foo.d containing the $(wildcard).

Using gcc -MP

gcc also has the -MP option, which attempts to deal with the problem of disappearing files by creating empty rules to "build" missing files. For example, it's possible to eliminate the sed magic completely, using the -MP option in place of -MD:

```
.PHONY: all
all: foo.o bar.o baz.o

SRCS = foo.c bar.c baz.c

%.o : %.c
→ @$(COMPILE.c) -MP -o $@ $<

-include $(SRCS:.c=.d)
```

The foo.d file will look like this:

```
foo.o : foo.h header.h common.h
foo.h :
header.h :
common.h :
```

If, for example, foo.h is deleted, make will not complain because it will find the empty rule (foo.h :) to build it, and the missing file error will be prevented. However, it is vital that the foo.d file be updated every time foo.o is built. If it's not, foo.d will still contain foo.h as a prerequisite, and foo.o will rebuild every time make is run because make will attempt to build foo.h (forcing a foo.o build) using the empty rule.

Atomic Rules in GNU make

A fundamental law of GNU make physics is that each rule builds one and only one file (called a *target*). There are exceptions to that rule (which we'll see in the rest of this section), but nevertheless, for any normal GNU make rule such as

```
a: b c
→ @command
```

there's only one file mentioned to the left of the :. That's the filename that gets put into the $@ automatic variable. It's expected that command will actually update that file.

This section explains what to do if a command updates more than one file and how to express that so GNU make knows that more than one file was updated and behaves correctly.

What Not to Do

Imagine a command that makes two files (a and b) from the same prerequisites in a single step. In this section, such a command is simulated with touch a b, but in reality it could be much more complex than that.

Listing 3-5 shows what not to do:

```
.PHONY: all
all: a b

a b: c d
→ touch a b
```

Listing 3-5: What not to do

At first glance Listing 3-5 looks correct; it seems to say that a and b are built from c and d by a single command. If you run this in make, you can get output like this (especially if you use the -j option to run a parallel build):

```
$ make
touch a b
touch a b
```

The command was run twice. In this case that's harmless, but for a real command that does real work, running twice is almost certainly the wrong thing to do. Also, if you use the -j option to run in parallel, you can end up with the command running more than once and simultaneously with itself.

The reason is that GNU make actually interprets the makefile as:

```
.PHONY: all
all: a b

a: c d
→ touch a b

b: c d
→ touch a b
```

There are two separate rules (one declares that it builds a; the other says it builds b) that both build a and b.

Using Pattern Rules

GNU make does have a way to build more than one target in a single rule using a pattern rule. Pattern rules can have an arbitrary number of target patterns and still be treated as a single rule.

For example:

```
%.foo %.bar %.baz:
→ command
```

This means that files with the extensions .foo, .bar, and .baz (and of course the same prefix that will match against the %) will be built with a single invocation of command.

Suppose that the makefile looked like this:

```
.PHONY: all
all: a.foo a.bar a.baz

%.foo %.bar %.baz:
→ command
```

Then, command would be invoked just once. In fact, it's enough to specify that just one of the targets and the pattern rule will run:

```
.PHONY: all
all: a.foo

%.foo %.bar %.baz:
→ command
```

This can be very useful. For example:

```
$(OUT)/%.lib $(OUT)/%.dll: $(VERSION_RESOURCE)
→ link /nologo /dll /fixed:no /incremental:no    \
   /map:'$(call to_dos,$(basename $@).map)'      \
   /out:'$(call to_dos,$(basename $@).dll)'      \
   /implib:'$(call to_dos,$(basename $@).lib)'   \
        $(LOADLIBES) $(LDLIBS)                    \
   /pdb:'$(basename $@).pdb'                      \
   /machine:x86                                   \
   $^
```

This is an actual rule from a real makefile that builds a .lib and its associated .dll in one go.

Of course, if the files don't have a common part in their names, using a pattern rule won't work. It doesn't work for the simple example at the beginning of this section, but there is an alternative.

Using a Sentinel File

A possible workaround to using a pattern rule is to introduce a single file to indicate whether any of the targets of a multi-target rule have been built.

Creating a single "indicator" file turns multiple files into a single file, and GNU make understands single files. Here's Listing 3-5, rewritten:

```
.PHONY: all
all: a b

a b: .sentinel
→ @:

.sentinel: c d
→ touch a b
→ touch .sentinel
```

The rule to build a and b can be run only once because only one prerequisite is specified (.sentinel). If c or d are newer, .sentinel gets rebuilt (and hence a and b are rebuilt). If the makefile asks for either a or b, they are rebuilt via the .sentinel file.

The funny @: command in the a b rule just means that there are commands to build a and b but they do nothing.

It would be nice to make this transparent. That's where the atomic function comes in. The atomic function sets up the sentinel file automatically, based on the names of the targets to be built, and creates the necessary rules:

```
sp :=
sp +=
sentinel = .sentinel.$(subst $(sp),_,$(subst /,_,$1))
atomic = $(eval $1: $(call sentinel,$1) ; @:)$(call sentinel,$1): $2 ; touch $$@

.PHONY: all
all: a b

$(call atomic,a b,c d)
→ touch a b
```

All we've done is replace the original a b : c d rule with a call to atomic. The first argument is the list of targets that need to be built atomically; the second argument is the list of prerequisites.

atomic uses the sentinel function to create a unique sentinel filename (in the case of targets a b the sentinel filename is .sentinel.a_b) and then sets up the necessary rules.

Expanding atomic in this makefile would be the same as doing this:

```
.PHONY: all
all: a b

a b: .sentinel.a_b ; @:

.sentinel.a_b: c d ; touch $@
→ touch a b
```

There's one flaw with this technique. If you delete a or b, you must also delete the related sentinel file or the files won't get rebuilt.

To work around this, you can have the makefile delete the sentinel file if necessary by checking to see if any of the targets being built are missing. Here's the updated code:

```
sp :=
sp +=
sentinel = .sentinel.$(subst $(sp),_,$(subst /,_,$1))
atomic = $(eval $1: $(call sentinel,$1) ; @:)$(call sentinel,$1): \
$2 ; touch $$@ $(foreach t,$1,$(if $(wildcard $t),,$(shell rm -f \
$(call sentinel,$1))))

.PHONY: all
all: a b

$(call atomic,a b,c d)
→ touch a b
```

Now atomic runs through the targets. If any are missing—detected by the $(wildcard)—the sentinel file is deleted.

Painless Non-recursive make

Once a makefile project reaches a certain size (usually when it has dependencies on subprojects), it's inevitable that the build master writes a rule that contains a call to $(MAKE). And right there the build master has created a recursive make: a make that executes an entire other make process. It's incredibly tempting to do this because conceptually, recursive make is simple: if you need to build a subproject, just go to its directory and run make via $(MAKE).

But it has one major flaw: once you start a separate make process, all information about dependencies is lost. The parent make doesn't know whether the subproject make really needed to happen, so it has to run it every time, and that can be slow. Fixing that problem isn't easy, but non-recursive makes are powerful once implemented.

One common objection to using non-recursive make is that with recursive make it's possible to go to anywhere in a source code tree and type make. Doing so typically builds the objects that are defined by the makefile at that level in the tree (and possibly below that, if the makefile recurses).

Non-recursive make systems (based on include statements instead of make invocations) often do not offer this flexibility, and GNU make must be run from the top-level directory. Even though non-recursive GNU make is typically more efficient (running from the top-level directory should be quick), it's important to be able to give developers the same level of functionality as a recursive make system.

This section outlines a pattern for a non-recursive GNU make system that supports the familiar make-anywhere style common to recursive GNU make systems. Typing make in a directory will build everything in that directory and below, but there are no recursive $(MAKE) invocations. The single make that runs knows about all the dependencies across projects and subprojects, and it can build efficiently.

A Simple Recursive Make

Imagine a project with the following subdirectories:

```
/src/
/src/library/
/src/executable/
```

/src/ is the top-level directory and is where you'd type make to get a full build. Inside /src/ is a library/ directory that builds a library called lib.a from source files lib1.c and lib2.c:

```
/src/library/lib1.c
/src/library/lib2.c
```

The /src/executable/ directory builds an executable file called exec from two source files (foo.c and bar.c) and links with the library lib.a:

```
/src/executable/foo.c
/src/executable/bar.c
```

The classic recursive make solution is to put a makefile in each subdirectory. Each makefile contains rules to build that directory's objects, and a top-level makefile recurses into each subdirectory. Here are the contents of such a recursive makefile (/src/makefile):

```
SUBDIRS = library executable

.PHONY: all
all:
→ for dir in $(SUBDIRS); do \
→ $(MAKE) -C $$dir;         \
→ done
```

This enters each directory in turn and runs make to build first the library and then the executable. The dependency between the executable and the library (that is, the fact that the library needs to be built before the executable) is implicit in the order in which the directories are specified in SUBDIRS.

Here's an example of an improvement on using a for loop using phony targets for each directory:

```
SUBDIRS = library executable

.PHONY: $(SUBDIRS)
$(SUBDIRS):
→ $(MAKE) -C $@

.PHONY: all
all: $(SUBDIRS)

executable: library
```

You unwind the loop inside the rule for all, create separate rules for each subdirectory, and explicitly specify the dependency between executable and library. This code is much clearer, but it's still recursive with separate make invocations for each subdirectory.

A Flexible Non-recursive make System

When moving to non-recursive make, the ideal top-level makefile would look like Listing 3-6.

```
SUBDIRS = library executable

include $(addsuffix /makefile,$(SUBDIRS))
```

Listing 3-6: A small non-recursive makefile

This simply says to include the makefile from each subdirectory. The trick is to make that work! Before you see how, here are the skeletons of the contents of the makefiles in the library and executable subdirectories:

```
# /src/library/Makefile

include root.mak
include top.mak

SRCS := lib1.c lib2.c
BINARY := lib
BINARY_EXT := $(_LIBEXT)
include bottom.mak
```

and

```
# /src/executable/Makefile

include root.mak
include top.mak
```

```
SRCS := foo.c foo.c
BINARY := exec
BINARY_EXT := $(_EXEEXT)

include bottom.mak
```

Each of those makefiles specifies the source files to be built (in the SRCS variable), the name of the final linked binary (in the BINARY variable), and the type of the binary (using the BINARY_EXT variable, which is set from special variables _LIBEXT and _EXEEXT).

Both the makefiles include the common makefiles root.mak, top.mak, and bottom.mak, which are located in the /src/ directory.

Because the .mak included makefiles are not in the subdirectories, GNU make needs to go looking for them. To find the .mak files in /src, do this:

```
$ make -I /src
```

Here, you use the -I command line option that adds a directory to the include search path.

It's unfortunate to ask a user to add anything to the make command line. To avoid that, you can create a simple method of automatically walking up the source tree to find the .mak files. Here's the actual makefile for /src/ library:

```
sp :=
sp +=
_walk = $(if $1,$(wildcard /$(subst $(sp),/,$1)/$2) $(call _walk,$(wordlist 2,$(words $1),x $1),$2))
_find = $(firstword $(call _walk,$(strip $(subst /, ,$1)),$2))
_ROOT := $(patsubst %/root.mak,%,$(call _find,$(CURDIR),root.mak))

include $(_ROOT)/root.mak
include $(_ROOT)/top.mak

SRCS := lib1.c lib2.c
BINARY := lib
BINARY_EXT := $(_LIBEXT)

include $(_ROOT)/bottom.mak
```

The _find function walks up a directory tree starting from the directory in $1, looking for the file named $2. The actual find is achieved by calling the _walk function, which walks up the tree, finding every instance of the file $2 in each of the successively shorter paths from $1.

The block of code at the start of the makefile finds the location of root.mak, which is in the same directory as top.mak and bottom.mak (namely, /src), and saves that directory in _ROOT.

Then, the makefile can use $(_ROOT)/ to include the root.mak, top.mak, and bottom.mak makefiles without any need to type anything other than make.

Here are the contents of the first included makefile (root.mak):

```
_push = $(eval _save$1 := $(MAKEFILE_LIST))
_pop = $(eval MAKEFILE_LIST := $(_save$1))
_INCLUDE = $(call _push,$1)$(eval include $(_ROOT)/$1/Makefile)$(call _pop,$1)
DEPENDS_ON = $(call _INCLUDE,$1)
DEPENDS_ON_NO_BUILD = $(eval _NO_RULES := T)$(call _INCLUDE,$1)$(eval _NO_RULES :=)
```

For the moment, ignore its contents and return to what these functions are used for when looking at dependencies between modules. The real work begins with top.mak:

```
_OUTTOP ?= /tmp/out

.PHONY: all
all:

_MAKEFILES := $(filter %/Makefile,$(MAKEFILE_LIST))
_INCLUDED_FROM := $(patsubst $(_ROOT)/%,%,$(if $(_MAKEFILES), \
$(patsubst %/Makefile,%,$(word $(words $(_MAKEFILES)),$(_MAKEFILES)))))
ifeq ($(_INCLUDED_FROM),)
_MODULE := $(patsubst $(_ROOT)/%,%,$(CURDIR))
else
_MODULE := $(_INCLUDED_FROM)
endif
_MODULE_PATH := $(_ROOT)/$(_MODULE)
_MODULE_NAME := $(subst /,_,$(_MODULE))
$(_MODULE_NAME)_OUTPUT := $(_OUTTOP)/$(_MODULE)

_OBJEXT := .o
_LIBEXT := .a
_EXEEXT :=
```

The _OUTTOP variable defines the top-level directory into which all binary output (object files and so on) will be placed. Here it has the default value of /tmp/out, and it's defined with ?= so it can be overridden on the command line.

Next, top.mak sets up the default target for GNU make as the classic all. Here it has no dependencies, but they are added later for each module that will be built.

Thereafter, a number of variables end up setting the _MODULE_PATH to the full path to the module directory being built. For example, when building the library module, _MODULE_PATH would be /src/library. Setting this variable is complex because determining the module directory has to be independent of the directory from which GNU make was executed (so that the library can be built from the top-level, for a make all, or from the individual library directory, for an individual developer build, or the library can even be included as a dependency on a different module).

The _MODULE_NAME is simply the path relative to the root of the tree with / replaced by _. In Listing 3-5, the two modules have _MODULE_NAMEs: library and executable. But if library had a subdirectory containing a module called sublibrary, then its _MODULE_NAME would be library_sublibrary.

The _MODULE_NAME is also used to create the $(_MODULE_NAME)_OUTPUT special variable, which has a computed name based on _MODULE_NAME. So for the library module, the variable library_OUTPUT is created with the full path of the directory into which library's object files should be written. The output path is based on _OUTTOP and the relative path to the module being built. As a result, the /tmp/out tree mirrors the source tree.

Finally, some standard definitions of extensions used on filenames are set up. Definitions for Linux systems are used here, but these can easily be changed for systems such as Windows that don't use .o for an object file or .a for a library.

bottom.mak uses these variables to set up the rules that will actually build the module:

```
$(_MODULE_NAME)_OBJS := $(addsuffix $(_OBJEXT),$(addprefix \
$($(_MODULE_NAME)_OUTPUT)/,$(basename $(SRCS)))) $(DEPS)
$(_MODULE_NAME)_BINARY := $($(_MODULE_NAME)_OUTPUT)/$(BINARY)$(BINARY_EXT)

ifneq ($(_NO_RULES),T)
ifneq ($($(_MODULE_NAME)_DEFINED),T)
all: $($(_MODULE_NAME)_BINARY)

.PHONY: $(_MODULE_NAME)
$(_MODULE_NAME): $($(_MODULE_NAME)_BINARY)
_IGNORE := $(shell mkdir -p $($(_MODULE_NAME)_OUTPUT))

_CLEAN := clean-$(_MODULE_NAME)
.PHONY: clean $(_CLEAN)
clean: $(_CLEAN)
$(_CLEAN):
→ rm -rf $($(patsubst clean-%,%,$@)_OUTPUT)

$($(_MODULE_NAME)_OUTPUT)/%.o: $(_MODULE_PATH)/%.c
→ @$(COMPILE.c) -o '$@' '$<'
$($(_MODULE_NAME)_OUTPUT)/$(BINARY).a: $($(_MODULE_NAME)_OBJS)
→ @$(AR) r '$@' $^
→ @ranlib '$@'
$($(_MODULE_NAME)_OUTPUT)/$(BINARY)$(_EXEEXT): $($(_MODULE_NAME)_OBJS)
→ @$(LINK.cpp) $^ -o'$@'

$(_MODULE_NAME)_DEFINED := T
endif
endif
```

The first thing bottom.mak does is set up two variables with computed names: $(_MODULE_NAME)_OBJS (which is the list of object files in the module computed from the SRCS variable by transforming the extension) and $(_MODULE_NAME)_BINARY (which is the name of the binary file created by the module; this would typically be the library or executable being built).

We include the DEPS variable, so the $(_MODULE_NAME)_OBJS variable also includes any object files that the module needs but doesn't build. Later you'll see how this is used to define a dependency between the library and executable.

Next, if rules for this module have not previously been set up (controlled by the $(_MODULE_NAME)_DEFINED variable) and have not been explicitly disabled by the _NO_RULES variable, the actual rules to build the module are defined.

In this example, rules for Linux are shown. This is where you'd change this example for another operating system.

all has the current binary, from $(_MODULE_NAME)_BINARY, added as a prerequisite so that the module gets built when a full build is done. Then there's a rule that associates the module name with the module binary so that it's possible to type something like make library at the top level of the build to build just the library.

Then there's a general clean rule and a module-specific clean (for the library module there's a rule called clean-library to just clean its objects). clean is implemented as a simple rm -rf because all the output is organized in a specific subdirectory of _OUTTOP.

After that a $(shell) is used to set up the directory where the module's output will go. Finally, specific rules associate the object files in this module's output directory with source files in this module's source directory.

With all that infrastructure in place, we can finally come to the makefile in the executable directory:

```
sp :=
sp +=
_walk = $(if $1,$(wildcard /$(subst $(sp),/,$1)/$2) $(call _walk,$(wordlist 2,$(words $1),x $1),$2))
_find = $(firstword $(call _walk,$(strip $(subst /, ,$1)),$2))
_ROOT := $(patsubst %/root.mak,%,$(call _find,$(CURDIR),root.mak))

include $(_ROOT)/root.mak

$(call DEPENDS_ON,library)

include $(_ROOT)/top.mak

SRCS := foo.c bar.c
BINARY := exec
BINARY_EXT := $(_EXEEXT)
DEPS := $(library_BINARY)

include $(_ROOT)/bottom.mak
```

This looks a lot like the makefile for the library, but there are differences. Because the executable needs the library, the DEPS line specifies that the executable depends on the binary file created by the library. And because each module has unique variables for objects and binaries, it's easy to define that dependency by referring to $(library_BINARY), which will expand to the full path to the library file created by the library module.

To ensure that $(library\_BINARY)$ is defined, it's necessary to include the makefile from the library directory. The root.mak file provides two functions that make this trivial: DEPENDS_ON and DEPENDS_ON_NO_BUILD.

DEPENDS_ON_NO_BUILD just sets up the variables for the specified module so they can be used in the makefile. If that function were used in the executable makefile, the library (lib.a) would have to exist for the executable to build successfully. On the other hand, DEPENDS_ON is used here to ensure that the library will get built if necessary.

DEPENDS_ON_NO_BUILD provides functionality similar to a classic recursive build, which doesn't know how to build that library but depends on it. DEPENDS_ON is more flexible because without recursion, you can specify a relationship and make sure that code is built.

Using the Non-recursive make System

The non-recursive make system provides great flexibility. Here are a few examples that illustrate that the non-recursive make system is just as flexible as a recursive one (and more so!).

Building everything from the top level is a simple make (in these examples, we use the command make -n so the commands are clearly shown):

```
$ cd /src
$ make -n
cc  -c -o '/tmp/out/library/lib1.o' '/home/jgc/doc/nonrecursive/library/lib1.c'
cc  -c -o '/tmp/out/library/lib2.o' '/home/jgc/doc/nonrecursive/library/lib2.c'
ar r '/tmp/out/library/lib.a' /tmp/out/library/lib1.o /tmp/out/library/lib2.o
ranlib '/tmp/out/library/lib.a'
cc  -c -o '/tmp/out/executable/foo.o' '/home/jgc/doc/nonrecursive/executable/foo.c'
cc  -c -o '/tmp/out/executable/bar.o' '/home/jgc/doc/nonrecursive/executable/bar.c'
g++  /tmp/out/executable/foo.o /tmp/out/executable/bar.o /tmp/out/library/lib.a -o'/tmp/out/
executable/exec'
```

Cleaning everything is simple too:

```
$ cd /src
$ make -n clean
rm -rf /tmp/out/library
rm -rf /tmp/out/executable
```

From the top-level directory, it's possible to ask for any individual module to be built or cleaned:

```
$ cd /src
$ make -n clean-library
rm -rf /tmp/out/library
$ make -n library
cc  -c -o '/tmp/out/library/lib1.o' '/home/jgc/doc/nonrecursive/library/lib1.c'
cc  -c -o '/tmp/out/library/lib2.o' '/home/jgc/doc/nonrecursive/library/lib2.c'
ar r '/tmp/out/library/lib.a' /tmp/out/library/lib1.o /tmp/out/library/lib2.o
ranlib '/tmp/out/library/lib.a'
```

And if we ask that the executable module be built, the library gets built at the same time because of the dependency:

```
$ cd /src
$ make -n executable
cc  -c -o '/tmp/out/executable/foo.o' '/home/jgc/doc/nonrecursive/executable/foo.c'
cc  -c -o '/tmp/out/executable/bar.o' '/home/jgc/doc/nonrecursive/executable/bar.c'
cc  -c -o '/tmp/out/library/lib1.o' '/home/jgc/doc/nonrecursive/library/lib1.c'
cc  -c -o '/tmp/out/library/lib2.o' '/home/jgc/doc/nonrecursive/library/lib2.c'
ar r '/tmp/out/library/lib.a' /tmp/out/library/lib1.o /tmp/out/library/lib2.o
ranlib '/tmp/out/library/lib.a'
g++  /tmp/out/executable/foo.o /tmp/out/executable/bar.o /tmp/out/library/lib.a -o'/tmp/out/
executable/exec'
```

Okay, so much for the top level. If we pop down into the library module, we can build or clean it just as easily:

```
$ cd /src/library
$ make -n clean
rm -rf /tmp/out/library
$ make -n
cc  -c -o '/tmp/out/library/lib1.o' '/home/jgc/doc/nonrecursive/library/lib1.c'
cc  -c -o '/tmp/out/library/lib2.o' '/home/jgc/doc/nonrecursive/library/lib2.c'
ar r '/tmp/out/library/lib.a' /tmp/out/library/lib1.o /tmp/out/library/lib2.o
ranlib '/tmp/out/library/lib.a'
```

Of course, doing this in the executable directory will build the library as well:

```
$ cd /src/executable
$ make -n
cc  -c -o '/tmp/out/library/lib1.o' '/home/jgc/doc/nonrecursive/library/lib1.c'
cc  -c -o '/tmp/out/library/lib2.o' '/home/jgc/doc/nonrecursive/library/lib2.c'
ar r '/tmp/out/library/lib.a' /tmp/out/library/lib1.o /tmp/out/library/lib2.o
ranlib '/tmp/out/library/lib.a'
cc  -c -o '/tmp/out/executable/foo.o' '/home/jgc/doc/nonrecursive/executable/foo.c'
cc  -c -o '/tmp/out/executable/bar.o' '/home/jgc/doc/nonrecursive/executable/bar.c'
g++  /tmp/out/executable/foo.o /tmp/out/executable/bar.o /tmp/out/library/lib.a -o'/tmp/out/
executable/exec'
```

What About Submodules?

Suppose that the source tree was actually

```
/src/
/src/library/
/src/library/sublibrary
/src/executable/
```

where there's an additional sublibrary under the `library` that builds `slib.a` from `slib1.c` and `slib2.c` using the following makefile:

```
sp :=
sp +=
_walk = $(if $1,$(wildcard /$(subst $(sp),/,$1)/$2) $(call _walk,$(wordlist 2,$(words $1),x $1),$2))
_find = $(firstword $(call _walk,$(strip $(subst /, ,$1)),$2))
_ROOT := $(patsubst %/root.mak,%,$(call _find,$(CURDIR),root.mak))

include $(_ROOT)/root.mak
include $(_ROOT)/top.mak

SRCS := slib1.c slib2.c
BINARY := slib
BINARY_EXT := $(_LIBEXT)

include $(_ROOT)/bottom.mak
```

To specify that `library` has a dependency of `sublibrary` is as simple as adding a `DEPENDS_ON` call to the makefile in the `library` directory:

```
sp :=
sp +=
_walk = $(if $1,$(wildcard /$(subst $(sp),/,$1)/$2) $(call _walk,$(wordlist 2,$(words $1),x $1),$2))
_find = $(firstword $(call _walk,$(strip $(subst /, ,$1)),$2))
_ROOT := $(patsubst %/root.mak,%,$(call _find,$(CURDIR),root.mak))

include $(_ROOT)/root.mak

$(call DEPENDS_ON,library/sublibrary)

include $(_ROOT)/top.mak

SRCS := lib1.c lib2.c
BINARY := lib
BINARY_EXT := $(_LIBEXT)

include $(_ROOT)/bottom.mak
```

In this example, there's no `DEPS` line, so the `library` doesn't depend on `sublibrary` at the object level. We're simply declaring `sublibrary` as a submodule of `library` that needs to be built if `library` is.

Going back and repeating the previous examples, we see that the `sublibrary` has been successfully included in the `library` build (and automatically in the executable build).

Here's the full build from the top, followed by a clean:

```
$ cd /src
$ make -n
cc  -c -o '/tmp/out/library/sublibrary/slib1.o' '/home/jgc/doc/nonrecursive/library/sublibrary/
slib1.c'
```

```
cc  -c -o '/tmp/out/library/sublibrary/slib2.o' '/home/jgc/doc/nonrecursive/library/sublibrary/
slib2.c'
ar r '/tmp/out/library/sublibrary/slib.a' /tmp/out/library/sublibrary/slib1.o /tmp/out/library/
sublibrary/slib2.o
ranlib '/tmp/out/library/sublibrary/slib.a'
cc  -c -o '/tmp/out/library/lib1.o' '/home/jgc/doc/nonrecursive/library/lib1.c'
cc  -c -o '/tmp/out/library/lib2.o' '/home/jgc/doc/nonrecursive/library/lib2.c'
ar r '/tmp/out/library/lib.a' /tmp/out/library/lib1.o /tmp/out/library/lib2.o
ranlib '/tmp/out/library/lib.a'
cc  -c -o '/tmp/out/executable/foo.o' '/home/jgc/doc/nonrecursive/executable/foo.c'
cc  -c -o '/tmp/out/executable/bar.o' '/home/jgc/doc/nonrecursive/executable/bar.c'
g++   /tmp/out/executable/foo.o /tmp/out/executable/bar.o /tmp/out/library/lib.a -o'/tmp/out/
executable/exec'
$ make -n clean
rm -rf /tmp/out/library/sublibrary
rm -rf /tmp/out/library
rm -rf /tmp/out/executable
```

Here, we ask for the sublibrary to be built:

```
$ cd /src
$ make -n clean-library_sublibrary
rm -rf /tmp/out/library/sublibrary
$ make -n library_sublibrary
cc  -c -o '/tmp/out/library/sublibrary/slib1.o' '/home/jgc/doc/nonrecursive/library/sublibrary/
slib1.c'
cc  -c -o '/tmp/out/library/sublibrary/slib2.o' '/home/jgc/doc/nonrecursive/library/sublibrary/
slib2.c'
ar r '/tmp/out/library/sublibrary/slib.a' /tmp/out/library/sublibrary/slib1.o /tmp/out/library/
sublibrary/slib2.o
ranlib '/tmp/out/library/sublibrary/slib.a'
```

And if we ask that the executable module be built, the library gets built
at the same time (and also the sublibrary) because of the dependency:

```
$ cd /src/executable
$ make -n executable
cc  -c -o '/tmp/out/library/sublibrary/slib1.o' '/home/jgc/doc/nonrecursive/library/sublibrary/
slib1.c'
cc  -c -o '/tmp/out/library/sublibrary/slib2.o' '/home/jgc/doc/nonrecursive/library/sublibrary/
slib2.c'
ar r '/tmp/out/library/sublibrary/slib.a' /tmp/out/library/sublibrary/slib1.o /tmp/out/library/
sublibrary/slib2.o
ranlib '/tmp/out/library/sublibrary/slib.a'
cc  -c -o '/tmp/out/library/lib1.o' '/home/jgc/doc/nonrecursive/library/lib1.c'
cc  -c -o '/tmp/out/library/lib2.o' '/home/jgc/doc/nonrecursive/library/lib2.c'
ar r '/tmp/out/library/lib.a' /tmp/out/library/lib1.o /tmp/out/library/lib2.o
ranlib '/tmp/out/library/lib.a'
cc  -c -o '/tmp/out/executable/foo.o' '/home/jgc/doc/nonrecursive/executable/foo.c'
cc  -c -o '/tmp/out/executable/bar.o' '/home/jgc/doc/nonrecursive/executable/bar.c'
g++   /tmp/out/executable/foo.o /tmp/out/executable/bar.o /tmp/out/library/lib.a -o'/tmp/out/
executable/exec'
```

Although not as simple to code as a recursive make, this non-recursive system is very flexible. It allows dependencies between individual binary files across modules, which is not possible with recursive make, and it allows this without losing the "go to any directory and type make" notion that engineers know.

GNU make is incredibly powerful (which is partly why it's still around after so many years), but when projects become large, makefiles can get unwieldy. With what you learned in this chapter, you can now simplify makefiles to work around GNU make's weaknesses so that large projects are made simpler and more reliable.

4

PITFALLS AND PROBLEMS

In this chapter, you'll learn how to deal with problems faced by makefile maintainers as projects get considerably larger. Tasks that seem easy with small makefiles become more difficult with large, sometimes recursive, make processes. As makefiles become more complex, it's easy to run into problems with edge cases or sometimes poorly understood behavior of GNU make.

Here you'll see a complete solution to the "recursive make problem," how to overcome GNU make's problems handling filenames that contain spaces, how to deal with cross-platform file paths, and more.

GNU make Gotcha: ifndef and ?=

It's easy to get tripped up by the two ways of checking whether a variable is defined, ifndef and ?=, because they do similar things, yet one has a deceptive name. ifndef doesn't really test whether a variable is defined; it only checks that the variable is not empty, whereas ?= does make its decision based on whether the variable is defined or not.

Compare these two ways of conditionally setting the variable FOO in a makefile:

```
ifndef FOO
FOO=New Value
endif
```

and

```
FOO ?= New Value
```

They look like they should do the same thing, and they do, well, almost.

What ?= Does

The ?= operator in GNU make sets the variable mentioned on its left side to the value on the right side if the left side is not defined. For example:

```
FOO ?= New Value
```

This makefile sets FOO to New Value.
But the following one does not:

```
FOO=Old Value
FOO ?= New Value
```

Neither does this one (even though FOO was initially empty):

```
FOO=
FOO ?= New Value
```

In fact, ?= is the same as the following makefile, which uses the GNU make $(origin) function to determine whether a variable is undefined:

```
ifeq ($(origin FOO),undefined)
FOO = New Value
endif
```

$(origin FOO) will return a string that shows whether and how FOO is defined. If FOO is undefined, then $(origin FOO) is the string undefined.

Note that variables defined with ?= are expanded, just like variables defined with the = operator. They are expanded when used but not when defined, just like a normal GNU make variable.

What ifndef Does

As mentioned earlier, ifndef tests whether a variable is empty but does not check to see whether the variable is defined. ifndef means *if the variable is undefined or is defined but is empty.* Thus, this:

```
ifndef FOO
FOO=New Value
endif
```

will set FOO to the New Value if FOO is undefined or FOO is empty. So ifndef can be rewritten as such:

```
ifeq ($(FOO),)
FOO=New Value
endif
```

because an undefined variable is always treated as having an empty value when read.

$(shell) and := Go Together

The suggestion in this section often speeds up makefiles with just the addition of a suitably placed colon. To understand how a single colon can make such a difference, you need to understand GNU make's $(shell) function and the difference between = and :=.

$(shell) Explained

$(shell) is GNU make's equivalent of the backtick (`) operator in the shell. It executes a command, flattens the result (turns all whitespace, including new lines, into spaces), and returns the resulting string.

For example, if you want to get the output of the date command into a variable called NOW, you write:

```
NOW = $(shell date)
```

If you want to count the number of files in the current directory and get that number into FILE_COUNT, do this:

```
FILE_COUNT = $(shell ls | wc -l )
```

Because $(shell) flattens output to get the names of all the files in the current directory into a variable, the following works:

```
FILES = $(shell ls)
```

The newline between files is replaced with a single space, making FILES a space-separated list of filenames.

It's common to see an execution of the pwd command to get the current working directory into a variable (in this case CWD):

```
CWD = $(shell pwd)
```

We'll look at the pwd command later when considering how to optimize an example makefile that wastes time getting the working directory over and over again.

The Difference Between = and :=

Ninety-nine percent of the time, you'll see variable definitions in makefiles that use the = form, like this:

```
FOO = foo
BAR = bar
FOOBAR = $(FOO) $(BAR)

all: $(FOOBAR)
❶ $(FOOBAR):
→ @echo $@ $(FOOBAR)

FOO = fooey
BAR = barney
```

Here, variables FOO, BAR, and FOOBAR are *recursively expanded* variables. That means that when the value of a variable is needed, any variables that it references are expanded at that point. For example, if the value of $(FOOBAR) is needed, GNU make gets the value of $(FOO) and $(BAR), puts them together with the space in between, and returns foo bar. Expansion through as many levels of variables as necessary is done when the variable is used.

In this makefile FOOBAR has two different values. Running it prints out:

```
$ make
foo fooey barney
bar fooey barney
```

The value of FOOBAR is used to define the list of prerequisites to the all rule and is expanded as foo bar; the same thing happens for the next rule ❶, which defines rules for foo and bar.

But when the rules are *run*, the value of FOOBAR as used in the echo produces fooey barney. (You can verify that the value of FOOBAR was foo bar when the rules were defined by looking at the value of $@, the target being built, when the rules are run).

Keep in mind the following two cases:

- When a rule is being defined in a makefile, variables will evaluate to their value *at that point* in the makefile.
- Variables used in recipes (that is, in the commands) have the final value: whatever value the variable had at the end of the makefile.

If the definition of FOOBAR is changed to use a := instead of =, running the makefile produces a very different result:

```
$ make
foo foo bar
bar foo bar
```

Now FOOBAR has the same value everywhere. This is because := forces the right side of the definition to be expanded at that moment during makefile parsing. Rather than storing $(FOO) $(BAR) as the definition of FOOBAR, GNU make stores the expansion of $(FOO) $(BAR), which at that point is foo bar. The fact that FOO and BAR are redefined later in the makefile is irrelevant; FOOBAR has already been expanded and set to a fixed string. GNU make refers to variables defined in this way as *simply expanded.*

Once a variable has become simply expanded, it remains that way unless it is redefined using the = operator. This means that when text is appended to a simply expanded variable, it is expanded before being added to the variable.

For example, this:

```
FOO=foo
BAR=bar
BAZ=baz
FOOBAR := $(FOO) $(BAR)
FOOBAR += $(BAZ)
BAZ=bazzy
```

results in FOOBAR being foo bar baz. If = had been used instead of :=, when $(BAZ) was appended, it would not have been expanded and the resulting FOOBAR would have been foo baz bazzy.

The Hidden Cost of =

Take a look at this example makefile:

```
CWD = $(shell pwd)
SRC_DIR=$(CWD)/src/
OBJ_DIR=$(CWD)/obj/
OBJS = $(OBJ_DIR)foo.o $(OBJ_DIR)bar.o $(OBJ_DIR)baz.o

$(OBJ_DIR)%.o: $(SRC_DIR)%.c ; @echo Make $@ from $<

all: $(OBJS)
→ @echo $? $(OBJS)
```

It gets the current working directory into CWD, defines a source and object directory as subdirectories of the CWD, defines a set of objects (foo.o, bar.o, and baz.o) to be built in the OBJ_DIR, sets up a pattern rule showing how to build a .o from a .c, and finally states that by default the makefile should build all the objects and print out a list of those that were out of date ($? is the list of prerequisites of a rule that were out of date) as well as a full list of objects.

You might be surprised to learn that this makefile ends up making eight shell invocations just to get the CWD value. Imagine how many times GNU make would make costly calls to the shell in a real makefile with hundreds or thousands of objects!

So many calls to $(shell) are made because the makefile uses recursively expanded variables: variables whose value is determined when the variable is used but not at definition time. OBJS references OBJ_DIR three times, which references CWD each time; every time OBJS is referenced, three calls are made to $(shell pwd). Any other reference to SRC_DIR or OBJ_DIR (for example, the pattern rule definition) results in another $(shell pwd).

But a quick fix for this is just to change the definition of CWD to simply expand by inserting a : to turn = into :=. Because the working directory doesn't change during the make, we can safely get it once:

```
CWD := $(shell pwd)
```

Now, a single call out to the shell is made to get the working directory. In a real makefile this could be a huge time-saver.

Because it can be difficult to follow through a makefile to see everywhere a variable is used, you can use a simple trick that will cause make to print out the exact line at which a variable is expanded. Insert $(warning Call to shell) in the definition of CWD so that its definition becomes this:

```
CWD = $(warning Call to shell)$(shell pwd)
```

Then you get the following output when you run make:

```
$ make
makefile:8: Call to shell
makefile:8: Call to shell
makefile:10: Call to shell
makefile:10: Call to shell
makefile:10: Call to shell
Make /somedir/obj/foo.o from /somedir/src/foo.c
Make /somedir/obj/bar.o from /somedir/src/bar.c
Make /somedir/obj/baz.o from /somedir/src/baz.c
makefile:11: Call to shell
makefile:11: Call to shell
makefile:11: Call to shell
/somedir/obj/foo.o /somedir/obj/bar.o /somedir/obj/baz.o /somedir/obj/foo.o
/somedir/obj/bar.o /somedir/obj/baz.o
```

The $(warning) doesn't change the value of CWD, but it does output a message to STDERR. From the output you can see the eight calls to the shell and which lines in the makefile caused them.

If CWD is defined using :=, the $(warning) trick verifies that CWD is expanded only once:

```
$ make
makefile:1: Call to shell
Make /somedir/obj/foo.o from /somedir/src/foo.c
Make /somedir/obj/bar.o from /somedir/src/bar.c
Make /somedir/obj/baz.o from /somedir/src/baz.c
/somedir/obj/foo.o /somedir/obj/bar.o /somedir/obj/baz.o /somedir/obj/foo.o
/somedir/obj/bar.o /somedir/obj/baz.o
```

A quick way to determine if a makefile uses the expensive combination of = and $(shell) is to run the command:

```
grep -n \$\(shell makefile | grep -v :=
```

This prints out the line number and details of every line in the makefile that contains a $(shell) and doesn't contain a :=.

$(eval) and Variable Caching

In the previous section, you learned how to use := to speed up makefiles by not repeatedly performing a $(shell). Unfortunately, it can be problematic to rework makefiles to use := because they may rely on being able to define variables in any order.

In this section, you'll learn how to use GNU make's $(eval) function to get the benefits of recursively expanded variables using = while getting the sort of speedup that's possible with :=.

About $(eval)

$(eval)'s argument is expanded and then parsed as if it were typed in as part of a makefile. As a result, within a $(eval) (which could be inside a variable definition) you can programmatically define variables, create rules (explicit or pattern), include other makefiles, and so on. It's a powerful function.

Here's an example:

```
set = $(eval $1 := $2)

$(call set,FOO,BAR)
$(call set,A,B)
```

This results in FOO having the value BAR and A having the value B. Obviously, this example could have been achieved without $(eval), but it's easy to see how you can use $(eval) to make programmatic changes to the definitions in a makefile.

An $(eval) Side Effect

One use of $(eval) is to create side effects. For example, here's a variable that is actually an auto-incrementing counter (it uses the arithmetic functions from the GMSL):

```
include gmsl

c-value := 0
counter = $(c-value)$(eval c-value := $(call plus,$(c-value),1))
```

Every time counter is used, its value is incremented by one. For example, the following sequence of $(info) functions outputs numbers in sequence starting from 0:

```
$(info Starts at $(counter))
$(info Then it's $(counter))
$(info And then it's $(counter))
```

Here's the output:

```
$ make
Starts at 0
Then it's 1
And then it's 2
```

You could use a simple side effect like this to find out how often a particular variable is reevaluated by GNU make. You might be surprised at the result. For example, when building GNU make, the variable srcdir from its makefile is accessed 48 times; OBJEXT is accessed 189 times, and that's in a very small project.

GNU make wastes time accessing an unchanging variable by looking at the same string repeatedly. If the variable being accessed is long (such as a long path) or contains calls to $(shell) or complex GNU make functions, the performance of variable handling could affect the overall runtime of a make.

That's especially important if you are trying to minimize build time by parallelizing the make or if a developer is running an incremental build requiring just a few files to be rebuilt. In both cases a long startup time by GNU make could be very inefficient.

Caching Variable Values

GNU make does provide a solution to the problem of reevaluating a variable over and over again: use := instead of =. A variable defined using := gets its value set once and for all, the right side is evaluated once, and the resulting value is set in the variable. Using := can cause a makefile to be parsed more quickly because the right side is evaluated only once. But it does introduce limitations, so it is rarely used. One limitation is that it requires variable definitions to be ordered a certain way. For example, if ordered this way:

```
FOO := $(BAR)
BAR := bar
```

the result in FOO would have a totally different value than if it was ordered this way:

```
BAR := bar
FOO := $(BAR)
```

In the first snippet FOO is empty, and in the second FOO is bar. Contrast that with the simplicity of the following:

```
FOO = $(BAR)
BAR = bar
```

Here, FOO is bar. Most makefiles are written in this style, and only very conscientious (and speed conscious) makefile authors use :=.

On the other hand, almost all of these recursively defined variables only ever have one value when used. The long evaluation time for a complex recursively defined variable is a convenience for the makefile author.

An ideal solution would be to cache variable values so the flexibility of the = style is preserved, but the variables are only evaluated once for speed. Clearly, this would cause a minor loss of flexibility, because a variable can't take two different values (which is sometimes handy in a makefile). But for most uses, it would provide a significant speed boost.

Speed Improvements with Caching

Consider the example makefile in Listing 4-1:

```
C := 1234567890 ABCDEFGHIJKLMNOPQRSTUVWXYZ
C += $C
C += $C
C += $C
C += $C
C += $C
C += $C
C += $C
C += $C
C += $C
C += $C
C += $C

FOO = $(subst 9,NINE,$C)$(subst 8,EIGHT,$C)$(subst 7,SEVEN,$C) \
$(subst 6,SIX,$C)$(subst 5,FIVE,$C)$(subst 4,FOUR,$C)        \
$(subst 3,THREE,$C)$(subst 2,TWO,$C)$(subst 1,ONE,$C)
_DUMMY := $(FOO)
```

```
--snip--

.PHONY: all
all:
```

Listing 4-1: In this makefile, FOO and C are uselessly evaluated over and over again.

It defines a variable C, which is a long string (it's actually 1234567890 repeated 2,048 times followed by the alphabet repeated 2,048 times plus spaces for a total of 77,824 characters). Here := is used so that C is created quickly. C is designed to emulate the sort of long strings that are generated within makefiles (for example, long lists of source files with paths).

Then a variable FOO is defined that manipulates C using the built-in $(subst) function. FOO emulates the sort of manipulation that occurs within makefiles (such as changing filename extensions from .c to .o).

Finally, $(FOO) is evaluated 200 times to emulate the use of FOO in a small but realistically sized makefile. The makefile does nothing; there's a dummy, empty all rule at the end.

On my laptop, using GNU make 3.81, this makefile takes about 3.1 seconds to run. That's a long time spent repeatedly manipulating C and FOO but not doing any actual building.

Using the counter trick from "An $(eval) Side Effect" on page 116, you can figure out how many times FOO and C are evaluated in this makefile. FOO was evaluated 200 times and C 1600 times. It's amazing how fast these evaluations can add up.

But the values of C and FOO need to be calculated only once, because they don't change. Let's say you alter the definition of FOO to use :=:

```
FOO := $(subst 9,NINE,$C)$(subst 8,EIGHT,$C)$(subst 7,SEVEN,$C) \
$(subst 6,SIX,$C)$(subst 5,FIVE,$C)$(subst 4,FOUR,$C)            \
$(subst 3,THREE,$C)$(subst 2,TWO,$C)$(subst 1,ONE,$C)
```

This drops the runtime to 1.8 seconds, C is evaluated nine times, and FOO is evaluated just once. But, of course, that requires using := with all its problems.

A Caching Function

An alternative caching function is this simple caching scheme:

```
cache = $(if $(cached-$1),,$(eval cached-$1 := 1)$(eval cache-$1 := $($1)))$(cache-$1)
```

First, a function called cache is defined, which automatically caches a variable's value the first time it is evaluated and retrieves it from the cache for each subsequent attempt to retrieve it.

cache uses two variables to store the cached value of a variable (when caching variable A, the cached value is stored in cache-A) and whether the variable has been cached (when caching variable A, the *has been cached flag* is cached-A).

First, it checks to see whether the variable has been cached; if it has, the $(if) does nothing. If it hasn't, the cached flag is set for that variable in the first $(eval) and then the value of the variable is expanded (notice the $($1), which gets the name of the variable and then gets its value) and cached. Finally, cache returns the value from cache.

To update the makefile, simply turn any reference to a variable into a call to the cache function. For example, you can modify the makefile from Listing 4-1 by changing all occurrences of $(FOO) to $(call cache,FOO) using a simple find and replace. The result is shown in Listing 4-2.

```
C := 1234567890 ABCDEFGHIJKLMNOPQRSTUVWXYZ
C += $C
C += $C
C += $C
C += $C
C += $C
C += $C
C += $C
C += $C
C += $C
C += $C
C += $C

FOO = $(subst 9,NINE,$C)$(subst 8,EIGHT,$C)$(subst 7,SEVEN,$C) \
$(subst 6,SIX,$C)$(subst 5,FIVE,$C)$(subst 4,FOUR,$C)          \
$(subst 3,THREE,$C)$(subst 2,TWO,$C)$(subst 1,ONE,$C)

_DUMMY := $(call cache,FOO)
--snip--

.PHONY: all
all:
```

Listing 4-2: A modified version of Listing 4-1 that uses the cache function

Running this on my machine shows that there's now one access of FOO, the same nine accesses of C, and a runtime of 2.4 seconds. It's not as fast as the := version (which took 1.8 seconds), but it's still 24 percent faster. On a big makefile, this technique could make a real difference.

Wrapping Up

The fastest way to handle variables is to use := whenever you can, but it requires care and attention, and is probably best done only in a new makefile (just imagine trying to go back and reengineer an existing makefile to use :=).

If you're stuck with =, the cache function presented here can give you a speed boost that developers doing incremental short builds will especially appreciate.

If it's only necessary to change a single variable definition, it's possible to eliminate the cache function. For example, here's the definition of FOO changed to magically switch from being recursively defined to a simple definition:

```
FOO = $(eval FOO := $(subst 9,NINE,$C)$(subst 8,EIGHT,$C)$(subst 7,SEVEN,$C) \
$(subst 6,SIX,$C)$(subst 5,FIVE,$C)$(subst 4,FOUR,$C)$(subst 3,THREE,$C)      \
$(subst 2,TWO,$C)$(subst 1,ONE,$C))$(value FOO)
```

The first time $(FOO) is referenced, the $(eval) happens, turning FOO from a recursively defined variable to a simple definition (using :=). The $(value FOO) at the end returns the value stored in FOO, making this process transparent.

The Trouble with Hidden Targets

Take a look at the makefile in Listing 4-3:

```
.PHONY: all
all: foo foo.o foo.c

foo:
→ touch $@ foo.c

%.o: %.c
→ touch $@
```

Listing 4-3: In this makefile, the rule to make foo also makes foo.c.

It contains a nasty trap for the unwary that can cause make to report odd errors, stop the -n option from working, and prevent a speedy parallel make. It can even cause GNU make to do the wrong work and update an up-to-date file.

On the face of it this makefile looks pretty simple. If you run it through GNU make, it'll build foo (which creates the files foo and foo.c) and then use the pattern at the bottom to make foo.o from foo.c. It ends up running the following commands:

```
touch foo foo.c
touch foo.o
```

But there's a fatal flaw. Nowhere does this makefile mention that the rule to make foo actually also makes foo.c. So foo.c is a *hidden target*, a file that was built but that GNU make is unaware of, and hidden targets cause an endless number of problems.

GNU make is very good at keeping track of targets, files that need to be built, and the dependencies between targets. But the make program is only as good as its inputs. If you don't tell make about a relationship between two files, it won't discover it on its own and it'll make mistakes because it assumes it has perfect knowledge about the files and their relationships.

In this example, make only works because it builds the prerequisites of all from left to right. First it encounters foo, which it builds, creating foo.c as a side effect, and then it builds foo.o using the pattern. If you change the order of the prerequisites of all so that it doesn't build foo first, the build will fail.

There are (at least!) five nasty side effects of hidden targets.

An Unexpected Error if the Hidden Target Is Missing

Suppose that foo exists, but foo.c and foo.o are missing:

```
$ rm -f foo.c foo.o
$ touch foo
$ make
No rule to make target `foo.c', needed by `foo.o'.
```

make tries to update foo.o, but because it doesn't know how to make foo.c (because it's not mentioned as the target of any rule), invoking GNU make results in an error.

The -n Option Fails

The helpful -n debugging option in GNU make tells it to print out the commands that it would run to perform the build without actually running them:

```
$ make -n
touch foo foo.c
No rule to make target `foo.c', needed by `foo.o'.
```

You've seen that make would actually perform two touch commands (touch foo foo.c followed by touch foo.o), but doing a make -n (with no foo* files present) results in an error. make doesn't know that the rule for foo makes foo.c, and because it hasn't actually run the touch command, foo.c is missing. Thus, the -n doesn't represent the actual commands that make would run, making it useless for debugging.

You Can't Parallelize make

GNU make provides a handy feature that allows it to run multiple jobs at once. If you have many compiles in a build, specifying the -j option (followed by a number indicating the number of jobs to run at the same time) can maximize CPU utilization and shorten the build.

Unfortunately, a hidden target spoils that plan. Here's the output from make -j3 running three jobs at once on our example makefile from Listing 4-3:

```
$ make -j3
touch foo foo.c
```

```
No rule to make target `foo.c', needed by `foo.o'.
Waiting for unfinished jobs....
```

GNU make tried to build foo, foo.o, and foo.c at the same time, and discovered that it didn't know how to build foo.c because it had no way of knowing that it should wait for foo to be made.

make Does the Wrong Work if the Hidden Target Is Updated

Suppose the file foo.c already exists when make is run. Because make doesn't know that the rule for foo will mess with foo.c, it'll get updated even though it's up-to-date. In Listing 4-2, foo.c is altered by a benign touch operation that only alters the file's timestamp, but a different operation could destroy or overwrite the contents of the file:

```
$ touch foo.c
$ rm -f foo foo.o
$ make
touch foo foo.c
touch foo.o
```

make rebuilds foo because it's missing and updates foo.c at the same time, even though it was apparently up-to-date.

You Can't Direct make to Build foo.o

You'd hope that typing make foo.o would result in GNU make building foo.o from foo.c and, if necessary, building foo.c. But make doesn't know how to build foo.c. That just happens by accident when building foo:

```
$ rm -f foo.c
$ make foo.o
No rule to make target `foo.c', needed by `foo.o'.
```

So if foo.c is missing, make foo.o results in an error.

Hopefully, you're now convinced that hidden targets are a bad idea and can lead to all sorts of build problems.

GNU make's Escaping Rules

Sometimes you'll need to insert a special character in a makefile. Perhaps you need a newline inside an $(error) message, a space character in a $(subst), or a comma as the argument to a GNU make function. Those three simple tasks can be frustratingly difficult to do in GNU make; this section takes you through simple syntax that eliminates the frustration.

GNU make's use of the tab character at the start of any line containing commands is a notorious language feature, but some other special characters can also trip you up. The ways GNU make handles $, %, ?, *, [, ~, \, and # are all special.

Dealing with $

Every GNU make user is familiar with $ for starting a variable reference. It's possible to write $(variable) (with parentheses) or ${variable} (with curly brackets) to get the value of variable, and if the variable name is a single character (such as a), you can drop the parentheses and just use $a.

To get a literal $, you write $$. So to define a variable containing a single $ symbol you'd write: dollar := $$.

Playing with %

Escaping % is not as simple as $, but it needs to be done in only three situations, and the same rules apply for each: in the vpath directive, in a $(patsubst), and in a pattern or static-pattern rule.

The three rules for % escaping are:

- You can escape % with a single \ character (that is, \% becomes a literal %).

- If you need to put a literal \ in front of a % (that is, you want the \ to not escape the %), escape it with \ (in other words, \\% becomes a literal \ followed by a % character that *will* be used for the pattern match).

- Don't worry about escaping \ anywhere else in a pattern. It will be treated as a literal. For example, \hello is \hello.

Wildcards and Paths

The symbols ?, *, [, and] get treated specially when they appear in a file-name. A makefile that has

```
*.c:
→ @command
```

will actually search for all .c files in the current directory and define a rule for each. The targets (along with prerequisites and files mentioned in the include directive) are globbed (the filesystem is searched and file-names matched against the wildcard characters) if they contain a wild-card character. The globbing characters have the same meaning as in the Bourne shell.

The ~ character is also handled specially in filenames and is expanded to the home directory of the current user.

All of those special filename characters can be escaped with a \. For example:

```
\*.c:
→ @command
```

This makefile defines a rule for the file named (literally) *.c.

Continuations

Other than the escaping function, you can also use the \ as a continuation character at the end of a line:

```
all:        \
prerequisite \
something else
→ @command
```

Here, the rule for all has three prerequisites: prerequisite, something, and else.

Comments

You can use the # character to start a comment, and you can make it a literal with a \ escape:

```
pound := \#
```

Here, $(pound) is a single character: #.

I Just Want a Newline!

GNU make does its best to insulate you from the newline character. You can't escape a newline—there's no syntax for special characters (for example, you can't write \n), and even the $(shell) function strips newlines from the returned value.

But you can define a variable that contains a newline using the define syntax:

```
define newline


endef
```

Note that this definition contains two blank lines, but using $(newline) will expand into only one newline, which can be useful for formatting error messages nicely:

```
$(error This is an error message$(newline)with two lines)
```

Because of GNU make's rather liberal variable naming rules, it's possible to define a variable called \n. So if you like to maintain a familiar look, you can do this:

```
define \n


endef

$(error This is an error message $(\n)with two lines)
```

We'll look more at special variable names in the next section.

Function Arguments: Spaces and Commas

A problem that many GNU make users run into is the handling of spaces and commas in GNU make function arguments. Consider the following use of $(subst):

```
spaces-to-commas = $(subst  ,,,$1)
```

This takes three arguments separated by commas: the from text, the to text, and the string to change.

It defines a function called spaces-to-commas to convert all spaces in its argument to commas (which might be handy for making a CSV file for example). Unfortunately, it doesn't work for two reasons:

- The first argument of the $(subst) is a space. GNU make strips all leading and trailing whitespace around function arguments. In this case, the first argument is interpreted as an empty string.

- The second argument is a comma. GNU make cannot distinguish between the commas used for argument separators and the comma as an argument. In addition, there's no way to escape the comma.

You can work around both issues if you know that GNU make does the whitespace stripping and separation of arguments before it does any expansion of the arguments. So if we can define a variable containing a space and a variable containing a comma, we can write the following to get the desired effect:

```
spaces-to-commas = $(subst $(space),$(comma),$1)
```

Defining a variable containing a comma is easy, as shown here:

```
comma := ,
```

But space is a bit harder. You can define a space in a couple of ways. One way is to use the fact that whenever you append to a variable (using +=), a space is inserted before the appended text:

```
space :=
space +=
```

Another way is to first define a variable that contains nothing, and then use it to surround the space so that it doesn't get stripped by GNU make:

```
blank :=
space := $(blank) $(blank)
```

You can also use this technique to get a literal tab character into a variable:

```
blank :=
tab := $(blank)→$(blank)
```

Much in the way that $(\n) was defined in the previous section, it's possible to define specially named space and comma variables. GNU make's rules are liberal enough to allow us to do this:

```
, := ,

blank :=
space := $(blank) $(blank)
$(space) := $(space)
```

The first line defines a variable called , (which can be used as $(,) or even $,) containing a comma.

The last three lines define a variable called space containing a space character and then use it to define a variable named (that's right, its name is a space character) containing a space.

With that definition it's possible to write $( ) or even $ (there's a space after that $) to get a space character. Note that doing this might cause problems in the future as make is updated, so playing tricks like this can be dangerous. If you're averse to risks, just use the variable named space and avoid $( ). Because whitespace is special in GNU make, pushing make's parser to the limit with tricks like $( ) might lead to breakages.

Using those definitions, the spaces-to-commas function can be written as:

```
spaces-to-commas = $(subst $( ),$(,),$1)
```

This strange-looking definition replaces spaces with commas using subst. It works because the $( ) will get expanded by subst and will itself be a space. That space will then be the first parameter (the string that will be replaced). The second parameter is $(,), which, when expanded, becomes a ,. The result is that spaces-to-commas turns spaces into commas without confusing GNU make with the actual space and comma characters.

The Twilight Zone

It's possible to take definitions like $( ) and $(\n) and go much further, defining variables with names like =, # or :. Here are other interesting variable definitions:

```
# Define the $= or $(=) variable which has the value =
equals := =
$(equals) := =

# Define the $# or $(#) variable which has the value #
hash := \#
$(hash) := \#
```

```
# Define the $: or $(:) variable which has the value :
colon := :
$(colon) := :

# Define the $($$) variable which has the value $
dollar := $$
$(dollar) := $$
```

These definitions probably aren't useful, but if you want to push GNU make syntax to its limits, try this:

```
+:=+
```

Yes, that defines a variable called + containing a +.

The Trouble with $(wildcard)

The function $(wildcard) is GNU make's globbing function. It's a useful way of getting a list of files inside a makefile, but it can behave in unexpected ways. It doesn't always provide the same answer as running ls. Read on to find out why and what to do about it.

$(wildcard) Explained

You can use $(wildcard) anywhere in a makefile or rule to get a list of files that match one or more *glob* style patterns. For example, $(wildcard *.foo) returns a list of files ending in .foo. Recall that a list is a string where list elements are separated by spaces, so $(wildcard *.foo) might return a.foo b.foo c.foo. (If a filename contains a space, the returned list may appear incorrect because there's no way to spot the difference between the list separator—a space—and the space in a filename.)

You can also call $(wildcard) with a list of patterns, so $(wildcard *.foo *.bar) returns all the files ending in .foo or .bar. The $(wildcard) function supports the following globbing operators: * (match 0 or more characters), ? (match 1 character), and [...] (matches characters, [123], or a range of characters, [a-z]).

Another useful feature of $(wildcard) is that if the filename passed to it does not contain a pattern, that file is simply checked for existence. If the file exists, its name is returned; otherwise, $(wildcard) returns an empty string. Thus, $(wildcard) can be combined with $(if) to create an if-exists function:

```
if-exists = $(if ($wildcard $1),$2,$3)
```

if-exists has three parameters: the name of the filename to check for, what to do if the file exists, and what to do if it does not. Here's a simple example of its use:

```
$(info a.foo is $(call if-exists,a.foo,there,not there))
```

This will print a.foo is there if a.foo exists, or it will print a.foo is not there if not.

Unexpected Results

Each of the following examples uses two variables to obtain a list of files ending in .foo in a particular directory: WILDCARD_LIST and LS_LIST each return the list of files ending in .foo by calling $(wildcard) and $(shell ls), respectively. The variable DIRECTORY holds the directory in which the examples look for files; for the current directory, DIRECTORY is left empty.

The starting makefile looks like this:

```
WILDCARD_LIST = wildcard returned \'$(wildcard $(DIRECTORY)*.foo)\'
LS_LIST = ls returned \'$(shell ls $(DIRECTORY)*.foo)\'

.PHONY: all
all:
→ @echo $(WILDCARD_LIST)
→ @echo $(LS_LIST)
```

With a single file a.foo in the current directory, running GNU make results in this:

```
$ touch a.foo
$ make
wildcard returned 'a.foo'
ls returned 'a.foo'
```

Now extend the makefile so it makes a file called b.foo using touch. The makefile should look like Listing 4-4:

```
WILDCARD_LIST = wildcard returned \'$(wildcard $(DIRECTORY)*.foo)\'
LS_LIST = ls returned \'$(shell ls $(DIRECTORY)*.foo)\'

.PHONY: all
all: b.foo
→ @echo $(WILDCARD_LIST)
→ @echo $(LS_LIST)

b.foo:
→ @touch $@
```

Listing 4-4: When you run this makefile, ls and $(wildcard) return different results.

Running this makefile through GNU make (with just the preexisting a.foo file) results in the following surprising output:

```
$ touch a.foo
$ make
wildcard returned 'a.foo'
ls returned 'a.foo b.foo'
```

The ls returns the correct list (because b.foo has been created by the time the all rule runs), but $(wildcard) does not; $(wildcard) appears to be showing the state before b.foo was created.

Working with the .foo files in a subdirectory (not in the current working directory) results in different output, as shown in Listing 4-5.

```
DIRECTORY=subdir/

.PHONY: all
all: $(DIRECTORY)b.foo
→ @echo $(WILDCARD_LIST)
→ @echo $(LS_LIST)

$(DIRECTORY)b.foo:
→ @touch $@
```

Listing 4-5: This time, ls and $(wildcard) return the same results.

Here, the makefile is updated so that it uses the DIRECTORY variable to specify the subdirectory subdir. There's a single preexisting file subdir/a.foo, and the makefile will create subdir/b.foo.

Running this makefile results in:

```
$ touch subdir/a.foo
$ make
wildcard returned 'subdir/a.foo subdir/b.foo'
ls returned 'subdir/a.foo subdir/b.foo'
```

Here, both $(wildcard) and ls return the same results, and both show the presence of the two .foo files: subdir/a.foo, which existed before make was run, and subdir/b.foo, which was created by the makefile.

Let's look at one final makefile (Listing 4-6) before I explain what's happening:

```
DIRECTORY=subdir/

$(warning Preexisting file: $(WILDCARD_LIST))

.PHONY: all
all: $(DIRECTORY)b.foo
→ @echo $(WILDCARD_LIST)
→ @echo $(LS_LIST)
```

```
$(DIRECTORY)b.foo:
→ @touch $@
```

Listing 4-6: A small change makes ls *and* $(wildcard) *return different results.*

In this makefile, $(warning) is used to print out a list of the .foo files that already exist in the subdirectory.

Here's the output:

```
$ touch subdir/a.foo
$ make
makefile:6: Preexisting file: wildcard returned 'subdir/a.foo'
wildcard returned 'subdir/a.foo'
ls returned 'subdir/a.foo subdir/b.foo'
```

Notice now that GNU make appears to be behaving like it does in Listing 4-4; the subdir/b.foo file that was made by the makefile is invisible to $(wildcard) and doesn't appear, even though it was created and ls found it.

Unexpected Results Explained

We get unexpected, and apparently inconsistent, results because GNU make contains its own cache of directory entries. $(wildcard) reads from that cache (not directly from disk like ls) to get its results. Knowing when that cache is filled is vital to understanding the results the $(wildcard) will return.

GNU make fills the cache only when it is forced to (for example, when it needs to read the directory entries to satisfy a $(wildcard) or other globbing request). If you know that GNU make fills the cache only when needed, then it's possible to explain the results.

In Listing 4-4, GNU make fills the cache for the current working directory when it starts. So the file b.foo doesn't appear in the output of $(wildcard) because it wasn't present when the cache was filled.

In Listing 4-5, GNU make didn't fill the cache with entries from subdir until they were needed. The entries were first needed for the $(wildcard), which is performed after subdir/b.foo is created; hence, subdir/b.foo does appear in the $(wildcard) output.

In Listing 4-6, the $(warning) happens at the start of the makefile and fills the cache (because it did a $(wildcard)); hence, subdir/b.foo was missing from the output of $(wildcard) for the duration of that make.

Predicting when the cache will be filled is very difficult. $(wildcard) will fill the cache, but so will use of a globbing operator like * in the target or prerequisite list of a rule. Listing 4-7 is a makefile that builds two files (subdir/b.foo and subdir/c.foo) and does a couple of $(wildcard)s:

```
DIRECTORY=subdir/

.PHONY: all
all: $(DIRECTORY)b.foo
→ @echo $(WILDCARD_LIST)
→ @echo $(LS_LIST)
```

```
$(DIRECTORY)b.foo: $(DIRECTORY)c.foo
→ @touch $@
→ @echo $(WILDCARD_LIST)
→ @echo $(LS_LIST)

$(DIRECTORY)c.foo:
→ @touch $@
```

Listing 4-7: When GNU make fills, the $(wildcard) cache can be difficult to understand.

The output may surprise you:

```
$ make
wildcard returned 'subdir/a.foo subdir/c.foo'
ls returned 'subdir/a.foo subdir/c.foo'
❶ wildcard returned 'subdir/a.foo subdir/c.foo'
ls returned 'subdir/a.foo subdir/b.foo subdir/c.foo'
```

Even though the first $(wildcard) is being done in the rule that makes subdir/b.foo and after the touch that created subdir/b.foo, there's no mention of subdir/b.foo in the output of $(wildcard) ❶. Nor is there mention of subdir/b.foo in the output of the ls.

The reason is that the complete block of commands is expanded into its final form before any of the lines in the rule are run. So the $(wildcard) and $(shell ls) are done before the touch has run.

The output of $(wildcard) is even more unpredictable if the make is run in parallel with the -j switch. In that case, the exact order in which the rules are run is not predictable, so the output of $(wildcard) can be even less predictable.

Here's what I recommend: don't use $(wildcard) in a rule; use $(wildcard) in the makefile only at parsing time (before any rules start running). If you restrict the use of $(wildcard) to parsing time, you can be assured of consistent results: $(wildcard) will show the state of the filesystem before GNU make was run.

Making Directories

One common problem faced by real-world makefile hackers is the need to build a hierarchy of directories before the build, or at least before commands that use those directories can run. The most common case is that the makefile hacker wants to ensure that the directories where object files will be created exist, and they want that to happen automatically. This section looks at a variety of ways to achieve directory creation in GNU make and points out a common trap for the unwary.

An Example Makefile

The following makefile builds an object file /out/foo.o from foo.c using the GNU make built-in variable COMPILE.C to make a .o file from a .c by running the compiler.

foo.c is in the same directory as the makefile, but foo.o is placed in /out/:

```
.PHONY: all
all: /out/foo.o

/out/foo.o: foo.c
→ @$(COMPILE.C) -o $@ $<
```

This example works fine as long as /out/ exists. But if it does not, you'll get an error from the compiler along the lines of:

```
$ make
Assembler messages:
FATAL: can't create /out/foo.o: No such file or directory
make: *** [/out/foo.o] Error 1
```

Obviously, what you want is for the makefile to automatically create /out/ if it is missing.

What Not to Do

Because GNU make excels at making things that don't exist, it seems obvious to make /out/ a prerequisite of /out/foo.o and have a rule to make the directory. That way if we need to build /out/foo.o, the directory will get created.

Listing 4-8 shows the reworked makefile with the directory as a prerequisite and a rule to build the directory using mkdir.

```
OUT = /out

.PHONY: all
all: $(OUT)/foo.o

$(OUT)/foo.o: foo.c $(OUT)/
→ @$(COMPILE.C) -o $@ $<

$(OUT)/:
→ mkdir -p $@
```

Listing 4-8: This makefile can end up doing unnecessary work.

For simplification, the name of the output directory is stored in a variable called OUT, and the -p option on the mkdir command is used so that it will build all the necessary parent directories. In this case the path is simple: it's just /out/, but -p means that mkdir could make a long chain of directories in one go.

This works well for this basic example, but there's a major problem. Because the timestamp on a directory is typically updated when the directory is updated (for example, when a file is created, deleted, or renamed), this makefile can end up doing too much work.

For example, just creating another file inside /out/ forces a rebuild of /out/foo.o. In a complex example, this could mean that many object files are rebuilt for no good reason, just because other files were rebuilt in the same directory.

Solution 1: Build the Directory When the Makefile Is Parsed

A simple solution to the problem in Listing 4-8 is to just create the directory when the makefile is parsed. A quick call to $(shell) can achieve that:

```
OUT = /out

.PHONY: all
all: $(OUT)/foo.o

$(OUT)/foo.o: foo.c
→ @$(COMPILE.C) -o $@ $<

$(shell mkdir -p $(OUT))
```

Before any targets are created or commands run, the makefile is read and parsed. If you put $(shell mkdir -p $(OUT)) somewhere in the makefile, GNU make will run the mkdir every time the makefile is loaded.

One possible disadvantage is that if many directories need to be created, this process could be slow. And GNU make is doing unnecessary work, because it will attempt to build the directories every time you type make. Some users also don't like this method because it creates all the directories, even if they're not actually used by the rules in the makefile.

A small improvement can be made by first testing to see whether the directory exists:

```
ifeq ($(wildcard $(OUT)/.),)
$(shell mkdir -p $(OUT))
endif
```

Here, $(wildcard) is used with a /. appended to check for the presence of a directory. If the directory is missing, $(wildcard) will return an empty string and the $(shell) will be executed.

Solution 2: Build the Directory When all Is Built

A related solution is to build the directory only when all is being built. This means that the directories won't get created every time the makefile is parsed (which could avoid unnecessary work when you type make clean or make depend):

```
OUT = /out

.PHONY: all
all: make_directories $(OUT)/foo.o

$(OUT)/foo.o: foo.c
→ @$(COMPILE.C) -o $@ $<

.PHONY: make_directories
make_directories: $(OUT)/

$(OUT)/:
→ mkdir -p $@
```

This solution is messy because you must specify make_directories as a prerequisite of any target that the user might specify after make. If you don't, you could run into the situation in which the directories have not been built. You should avoid this technique, especially because it will completely break parallel builds.

Solution 3: Use a Directory Marker File

If you look back at Listing 4-8, you'll notice one rather nice feature: it builds only the directory needed for a specific target. In a more complex example (where there were many such directories to be built) it would be nice to be able to use something like that solution while avoiding the problem of constant rebuilds as the timestamp on the directory changes.

To do that, you can store a special empty file, which I call a *marker* file, in the directory and use that as the prerequisite. Because it's a normal file, normal GNU make rebuilding rules apply and its timestamp is not affected by changes in its directory.

If you add a rule to build the marker file (and to ensure that its directory exists), you can specify a directory as a prerequisite by specifying the marker file as a proxy for the directory.

In our example, the marker file is called .f:

```
OUT = /out
.PHONY: all
all: $(OUT)/foo.o

$(OUT)/foo.o: foo.c $(OUT)/.f
→ @$(COMPILE.C) -o $@ $<
```

```
$(OUT)/.f:
→ mkdir -p $(dir $@)
→ touch $@
```

Notice how the rule to build $(OUT)/.f creates the directory, if necessary, and touches the .f file. Because the target is a file (.f), it can safely be used as a prerequisite in the $(OUT)/foo.o rule.

The $(OUT)/.f rule uses the GNU make function $(dir FILE) to extract the directory portion of the target (which is the path to the .f file) and passes that directory to mkdir.

The only disadvantage here is that it's necessary to specify the .f files for every rule that builds a target in a directory that might need to be created.

To make this easy to use, you can create functions that automatically make the rule to create a directory and that calculate the correct name for .f files:

```
marker = $1.f
make_dir = $(eval $1.f: ; @mkdir -p $$(dir $$@) ; touch $$@)

OUT = /out
.PHONY: all
all: $(OUT)/foo.o

$(OUT)/foo.o: foo.c $(call marker,$(OUT))
→ @$(COMPILE.C) -o $@ $<

$(call make-dir,$(OUT))
```

Here, marker and make-dir are used to simplify the makefile.

Solution 4: Use an Order-Only Prerequisite to Build the Directory

In GNU make 3.80 and later, another solution is to use an *order-only* prerequisite. An order-only prerequisite is built before the target as normal but does not cause the target to be rebuilt when the prerequisite is changed. Usually, when a prerequisite is rebuilt, the target will also be rebuilt because GNU make assumes that the target depends on the prerequisite. Order-only prerequisites are different: they get built before the target, but the target isn't updated just because an order-only prerequisite was built.

This is exactly what we would've liked in the original broken example in Listing 4-8—to make sure that the directory gets rebuilt as needed but doesn't rebuild the .o file every time the directory's timestamp changes.

Order-only prerequisites are any prerequisites that come after the bar symbol | and must be placed after any normal prerequisites.

In fact, just adding this single character to the broken example in Listing 4-8 can make it work correctly:

```
OUT = /out

.PHONY: all
all: $(OUT)/foo.o
```

```
$(OUT)/foo.o: foo.c | $(OUT)/
→ @$(COMPILE.C) -o $@ $<
```

❶ ```
$(OUT)/:
→ mkdir -p $@
```

The rule for $(OUT)/ ❶ will be run if the directory is missing, but changes to the directory will not cause $(OUT)/foo.o to be rebuilt.

### Solution 5: Use Pattern Rules, Second Expansion, and a Marker File

In a typical makefile (not simple examples in books like this), targets are usually built using pattern rules, like so:

```
OUT = /out
.PHONY: all
all: $(OUT)/foo.o

$(OUT)/%.o: %.c
→ @$(COMPILE.C) -o $@ $<
```

But we can change this pattern rule to build directories automatically using marker files.

In GNU make 3.81 and later, there is an exciting feature called *second expansion* (which is enabled by specifying the .SECONDEXPANSION target in the makefile). With second expansion, the prerequisite list of any rule undergoes a second expansion (the first expansion happens when the makefile is read) just before the rule is used. By escaping any $ signs with a second $, it's possible to use GNU make automatic variables (such as $@) in the prerequisite list.

Using a marker file for each directory and second expansion, you can create a makefile that automatically creates directories only when necessary with a simple addition to the prerequisite list of any rule:

```
OUT = /tmp/out

.SECONDEXPANSION:

all: $(OUT)/foo.o

$(OUT)/%.o: %.c $$(@D)/.f
→ @$(COMPILE.C) -o $@ $<

%/.f:
→ mkdir -p $(dir $@)
→ touch $@

.PRECIOUS: %/.f
```
```

The pattern rule used to make .o files has a special prerequisite $$(@D)/.f, which uses the second expansion feature to obtain the directory in which the target is to be built. It does this by applying the D modifier to $@, which gets the directory of the target (while $@ on its own obtains the name of the target).

That directory will be built by the %/.f pattern rule in the process of building a .f file. Notice that the .f files are marked as *precious* so that GNU make will not delete them. Without this line, the .f files are considered to be useless intermediate files and would be cleaned up by GNU make on exit.

Solution 6: Make the Directory in Line

It's also possible to make directories inside the rules that need them; this is called making directories *in line*. For example:

```
OUT = /out

.PHONY: all
all: $(OUT)/foo.o

$(OUT)/foo.o: foo.c
→ mkdir -p $(@D)
→ @$(COMPILE.C) -o $@ $<
```

Here I've modified the $(OUT)/foo.o rule so that it makes the directory using -p each time. This only works if a small number of rules need to create directories. Updating every rule to add the mkdir is laborious and likely to result in some rules being missed.

GNU make Meets Filenames with Spaces

GNU make treats the space character as a list separator; any string containing spaces can be thought of as a list of space-delimited words. This is fundamental to GNU make, and space-separated lists abound. Unfortunately, that presents a problem when filenames contain spaces. This section looks at how to work around the "spaces in filenames problem."

An Example Makefile

Suppose you are faced with creating a makefile that needs to deal with two files named foo bar and bar baz, with foo bar built from bar baz. Filenames that include spaces can be tricky to work with.

A naive way to write this in a makefile would be:

```
foo bar: bar baz
→ @echo Making $@ from $<
```

But that doesn't work. GNU make can't differentiate between cases where spaces are part of the filename and cases where they're not. In fact, the naively written makefile is exactly the same as:

```
foo: bar baz
→ @echo Making $@ from $<
bar: bar baz
→ @echo Making $@ from $<
```

Placing quotations marks around the filenames doesn't work either. If you try this:

```
"foo bar": "bar baz"
→ @echo Making $@ from $<
```

GNU make thinks you're talking about four files called "foo, bar", "bar, and baz". GNU make ignores the double quotes and splits the list by spaces as it normally would.

Escape Spaces with \

One way to deal with the spaces problem is to use GNU make's escaping operator, \, which you can use to escape sensitive characters (such as a literal # so that it doesn't start a comment or a literal % so that it isn't used as a wildcard).

Thus, use \ to escape spaces in rules for filenames with spaces. Our example makefile can then be rewritten as follows:

```
foo\ bar: bar\ baz
→ @echo Making $@ from $<
```

and it will work correctly. The \ is removed during the parsing of the makefile, so the actual target and prerequisite names correctly contain spaces. This will be reflected in the automatic variables (such as $@).

When foo bar needs updating, the simple makefile will output:

```
$ make
Making foo bar from bar baz
```

You can also use the same escaping mechanism inside GNU make's $(wildcard) function. To check for the existence of foo bar, you can use $(wildcard foo\ bar) and GNU make will treat foo bar as a single filename to look for in the filesystem.

Unfortunately, GNU make's other functions that deal with space-separated lists do not respect the escaping of spaces. The output of $(sort foo\ bar) for example, is the list bar foo\, not foo\ bar as you might expect. In fact, $(wildcard) is the only GNU make function that respects the \ character to escape a space.

This leads to a problem if you have to deal with the automatic variables that contain lists of targets. Consider this slightly more complicated example:

```
foo\ bar: bar\ baz a\ b
→ @echo Making $@ from $<
```

Now foo bar has two prerequisites bar baz and a b. What's the value of $^ (the list of all prerequisites) in this case? It's bar baz a b: the escaping is gone, and even if it weren't gone, the fact that only $(wildcard) respects the \ means that it would be useless. $^ is, from GNU make's perspective, a list with four elements.

Looking at the definitions of the automatic variables tells us which are safe to use in the presence of spaces in filenames. Table 4-1 shows each automatic variable and whether it is safe.

Table 4-1: Safety of Automatic Variables

Automatic variable	Is it safe?
$@	Yes
$<	Yes
$%	Yes
$*	Yes
$?	No
$^	No
$+	No

Those that are inherently lists ($?, $^, and $+) are not safe because GNU make lists are separated by spaces; the others are safe.

And it gets a little worse. Even though the first four automatic variables in the table are safe to use, their modified versions with D and F suffixes (which extract the directory and filename portions of the corresponding automatic variable) are not. This is because they are defined in terms of the dir and notdir functions.

Consider this example makefile:

```
/tmp/foo\ bar/baz: bar\ baz a\ b
→ @echo Making $@ from $<
```

The value of $@ is /tmp/foo bar/baz as expected, but the value of $(@D) is /tmp bar (as opposed to /tmp/foo bar) and the value of $(@F) is foo baz (instead of just baz).

Turn Spaces into Question Marks

Another way to deal with the spaces problem is to turn spaces into question marks. Here's the original makefile transformed:

```
foo?bar: bar?baz
→ @echo Making $@ from $<
```

Because GNU make does globbing of target and prerequisite names (and respects any spaces found), this will work. But the results are inconsistent.

If foo bar exists when this makefile runs, the pattern foo?bar will get turned into foo bar and that value will be used for $@. If that file were missing when the makefile is parsed, the pattern (and hence $@) remains as foo?bar.

Another problem also exists: ? could match something other than a space. If there's a file called foombar on the system, for example, the makefile may end up working on the wrong file.

To get around this problem, Robert Mecklenburg defines two functions to add and remove spaces automatically in *Managing Projects with GNU Make, 3rd edition* (O'Reilly, 2004). The sq function turns every space into a question mark (sq means space to question mark); the qs function does the opposite (it turns every question mark into a space). Here's the updated makefile using two functions (sq and qs) to add and remove question marks. This works unless any filename contains a question mark but requires wrapping all uses of the filenames in calls to sq and qs.

```
sp :=
sp +=
qs = $(subst ?,$(sp),$1)
sq = $(subst $(sp),?,$1)

$(call sq,foo bar): $(call sq,bar baz)
→ @echo Making $(call qs,$@) from $(call qs,$<)
```

Either way, because we still can't be sure whether automatic variables will have question marks in them, using the list-based automatic variables or any GNU make list functions is still impossible.

My Advice

Given that GNU make has difficulty with spaces in filenames, what can you do? Here's my advice:

Rename your files to avoid spaces if possible.
However, this is impossible for many people because the spaces in filenames may have been added by a third party.

Use 8.3 filenames.
If you are working with Windows, it may be possible to use short, 8.3 filenames, which allows you to still have spaces on disk but avoid them in the makefile.

Use \ for escaping.

If you need the spaces, escape them with \, which does give consistent results. Just be sure to avoid the automatic variables listed as not safe in Table 4-1.

If you use \ for escaping and you need to manipulate lists of filenames that contain spaces, the best thing to do is substitute spaces with some other character and then change them back again.

For example, the s+ and +s functions in the following code change escaped spaces to + signs and back again. Then you can safely manipulate lists of filenames using all the GNU make functions. Just be sure to remove the + signs before using these names in a rule.

```
space :=
space +=

s+ = $(subst \$(space),+,$1)
+s = $(subst +,\$(space),$1)
```

Here's an example using them to transform a list of source files with escaped spaces into a list of object files, which are then used to define the prerequisites of an all rule:

```
SRCS := a\ b.c c\ d.c e\ f.c
SRCS := $(call s+,$(SRCS))

OBJS := $(SRCS:.c=.o)

all: $(call +s,$(OBJS))
```

The source files are stored in SRCS with spaces in filenames escaped. So SRCS contains three files named a b.c, c d.c, and e f.c. GNU make's \ escaping is used to preserve the escaped spaces in each name. Transforming SRCS into a list of objects in OBJS is done in the usual manner using .c=.o to replace each .c extension with .o, but first SRCS is altered using the s+ function so the escaped spaces become + signs. As a result, GNU make will see SRCS as a list of three elements, a+b.c, c+d.c, and e+f.c, and changing the extension will work correctly. When OBJS is used later in the makefile, the + signs are turned back into escaped spaces using a call to the function +s.

Path Handling

Makefile creators often have to manipulate filesystem paths, but GNU make provides few functions for path manipulation. And cross-platform make is difficult due to differences in path syntax. This section explains ways to manipulate paths in GNU make and navigate through the cross-platform minefield.

Target Name Matching

Look at the following example makefile and suppose that ../foo is missing. Does the makefile manage to create it?

```
.PHONY: all
all: ../foo

../././foo:
→ touch $@
```

If you run that makefile with GNU make, you might be surprised to see the following error:

```
$ make
make: *** No rule to make target `../foo', needed by `all'. Stop.
```

If you change the makefile to this:

```
.PHONY: all
all: ../foo

./../foo:
→ touch $@
```

you'll find that it works as expected and performs a touch ../foo.

The first makefile fails because GNU make doesn't do path manipulation on target names, so it sees two different targets called ../foo and ../././foo, and fails to make the connection between the two. The second makefile works because I lied in the preceding sentence. GNU make does do a tiny bit of path manipulation: it will strip leading ./ from target names. So in the second makefile both targets are ../foo, and it works as expected.

The general rule with GNU make targets is that they are treated as literal strings without interpreting them in any way. Therefore, it's essential that when you're referring to a target in a makefile, you always ensure that the same string is used.

Working with Path Lists

It bears repeating that GNU make lists are just strings in which any whitespace is considered a list separator. Consequently, paths with spaces in them are not recommended because it makes using many of GNU make's built-in functions impossible, and spaces in paths cause problems with targets.

For example, suppose a target is /tmp/sub directory/target, and we write a rule for it like this:

```
/tmp/sub directory/target:
→ @do stuff
```

GNU make will actually interpret that as two rules, one for /tmp/sub and one for directory/target, just as if you'd written this:

```
/tmp/sub:
→ @do stuff
directory/target:
→ @do stuff
```

You can work around that problem by escaping the space with \, but that escape is poorly respected by GNU make (it works only in target names and the $(wildcard) function).

Unless you must use them, avoid spaces in target names.

Lists of Paths in VPATH and vpath

Another place that lists of paths appear in GNU make is when specifying the VPATH or in a vpath directive used to specify where GNU make finds prerequisites. For example, it's possible to set the VPATH to search for source files in a list of : or whitespace separated paths:

```
VPATH = ../src:../thirdparty/src /src

vpath %c ../src:../thirdparty/src /src
```

GNU make will split that path correctly at either colons or whitespace. On Windows systems, the native builds of GNU make use ; as the path separator for VPATH (and vpath) because : is needed for drive letters. On Windows, GNU make actually tries to be smart and splits paths on colons unless it looks like a drive letter (one letter followed by a colon). This drive letter intelligence actually creates a problem if you have a directory in the path whose name is a single letter: in that case you must use ; as the path separator. Otherwise, GNU make will think it's a drive:

```
VPATH = ../src;../thirdparty/src /src

vpath %c ../src;../thirdparty/src /src
```

On both POSIX and Windows systems, a space in a path is a separator in a VPATH and vpath. So using spaces is the best bet for cross-platform makefiles.

Using / or \

On POSIX systems / is the path separator, and on Windows systems it's \. It's common to see paths being built up in makefiles like this:

```
SRCDIR := src
MODULE_DIR := module_1

MODULE_SRCS := $(SRCDIR)/$(MODULE_DIR)
```

It would be ideal to remove the POSIX-only / there and replace it with something that would work with a different separator. One way to do that is to define a variable called / (GNU make lets you get away with using almost anything as a variable name) and use it in place of /:

```
/ := /

SRCDIR := src
MODULE_DIR := module_1

MODULE_SRCS := $(SRCDIR)$/$(MODULE_DIR)
```

If that makes you uncomfortable, just call it SEP:

```
SEP := /

SRCDIR := src
MODULE_DIR := module_1

MODULE_SRCS := $(SRCDIR)$(SEP)$(MODULE_DIR)
```

Now when you switch to Windows, you can just redefine / (or SEP) to \. It's difficult to assign a literal \ on its own as a variable value (because GNU make interprets it as a line continuation and it can't be escaped), so it's defined here using $(strip).

```
/ := $(strip \)

SRCDIR := src
MODULE_DIR := module_1

MODULE_SRCS := $(SRCDIR)$/$(MODULE_DIR)
```

However, note that the Windows builds of GNU make will also accept / as a path separator, so weird paths like c:/src are legal. Using those paths will simplify the makefile, but be careful when passing them to a native Windows tool that expects \ separated paths. If that's necessary, use this instead:

```
forward-to-backward = $(subst /,\,$1)
```

This simple function will convert a forward slash path to a back-slash path.

Windows Oddity: Case Insensitive but Case Preserving

On POSIX systems filenames are case sensitive; on Windows they are not. On Windows the files File, file, and FILE are all the same file. But an oddity with Windows is that the first time a file is accessed, the specific case used is recorded and preserved. Thus, if we touch File, it will appear as File in the filesystem (but can be accessed as FILE, file, or any other case combination).

By default, GNU make does case-sensitive target comparisons, so the following makefile does not do what you might expect:

```
.PHONY: all
all: File

file:
→ @touch $@
```

As is, this file causes an error, but you can compile GNU make on Windows to do case-insensitive comparisons instead (with the build HAVE_CASE_INSENSITIVE_FS option).

This oddity is more likely to arise when a target specified in a makefile is also found in a wildcard search because the operating system may return a different case than the case used in the makefile. The target names may differ in case, and that may cause an unexpected No rule to make error.

Built-in Path Functions and Variables

You can determine the current working directory in GNU make using the built-in CURDIR. Note that CURDIR will follow symlinks. If you are in /foo but /foo is actually a symlink to /somewhere/foo, CURDIR will report the directory as /somewhere/foo. If you need the non-symlink-followed directory name, use the value of the environment variable PWD:

```
CURRENT_DIRECTORY := $(PWD)
```

But be sure to grab its value before any other part of the makefile has changed PWD: it can be altered, just like any other variable imported from the environment.

You can also find the directory in which the current makefile is stored using the MAKEFILE_LIST variable that was introduced in GNU make 3.80. At the start of a makefile, it's possible to extract its directory as follows:

```
CURRENT_MAKEFILE := $(word $(words $(MAKEFILE_LIST)),$(MAKEFILE_LIST))
MAKEFILE_DIRECTORY := $(dir $(CURRENT_MAKEFILE))
```

GNU make has functions for splitting paths into components: dir, notdir, basename, and suffix.

Consider the filename /foo/bar/source.c stored in the variable FILE. You can use the functions dir, notdir, basename, and suffix to extract the directory, filename, and suffix. So to get the directory, for example, use $(dir $(FILE)). Table 4-2 shows each of these functions and its result.

Table 4-2: Results of dir, notdir, basename, and suffix

Function	Result
dir	/foo/bar/
notdir	source.c
basename	source
suffix	.c

You can see that the directory, the non-directory part, the suffix (or extension), and the non-directory part without the suffix have been extracted. These four functions make filename manipulation easy. If no directory was specified, GNU make uses the current directory (./). For example, suppose that FILE was just source.c. Table 4-3 shows the result for each function.

Table 4-3: Results of dir, notdir, basename, and suffix with No Directory Specified

Function	Result
dir	./
notdir	source.c
basename	source
suffix	.c

Because these functions are commonly used in conjunction with GNU make's automatic variables (like $@), GNU make provides a modifier syntax. Appending D or F to any automatic variable is equivalent to calling $(dir) or $(notdir) on it. For example, $(@D) is equivalent to $(dir $@) and $(@F) is the same as $(notdir $@).

Useful Functions in 3.81: abspath and realpath

realpath is a GNU make wrapper for the C library realpath function, which removes ./, resolves ../, removes duplicated /, and follows symlinks. The argument to realpath must exist in the filesystem. The path returned by realpath is absolute. If the path does not exist, the function returns an empty string.

For example, you could find the full path of the current directory like this: current := $(realpath ./).

abspath is similar but does not follow symlinks, and its argument does not have to refer to an existing file or directory.

Usman's Law

`make clean` doesn't make clean. That's Usman's law (named after a smart coworker of mine who spent months working with real-world makefiles). `make clean` is intended to return to a state in which everything will be rebuilt from scratch. Often it doesn't. Read on to find out why.

The Human Factor

The `clean` rule from the OpenSSL makefile looks like this:

```
clean:
→ rm -f *.o *.obj lib tags core .pure .nfs* *.old *.bak fluff $(EXE)
```

Notice how it's a long list of clearly human-maintained directories, patterns, and filenames that need to be deleted to get back to a clean state. Human maintenance means human error. Suppose someone adds a rule that creates a temporary file with a fixed name. That temporary file should be added to the `clean` rule, but it most likely won't be.

Usman's law strikes.

Poor Naming

Here's a snippet found in many automatically generated makefiles:

```
mostlyclean::
→ rm -f *.o

clean:: mostlyclean
→ -$(LIBTOOL) --mode=clean rm -f $(program) $(programs)
→ rm -f $(library).a squeeze *.bad *.dvi *.lj

extraclean::
→ rm -f *.aux *.bak *.bbl *.blg *.dvi *.log *.pl *.tfm *.vf *.vpl
→ rm -f *.*pk *.*gf *.mpx *.i *.s *~ *.orig *.rej *\#*
→ rm -f CONTENTS.tex a.out core mfput.* texput.* mpout.*
```

In this example, three sorts of `clean` appear to have different degrees of cleanliness: `mostlyclean`, `clean`, and `extraclean`.

`mostlyclean` just deletes the object files compiled from source. `clean` does that plus deletes the generated library and a few other files. You'd think that `extraclean` would delete more than the other two, but it actually deletes a different set of files. And I've seen makefiles with `reallyclean`, `veryclean`, `deepclean`, and even `partiallyclean` rules!

When you can't tell from the naming what does what, it can easily lead to potential problems down the line.

Usman's law strikes again.

Silent Failure

Here's another makefile snippet that works some of the time:

```
clean:
→ @-rm *.o &> /dev/null
```

The @ means that the command isn't echoed. The - means that any error returned is ignored and all output is redirected with &> to /dev/null, making it invisible. Because no -f is on the rm command, any failure (from say, permissions problems) will go totally unnoticed.

Usman's law strikes again.

Recursive Clean

Many makefiles are recursive, and make clean must be recursive too, so you see the following pattern:

```
SUBDIRS = library executable

.PHONY: clean
clean:
→ for dir in $(SUBDIRS); do \
→ $(MAKE) -C $$dir clean;  \
→ done
```

The problem with this is that it means make clean has to work correctly in every directory in SUBDIR, leading to more opportunity for error.

Usman's law strikes again.

Pitfalls and Benefits of GNU make Parallelization

Many build processes run for hours, so build managers commonly type make and go home for the night. GNU make's solution to this problem is parallel execution: a simple command line option that causes GNU make to run jobs in parallel using the dependency information in the makefile to run them in the correct order.

In practice, however, GNU make parallel execution is severely limited by the fact that almost all makefiles are written with the assumption that their rules will run in series. Rarely do makefile authors *think in parallel* when writing their makefiles. That leads to hidden traps that either cause the build to fail with a fatal error or, worse, build "successfully" but result in incorrect binaries when GNU make is run in parallel mode.

This section looks at GNU make's parallel pitfalls and how to work around them to get maximum parallelism.

Using -j (or -jobs)

To start GNU make in parallel mode, you can specify either the -j or --jobs option on the command line. The argument to the option is the maximum number of processes that GNU make will run in parallel.

For example, typing make --jobs=4 allows GNU make to run up to four subprocesses in parallel, which would give a theoretical maximum speedup of 4×. However, the theoretical time is severely limited by restrictions in the makefile. To calculate the maximum actual speedup, you use Amdahl's law (which is covered in "Amdahl's Law and the Limits of Parallelization" on page 154).

One simple but annoying problem found in parallel GNU make is that because the jobs are no longer run serially (and the order depends on the timing of jobs), the output from GNU make will be sorted randomly depending on the actual order of job execution.

Fortunately, that problem has been addressed in GNU make 4.0 with the --output-sync option described in Chapter 1.

Consider the example in Listing 4-9:

```
.PHONY: all
all: t5 t4 t1
→ @echo Making $@

t1: t3 t2
→ touch $@

t2:
→ cp t3 $@

t3:
→ touch $@

t4:
→ touch $@

t5:
→ touch $@
```

Listing 4-9: A simple makefile to illustrate parallel making

It builds five targets: t1, t2, t3, t4, and t5. All are simply touched except for t2, which is copied from t3.

Running Listing 4-9 through standard GNU make without a parallel option gives the output:

```
$ make
touch t5
touch t4
touch t3
cp t3 t2
touch t1
Making all
```

The order of execution will be the same each time because GNU make will follow the prerequisites depth first and from left to right. Note that the left-to-right execution (in the all rule for example, t5 is built before t4, which is built before t1) is part of the POSIX make standard.

Now if make is run in parallel mode, it's clear that t5, t4, and t1 can be run at the same time because there are no dependencies between them. Similarly, t3 and t2 do not depend on each other, so they can be run in parallel.

The output of a parallel run of Listing 4-9 might be:

```
$ make --jobs=16
touch t4
touch t5
touch t3
cp t3 t2
touch t1
Making all
```

Or even:

```
$ make --jobs=16
touch t3
cp t3 t2
touch t4
touch t1
touch t5
Making all
```

This makes any process that examines log files to check for build problems (such as diffing log files) difficult. Unfortunately, there's no easy solution for this in GNU make without the --output-sync option, so you'll just have to live with it unless you upgrade to GNU make 4.0.

Missing Dependencies

The example in Listing 4-9 has an additional problem. The author fell into the classic left-to-right trap when writing the makefile, so when it's run in parallel, it's possible for the following to happen:

```
$ make --jobs=16
touch t5
touch t4
cp t3 t2
cp: cannot stat `t3': No such file or directory
make: *** [t2] Error 1
```

The reason is that when run in parallel, the rule to build t2 can occur before the rule to build t3, and t2 needs t3 to have already been built. This didn't happen in the serial case because of the left-to-right assumption: the rule to build t1 is t1: t3 t2, which implies that t3 will be built before t2.

But no actual dependency exists in the makefile that states that t3 must be built before t2. The fix is simple: just add t2: t3 to the makefile.

This is a simple example of the real problem of missing or implicit (left-to-right) dependencies that plagues makefiles when run in parallel. If a makefile breaks when run in parallel, it's worth looking for missing dependencies straightaway because they are very common.

The Hidden Temporary File Problem

Another way GNU make can break when running in parallel is if multiple rules use the same temporary file. Consider the example makefile in Listing 4-10:

```
TMP_FILE := /tmp/scratch_file

.PHONY: all
all: t

t: t1 t2
→ cat t1 t2 > $@

t1:
→ echo Output from $@ > $(TMP_FILE)
→ cat $(TMP_FILE) > $@

t2:
→ echo Output from $@ > $(TMP_FILE)
→ cat $(TMP_FILE) > $@
```

Listing 4-10: A hidden temporary file that breaks parallel builds

Run without a parallel option, GNU make produces the following output:

```
$ make
echo Output from t1 > /tmp/scratch_file
cat /tmp/scratch_file > t1
echo Output from t2 > /tmp/scratch_file
cat /tmp/scratch_file > t2
cat t1 t2 > t
```

and the t file contains:

```
Output from t1
Output from t2
```

But run in parallel, Listing 4-10 gives the following output:

```
$ make --jobs=2
echo Output from t1 > /tmp/scratch_file
echo Output from t2 > /tmp/scratch_file
cat /tmp/scratch_file > t1
cat /tmp/scratch_file > t2
cat t1 t2 > t
```

Now t contains:

```
Output from t2
Output from t2
```

This occurs because no dependency exists between t1 and t2 (because neither requires the output of the other), so they can run in parallel. In the output, you can see that they are running in parallel but that the output from the two rules is interleaved. Because the two echo statements ran first, t2 overwrote the output of t1, so the temporary file (shared by both rules) had the wrong value when it was finally cated to t1, resulting in the wrong value for t.

This example may seem contrived, but the same thing happens in real makefiles when run in parallel, resulting in either broken builds or the wrong binary being built. The yacc program for example, produces temporary files called y.tab.c and y.tab.h. If more than one yacc is run in the same directory at the same time, the wrong files could be used by the wrong process.

A simple solution for the makefile in Listing 4-10 is to change the definition of TMP_FILE to TMP_FILE = /tmp/scratch_file.$@, so its name will depend on the target being built. Now a parallel run would look like this:

```
$ make --jobs=2
echo Output from t1 > /tmp/scratch_file.t1
echo Output from t2 > /tmp/scratch_file.t2
cat /tmp/scratch_file.t1 > t1
cat /tmp/scratch_file.t2 > t2
cat t1 t2 > t
```

A related problem occurs when multiple jobs in the makefile write to a shared file. Even if they never read the file (for example, they might write to a log file), locking the file for write access can cause competing jobs to stall, reducing the overall performance of the parallel build.

Consider the example makefile in Listing 4-11 that uses the lockfile command to lock a file and simulate write locking. Although the file is locked, each job waits for a number of seconds:

```
LOCK_FILE := lock.me

.PHONY: all
all: t1 t2
→ @echo done.

t1:
→ @lockfile $(LOCK_FILE)
→ @sleep 10
→ @rm -f $(LOCK_FILE)
→ @echo Finished $@
```

```
t2:
→ @lockfile $(LOCK_FILE)
→ @sleep 20
→ @rm -f $(LOCK_FILE)
→ @echo Finished $@
```

Listing 4-11: Locking on shared files can lock a parallel build and make it run serially.

Running Listing 4-11 in a serial build takes about 30 seconds:

```
$ time make
Finished t1
Finished t2
done.
make 0.01s user 0.01s system 0% cpu 30.034 total
```

But it isn't any faster in parallel, even though t1 and t2 should be able to run in parallel:

```
$ time make -j4
Finished t1
Finished t2
done.
make -j4 0.01s user 0.02s system 0% cpu 36.812 total
```

It's actually slower because of the way lockfile detects lock availability. As you can imagine, write locking a file could cause similar delays in otherwise parallel-friendly makefiles.

Related to the file locking problem is a danger concerning archive (ar) files. If multiple ar processes were to run simultaneously on the same archive file, the archive could be corrupted. Locking around archive updates is necessary in a parallel build; otherwise, you'll need to prevent your dependencies from running multiple ar commands on the same file at the same time.

One way to prevent parallelism problems is to specify .NOTPARALLEL in a makefile. If this is seen, the entire make execution will be run in series and the -j or --jobs command line option will be ignored. .NOTPARALLEL is a very blunt tool because it affects an entire invocation of GNU make, but it could be handy in a recursive make situation with, for example, a third-party makefile that is not parallel safe.

The Right Way to Do Recursive make

GNU make is smart enough to share parallelism across sub-makes if a makefile using $(MAKE) is careful about how it calls sub-makes. GNU make has a message passing mechanism that works across most platforms (Windows support was added in GNU make 4.0) and enables sub-makes to use all the available jobs specified through -j or --jobs by passing tokens across pipes between the make processes.

The only serious gotcha is that you must write your makefile in a way that actually allows your sub-makes to run in parallel. The classic recursive make style that uses a shell for loop to process each sub-make doesn't allow for more than one sub-make to run at once. For example:

```
SUBDIRS := foo bar baz

.PHONY: all
all:
→ for d in $(SUBDIRS);      \
→ do                        \
→  $(MAKE) -directory=$$d;  \
→ done
```

This code has a big problem: if sub-make fails, the make will look like it has succeeded. It's possible to fix that, but the fixes become more and more complicated: other approaches are better.

When run in parallel mode, the all rule walks through each subdirectory and waits for its $(MAKE) to complete. Even though each of those sub-makes will be able to run in parallel, the overall make does not, meaning a less than ideal speedup. For example, if the make in the bar directory is capable of running only four jobs at once, then running on a 16-core machine won't make the build any faster than on one with just 4 cores.

The solution is to remove the for loop and replace it with a single rule for each directory:

```
SUBDIRS := foo bar baz

.PHONY: all $(SUBDIRS)
all: $(SUBDIRS)

$(SUBDIRS):
→ $(MAKE) --directory=$@
```

Each directory is considered to be a phony target, because the directory doesn't actually get built.

Now each directory can run while the others are running, and parallelism is maximized; it's even possible to have dependencies between directories causing some sub-makes to run before others. Directory dependencies can be handy when it's important that one sub-make runs before another.

Amdahl's Law and the Limits of Parallelization

Additionally, there are real limits to the amount of parallelization that is possible in a project. Look at Listing 4-12:

```
.PHONY: all
all: t
→ @echo done
```

```
t: t1 t2 t3 t4 t5 t6 t7 t8 t9 t10 t11 t12
→ @sleep 10
→ @echo Made $@

t1:
→ @sleep 11
→ @echo Made $@

t2:
→ @sleep 4
→ @echo Made $@

t3: t5
→ @sleep 7
→ @echo Made $@

t4:
→ @sleep 9
→ @echo Made $@

t5: t8
→ @sleep 10
→ @echo Made $@

t6:
→ @sleep 2
→ @echo Made $@

t7:
→ @sleep 12
→ @echo Made $@

t8:
→ @sleep 3
→ @echo Made $@

t9: t10
→ @sleep 4
→ @echo Made $@

t10:
→ @sleep 6
→ @echo Made $@

t11: t12
→ @sleep 1
→ @echo Made $@

t12:
→ @sleep 9
→ @echo Made $@
```

Listing 4-12: A makefile with sleep *used to simulate jobs that take time to complete*

When run in series, it takes about 88 seconds to complete:

```
$ time make
Made t1
Made t2
Made t8
Made t5
Made t3
Made t4
Made t6
Made t7
Made t10
Made t9
Made t12
Made t11
Made t
done
make 0.04s user 0.03s system 0% cpu 1:28.68 total
```

What's the maximum speedup possible, assuming as many CPUs are available as desired? Working through the makefile step by step, you'll see that t takes 10 seconds to build and everything else must be built before that. t1, t2, t4, t6, and t7 are all independent, and the longest of them takes 12 seconds. t3 waits for t5, which needs t8: that chain takes a total of 20 seconds. t9 needs t10 for a total of 10 seconds, and t11 needs t12 for another 10 seconds.

So the longest serial part of this build is the sequence t, t3, t5, t8, which takes a total of 30 seconds. This build can never go faster than 30 seconds (or 2.93 times faster than the serial 88 second time). How many processors are needed to achieve that speedup?

In general, the maximum speedup achievable is governed by Amdahl's law: if F is the fraction of the build that cannot be parallelized and N is the number of available processors, then the maximum speedup achievable is 1 / (F + (1 - F) / N).

In the Listing 4-12 example, 34 percent of the build can't be parallelized. Table 4-4 shows the results of applying Amdahl's law:

Table 4-4: Maximum Speedup Based on Number of Processors

Number of processors	Maximum speedup
2	1.49x
3	1.79x
4	1.98x
5	2.12x
6	2.22x
7	2.30x
8	2.37x
9	2.42x

Number of processors	Maximum speedup
10	2.46x
11	2.50x
12	2.53x

For this small build, the maximum speedup Amdahl's law predicts has a plateau starting at around eight processors. The actual plateau is further limited by the fact that only 13 possible jobs are in the build.

Looking at the structure of the build, we can see that eight processors is the maximum because five jobs can run in parallel without any dependencies: t1, t2, t4, t6, and t7. Then three small chains of jobs can each use one processor at a time: t3, t5, and t8; t9 and t10; and t11 and t12. Building t can reuse one of the eight processors because they'll all be idle at that point.

A real-world instance of Amdahl's law significantly impacting build times occurs with languages that have a linking step, such as C and C++. Typically, all the objects files are built before the link step and then a single (often huge) link process has to run. That link process is often not parallelizable and becomes the limiting factor on build parallelization.

Making $(wildcard) Recursive

The built-in $(wildcard) function is not recursive: it only searches for files in a single directory. You can have multiple globbing patterns in a $(wildcard) and use that to look in subdirectories. For example, $(wildcard */*.c) finds all the .c files in all subdirectories of the current directory. But if you need to search an arbitrary tree of directories, there's no built-in way to do it.

Fortunately, it's pretty easy to make a recursive version of $(wildcard), like this:

```
rwildcard=$(foreach d,$(wildcard $1*),$(call rwildcard,$d/,$2) $(filter $(subst *,%,$2),$d))
```

The function rwildcard takes two parameters: the first is the directory from which to start searching (this parameter can be left empty to start from the current directory), and the second is the glob pattern for the files to find in each directory.

For example, to find all .c files in the current directory (along with its subdirectories), use this:

```
$(call rwildcard,,*.c)
```

Or to find all .c files in /tmp, use this:

```
$(call rwildcard,/tmp/,*.c)
```

rwildcard also supports multiple patterns. For example:

```
$(call rwildcard,/src/,*.c *.h)
```

This finds all .c and .h files under /src/.

Which Makefile Am I In?

A common request is: Is there a way to find the name and path of the current makefile? By *current*, people usually mean the makefile that GNU make is currently parsing. There's no built-in way to quickly get the answer, but there is a way using the GNU make variable MAKEFILE_LIST.

MAKEFILE_LIST is the list of makefiles currently loaded or included. Each time a makefile is loaded or included, the MAKEFILE_LIST is appended with its path and name. The paths and names in the variable are relative to the current working directory (where GNU make was started or where it moved to with the -C or --directory option), but you can access the current directory from the CURDIR variable.

So using that, you can define a GNU make function (let's call it where-am-i) that will return the current makefile (it uses $(word) to get the last makefile name from the list):

```
where-am-i = $(CURDIR)/$(word $(words $(MAKEFILE_LIST)),$(MAKEFILE_LIST))
```

Then, whenever you want to find the full path to the current makefile, write the following at the top of the makefile:

```
THIS_MAKEFILE := $(call where-am-i)
```

It's important that this line goes at the top because any include statement in the makefile will change the value of MAKEFILE_LIST, so you want to grab the location of the current makefile before that happens.

Listing 4-13 shows an example makefile that uses where-am-i and includes another makefile from the foo/ subdirectory, which, in turn, includes a makefile from the foo/bar/ directory.

```
where-am-i = $(CURDIR)/$(word ($words $(MAKEFILE_LIST)),$(MAKEFILE_LIST)

include foo/makefile
```

Listing 4-13: A makefile that can determine where it is located on the filesystem

The contents of foo/makefile is shown in Listing 4-14.

```
THIS_MAKEFILE := $(call where-am-i)
$(warning $(THIS_MAKEFILE))

include foo/bar/makefile
```

Listing 4-14: A makefile included by Listing 4-13

The contents of foo/bar/makefile is shown in Listing 4-15.

```
THIS_MAKEFILE := $(call where-am-i)
$(warning $(THIS_MAKEFILE))
```

Listing 4-15: A makefile included by Listing 4-14

Putting the three makefiles in Listings 4-13, 4-14 and 4-15 in /tmp (and subdirectories) and running GNU make gives the output:

```
foo/makefile:2: /tmp/foo/makefile
foo/bar/makefile:2: /tmp/foo/bar/makefile
```

In this chapter, we've looked at common problems that makefile creators and maintainers run into when working on real makefiles. In any sizable project that uses make, you are likely to run into one or more (perhaps even all!) of them.

5

PUSHING THE ENVELOPE

In this chapter, you'll find techniques that you usually won't need but can, from time to time, be very useful. For example, sometimes it's useful to extend GNU make's language by creating new functions in C or even Guile. This chapter shows how to do that and more.

Doing Arithmetic

GNU make has no built-in arithmetic capability. But it is possible to create functions for addition, subtraction, multiplication, and division of integers. You can also create functions for integer comparisons, such as greater than or not equal. These functions are implemented entirely using GNU make's built-in list and string manipulation functions: $(subst), $(filter), $(filter-out), $(words), $(wordlist), $(call), $(foreach), and $(if). After we define our arithmetic functions, we'll implement a simple calculator in GNU make.

To create an arithmetic library, we first need a representation of numbers. A simple way to represent a number is with a list containing that number of items. For example, for the arithmetic library, a number is a list of letter xs. So the number 5 is represented by x x x x x.

Given this representation, we can use the $(words) function to convert from the internal form (all xs) to a human-readable form. For example, the following will output 5:

```
five := x x x x x

all: ; @echo $(words $(five))
```

Let's create a user-defined function decode to translate from the x representation to a number:

```
decode = $(words $1)
```

To use decode in a makefile, we need to use the GNU make function $(call), which can call a user-defined function with a set of arguments:

```
five := x x x x x

all: ; @echo $(call decode,$(five))
```

The arguments will be stored in temporary variables called $1, $2, $3, and so on. In decode, which takes one argument—the number to decode—we just use $1.

Addition and Subtraction

Now that we have a representation, we can define functions for addition, increment (by 1), and decrement (by 1):

```
plus = $1 $2
increment = x $1
decrement = $(wordlist 2,$(words $1),$1)
```

The plus function makes a list of its two arguments; concatenation is enough to implement addition with the x representation. The increment function adds a single x to its argument. decrement strips the first x off its argument by asking for the entire string of xs starting from index 2. For example, the following code will output 11:

```
two := x x
three := x x x
four := x x x x
five := x x x x x
six := x x x x x x

all: ; @echo $(call decode,$(call plus,$(five),$(six)))
```

Notice the nested calls to plus inside a call to decode so that we output the number 11 instead of a list of 11 xs.

We can create another simple function, double, which doubles its argument:

```
double = $1 $1
```

Implementing subtraction is more challenging that addition. But before we do that, let's implement max and min functions:

```
max = $(subst xx,x,$(join $1,$2))
min = $(subst xx,x,$(filter xx,$(join $1,$2)))
```

The max function uses two GNU make built-in functions: $(join) and $(subst). $(join LIST1,LIST2) takes two lists as arguments and joins the two lists together by concatenating the first element of LIST1 with the first element of LIST2 and so on through the list. If one list is longer than the other, the remaining items are just appended.

$(subst FROM,TO,LIST) runs through a list and substitutes elements that match a FROM pattern with the TO value. To see how max works, consider the sequence of events in computing $(call max,$(five),$(six)):

```
$(call max,$(five),$(six))
→ $(call max,x x x x x,x x x x x x)
→ $(subst xx,x,$(join x x x x x,x x x x x x))
→ $(subst xx,x,xx xx xx xx xx x)
→ x x x x x x
```

First, $(join) joins the list with five xs with the list with six xs, resulting in a list with six elements, the first five of which are xx. Then, $(subst) turns the first five xxs into xs. The final result is six xs, which is the maximum.

To implement min, we use a similar trick, but we keep only the xxs and throw away the xs:

```
$(call min,$(five),$(six))
→ $(call min,x x x x x,x x x x x x)
→ $(subst xx,x,$(filter xx,$(join x x x x x,x x x x x x)))
→ $(subst xx,x,$(filter xx,xx xx xx xx xx x))
→ $(subst xx,x,xx xx xx xx xx)
→ x x x x x
```

The xxs represent where the two lists could be joined. The shorter of the two lists will have only xxs. The $(filter PATTERN,LIST) function runs through the list and removes elements that do not match the pattern.

A similar pattern works for subtraction:

```
subtract = $(if $(call gte,$1,$2),              \
       $(filter-out xx,$(join $1,$2)),          \
       $(warning Subtraction underflow))
```

For a moment, ignore the $(warning) and $(if) parts of the definition, and focus on $(filter-out). $(filter-out) is the opposite of $(filter): it removes elements from a list that match the pattern. For example, we can see that the $(filter-out) here implements subtraction:

```
$(filter-out xx,$(join $(six),$(five)))
→ $(filter-out xx,$(join x x x x x x,x x x x x))
→ $(filter-out xx,xx xx xx xx xx x)
→ x
```

Unfortunately, this would also work if five and six were reversed, so we first need to check that the first argument is greater than or equal to the second. In the subtract definition, the special function gte (*greater than or equal*) returns a non-empty string if its first argument is greater than its second. We use gte to decide whether to do the subtraction or output a warning message using $(warning).

The gte function is implemented using two other functions for *greater than* (gt) and *equal* (eq):

```
gt = $(filter-out $(words $2),$(words $(call max,$1,$2)))
eq = $(filter $(words $1),$(words $2))
gte = $(call gt,$1,$2)$(call eq,$1,$2)
```

gte will return a non-empty string if either gt or eq returns a non-empty string.

The eq function is a bit of a mind-bender. It works out the number of elements in its two arguments, treats one argument as a pattern and the other as a list, and uses $(filter) to decide whether they are the same. Here's an example where they are equal:

```
$(call eq,$(five),$(five))
→ $(call eq,x x x x x,x x x x x)
→ $(filter $(words x x x x x),$(words x x x x x))
→ $(filter 5,5)
→ 5
```

The eq function converts both $(five)s to a list of five xs. These are then both converted to the number 5 using $(words). The two 5s are fed to $(filter). Because the two arguments of $(filter) are the same, the result is 5 and because 5 is not an empty string, it is interpreted as meaning *true*.

Here's what happens when they are not:

```
$(call eq,$(five),$(six))
→ $(call eq,x x x x x,x x x x x x)
→ $(filter $(words x x x x x),$(words x x x x x x))
→ $(filter 5,6)
```

This proceeds as for $(call eq,$(five),$(five)) but with $(six) in place of one of the $(five)s. Since $(filter 5,6) is an empty string, the result is false.

So the $(filter) function acts as a kind of string equality operator; the two strings in our case are the lengths of the two number strings. The gt function is implemented in a similar way: it returns a non-empty string if the length of the first number string is not equal to the maximum of the two number strings. Here's an example:

```
$(call gt,$(six),$(five))
→ $(call gt,x x x x x x,x x x x x)
→ $(filter-out $(words x x x x x),
  $(words $(call max,x x x x x x,x x x x x)))
→ $(filter-out $(words x x x x x),$(words x x x x x x))
→ $(filter-out 5,6)
→ 6
```

The gt function works in a manner similar to eq (described previously) but uses $(filter-out) instead of $(filter). It converts both x-representation numbers to digits but compares—using $(filter-out)—the first of them against the max of the two. When the first number is greater than the second, two different numbers are fed to $(filter-out). Because they are different, $(filter-out) returns a non-empty string indicating true.

Here's an example in which the first number is less than the second:

```
$(call gt,$(five),$(six))
→ $(call gt,x x x x x,x x x x x x)
→ $(filter-out $(words x x x x x x),
  $(words $(call max,x x x x x,x x x x x x)))
→ $(filter-out $(words x x x x x x),$(words x x x x x x))
→ $(filter-out 6,6)
```

Here, because the max of the two numbers is the same as the second number (because it's the largest), $(filter-out) is fed the same number and returns an empty string indicating false.

Similarly, we can define *not-equal* (ne), *less-than* (lt), and *less-than-or-equal* (lte) operators:

```
lt = $(filter-out $(words $1),$(words $(call max,$1,$2)))
ne = $(filter-out $(words $1),$(words $2))
lte = $(call lt,$1,$2)$(call eq,$1,$2)
```

lte is defined in terms of lt and eq. Because a non-empty string means *true*, lte just concatenates the values returned by lt and eq; if either returned true, then lte returns true.

Multiplication and Division

We'll have a pretty powerful arithmetic package after we define just three more functions: multiply, divide, and encode. encode is a way to create a number string of xs from an integer; we'll leave that for last and then implement our calculator.

Multiplication uses the $(foreach VAR,LIST,DO) function. It sets that variable named VAR to each element of LIST and does whatever DO says. So multiplication is easy to implement:

```
multiply = $(foreach a,$1,$2)
```

multiply just strings together its second argument for however many xs there are in the first argument. For example:

```
$(call multiply,$(two),$(three))
→ $(call multiply,x x,x x x)
→ $(foreach a,x x,x x x)
→ x x x x x x
```

divide is the most complex function of the lot because it requires recursion:

```
divide = $(if $(call gte,$1,$2),                \
    x $(call divide,$(call subtract,$1,$2),$2),)
```

If its first argument is less than its second, division returns 0 because the ELSE part of the $(if) is empty (see the ,) at the end). If division is possible, divide works by repeated subtraction of the second argument from the first, using the subtract function. Each time it subtracts, it adds an x and calls divide again. Here's an example:

```
$(call divide,$(three),$(two))
→ $(call divide,x x x,x x)
→ $(if $(call gte,x x x,x x),
   x $(call divide,$(call subtract,x x x,x x),x x),)

→ x $(call divide,$(call subtract,x x x,x x),x x)
→ x $(call divide,x,x x)
→ x $(if $(call gte,x,x x),
   x $(call divide,$(call subtract,x,x x),x x),)

→ x
```

First, gte returns a non-empty string, so recursion happens. Next, gte returns an empty string, so no more recursion occurs.

We can avoid recursion in the special case of division by 2; we define the halve function to be the opposite of double:

```
halve = $(subst xx,x,        \
    $(filter-out xy x y,     \
      $(join $1,$(foreach a,$1,y x))))
```

By now you've seen all the functions used in halve. Work through an example, say $(call halve,$(five)), to see how it works.

The only tricky thing to do is turn a number a user enters into a string of xs. The encode function does this by deleting a substring of xs from a predefined list of xs:

```
16 := x x x x x x x x x x x x x x x x
input_int := $(foreach a,$(16),          \
        $(foreach b,$(16),               \
          $(foreach c,$(16),$(16))))))

encode = $(wordlist 1,$1,$(input_int))
```

Here we are limited to entering numbers up to 65536. We can fix that by changing the number of xs in input_int. Once we have the number in the encoding, only available memory limits the size of integers we can work with.

Using Our Arithmetic Library: A Calculator

To really show off this library, here's an implementation of a Reverse Polish Notation calculator written entirely in GNU make functions:

```
stack :=

push = $(eval stack := $$1 $(stack))
pop = $(word 1,$(stack))$(eval stack := $(wordlist 2,$(words $(stack)),$(stack)))
pope = $(call encode,$(call pop))
pushd = $(call push,$(call decode,$1))
comma := ,
calculate = $(foreach t,$(subst $(comma), ,$1),$(call handle,$t))$(stack)
seq = $(filter $1,$2)
handle = $(call pushd,                              \
    $(if $(call seq,+,$1),                          \
      $(call plus,$(call pope),$(call pope)),       \
      $(if $(call seq,-,$1),                        \
      $(call subtract,$(call pope),$(call pope)), \
        $(if $(call seq,*,$1),                      \
      $(call multiply,$(call pope),$(call pope)), \
        $(if $(call seq,/,$1),                      \
        $(call divide,$(call pope),$(call pope)), \
          $(call encode,$1))))))
```

```
.PHONY: calc
calc: ; @echo $(call calculate,$(calc))
```

The operators and numbers are passed into GNU make in the calc variable, separated by commas. For example:

```
$ make calc="3,1,-,3,21,5,*,+,/"
54
```

Clearly, this is not what GNU make was designed for, but it does show the power of GNU make functions. Here's the complete commented makefile:

```
# input_int consists of 65536 x's built from the 16 x's in 16

16 := x x x x x x x x x x x x x x x x
input_int := $(foreach a,$(16),$(foreach b,$(16),$(foreach c,$(16),$(16))))

# decode turns a number in x's representation into an integer for human
# consumption

decode = $(words $1)

# encode takes an integer and returns the appropriate x's
# representation of the number by chopping $1 x's from the start of
# input_int

encode = $(wordlist 1,$1,$(input_int))

# plus adds its two arguments, subtract subtracts its second argument
# from its first if and only if this would not result in a negative result

plus = $1 $2

subtract = $(if $(call gte,$1,$2),        \
        $(filter-out xx,$(join $1,$2)), \
        $(warning Subtraction underflow))

# multiply multiplies its two arguments and divide divides its first
# argument by its second

multiply = $(foreach a,$1,$2)
divide = $(if $(call gte,$1,$2),x $(call divide,$(call subtract,$1,$2),$2),)

# max returns the maximum of its arguments and min the minimum

max = $(subst xx,x,$(join $1,$2))
min = $(subst xx,x,$(filter xx,$(join $1,$2)))

# The following operators return a non-empty string if their result is true:
#
# gt    First argument is greater than second argument
# gte   First argument is greater than or equal to second argument
# lt    First argument is less than second argument

# lte   First argument is less than or equal to second argument
# eq    First argument is numerically equal to the second argument
# ne    First argument is not numerically equal to the second argument

gt = $(filter-out $(words $2),$(words $(call max,$1,$2)))
lt = $(filter-out $(words $1),$(words $(call max,$1,$2)))
eq = $(filter $(words $1),$(words $2))
ne = $(filter-out $(words $1),$(words $2))
gte = $(call gt,$1,$2)$(call eq,$1,$2)
```

```makefile
lte = $(call lt,$1,$2)$(call eq,$1,$2)

# increment adds 1 to its argument, decrement subtracts 1. Note that
# decrement does not range check and hence will not underflow, but
# will incorrectly say that 0 - 1 = 0

increment = $1 x
decrement = $(wordlist 2,$(words $1),$1)

# double doubles its argument, and halve halves it

double = $1 $1
halve = $(subst xx,x,$(filter-out xy x y,$(join $1,$(foreach a,$1,y x))))

# This code implements a Reverse Polish Notation calculator by
# transforming a comma-separated list of operators (+ - * /) and
# numbers stored in the calc variable into the appropriate calls to
# the arithmetic functions defined in this makefile.

# This is the current stack of numbers entered into the calculator. The push
# function puts an item onto the top of the stack (the start of the list), and
# pop removes the top item.

stack :=

push = $(eval stack := $$1 $(stack))
pop = $(word 1,$(stack))$(eval stack := $(wordlist 2,$(words $(stack)),$(stack)))

# pope pops a number off the stack and encodes it
# and pushd pushes a number onto the stack after decoding

pope = $(call encode,$(call pop))
pushd = $(call push,$(call decode,$1))

# calculate runs through the input numbers and operations and either
# pushes a number on the stack or pops two numbers off and does a
# calculation followed by pushing the result back. When calculate is
# finished, there will be one item on the stack, which is the result.

comma := ,
calculate=$(foreach t,$(subst $(comma), ,$1),$(call handle,$t))$(stack)

# seq is a string equality operator that returns true (a non-empty
# string) if the two strings are equal

seq = $(filter $1,$2)

# handle is used by calculate to handle a single token. If it's an
# operator, the appropriate operator function is called; if it's a
# number, it is pushed.

handle = $(call pushd,                               \
      $(if $(call seq,+,$1),                         \
        $(call plus,$(call pope),$(call pope)),      \
        $(if $(call seq,-,$1),                       \
```

```
        $(call subtract,$(call pope),$(call pope)), \
          $(if $(call seq,*,$1),                    \
        $(call multiply,$(call pope),$(call pope)), \
           $(if $(call seq,/,$1),                   \
        $(call divide,$(call pope),$(call pope)),  \
             $(call encode,$1)))))))

.PHONY: calc
calc: ; @echo $(call calculate,$(calc))
```

You'll get a closer look at these techniques in Chapter 6 when you learn about the GNU Make Standard Library.

Making an XML Bill of Materials

With standard GNU make output, it's difficult to answer the question of what got built and why. This section presents a simple technique to get GNU make to create an XML file containing a *bill of materials (BOM)*. The BOM contains the names of all the files built by the makefile and is nested to show the prerequisites of each file.

An Example Makefile and BOM

Listing 5-1 shows an example makefile. We'll look at its BOM and then work backward to see how the BOM JSON file was generated.

```
all: foo bar
→ @echo Making $@

foo: baz
→ @echo Making $@

bar:
→ @echo Making $@

baz:
→ @echo Making $@
```

Listing 5-1: A simple makefile to illustrate the BOM

This makes all from foo and bar. In turn, foo is made from baz. Running this code in GNU make produces the following output:

```
$ make
Making baz
Making foo
Making bar
Making all
```

From the output, it's impossible to identify the tree-ordering of the build or which files depend on which. In this case, the makefile is small and relatively easy to trace by hand; in a real makefile, hand tracing is almost impossible.

It would be nice to produce output like that shown in Listing 5-2 that shows what was built and why:

```
<rule target="all">
<prereq>
 <rule target="foo">
  <prereq>
   <rule target="baz" />
  </prereq>
 </rule>
 <rule target="bar" />
</prereq>
</rule>
```

Listing 5-2: An XML document showing the structure of the example makefile

Here, each rule run by the makefile has a <rule> tag added with a target attribute giving the name of the target that the rule built. If the rule had any prerequisites, within the <rule>/</rule> pair a list of prerequisite rules would be enclosed in <prereq>/</prereq>.

You can see the structure of the makefile reflected in the nesting of the tags. Loading the XML document into an XML editor (or simply into a web browser) allows you to expand and contract the tree at will to explore the structure of the makefile.

How It Works

To create the output shown in Listing 5-2, the example makefile is modified to include a special bom makefile using the standard include bom method. With that included, we can generate the XML output by running GNU make using a command line, such as make bom-all.

bom-all instructs GNU make to build the BOM starting with the all target. It's as if you typed make all, but now an XML document will be created.

By default, the XML document has the same name as the makefile but with .xml appended. If the example makefile was in example.mk, the XML document created would be called example.mk.xml.

Listing 5-3 shows the contents of the bom makefile to include:

```
❶ PARENT_MAKEFILE := $(word $(words $(MAKEFILE_LIST)),x $(MAKEFILE_LIST))
❷ bom-file := $(PARENT_MAKEFILE).xml

❸ bom-old-shell := $(SHELL)
❹ SHELL = $(bom-run)$(bom-old-shell)

bom-%: %
❺ → @$(shell rm -f $(bom-file))$(call bom-dump,$*)
```

```
   bom-write = $(shell echo '$1' >> $(bom-file))
❻ bom-dump = $(if $(bom-prereq-$1),$(call bom-write,<rule target="$1">)      \
   $(call bom-write,<prereq>)$(foreach p,$(bom-prereq-$1),                    \
   $(call bom-dump,$p))$(call bom-write,</prereq>)$(call bom-write,</rule>), \
   $(call bom-write,<rule target="$1" />))

❼ bom-run = $(if $@,$(eval bom-prereq-$@ := $^))
```

Listing 5-3: The bom makefile that creates XML BOMs

First we determine the correct name for the XML file by extracting the name of the makefile that included bom into PARENT_MAKEFILE ❶, appending .xml, and storing the resulting name in bom-file ❷.

Then we use a trick that's appeared in this book a number of times: the SHELL hack. GNU make will expand the value of $(SHELL) for every rule that's run in the makefile. And at the time that $(SHELL) is expanded, the per-rule automatic variables (such as $@) have already been set. So by modifying SHELL, we can perform some task for every rule in the makefile as it runs.

At ❸, we store the original value of SHELL in bom-old-shell using an immediate assignment (:=), and we then redefine SHELL to be the expansion of $(bom-run) and the original shell at ❹. Because $(bom-run) actually expands to an empty string, the effect is that bom-run is expanded for each rule in the makefile, but the actual shell used is unaffected.

bom-run is defined at ❼. It uses $(eval) to store the relationship between the current target being built (the $(if) ensures that $@ is defined) and its prerequisites. For example, when foo is being built, a call will be made to bom-run with $@ set to foo and $^ (the list of all prerequisites) set to baz. bom-run will set the value of bom-prereq-foo to baz. Later, the values of these bom-prereq-X variables are used to print out the XML tree.

At ❺, we define the pattern rule that handles the bom-% target. Because the prerequisite of bom-% is %, this pattern rule has the effect of building the target matching the % and then building bom-%. In our example, running make bom-all matches against this pattern rule to build all and then run the commands associated with bom-% with $* set to all.

bom-%'s commands first delete the bom-file and then recursively dump out the XML starting from $*. In this example, where the user did make bom-all, the bom-% commands call bom-dump with the argument all.

We define bom-dump at ❻. It's fairly routine: it uses a helper function bom-write to echo fragments of XML to the bom-file and calls itself for each of the targets in the prerequisites of each target it is dumping. Prerequisites are extracted from the bom-prereq-X variables created by bom-run.

Gotchas

The technique in Listing 5-3 comes with a few gotchas. One gotcha is that the technique can end up producing enormous amounts of output. This is because it will print the entire tree below any target. If a target appears multiple times in the tree, a large tree can be repeated many times in the output. Even for small projects, this can make the dump time for the XML very lengthy.

As a workaround, we can change the definition of `bom-dump` to just dump the prerequisite information once for each target. This is much faster than the approach in Listing 5-3 and could be processed by a script like the following to help understand the structure of the make:

```
bom-%: %
→ @$(shell rm -f $(bom-file))$(call bom-write,<bom>)$(call bom-dump,$*)$(call bom-write,</bom>)

bom-write = $(shell echo '$1' >> $(bom-file))

bom-dump = $(if $(bom-prereq-$1),$(call bom-write,<rule target="$1">) \
$(call bom-write,<prereq>)$(foreach p,$(bom-prereq-$1),              \
$(call bom-write,<rule target="$p" />))$(call bom-write,</prereq>)   \
$(call bom-write,</rule>),$(call bom-write,<rule target="$1" />))    \
$(foreach p,$(bom-prereq-$1),$(call bom-dump,$p))$(eval bom-prereq-$1 := )
```

For the example makefile in Listing 5-1, the XML document now looks like this:

```
<bom>
<rule target="all">
 <prereq>
  <rule target="foo" />
  <rule target="bar" />
 </prereq>
</rule>
<rule target="foo">
 <prereq>
  <rule target="baz" />
 </prereq>
</rule>
<rule target="baz" />
<rule target="bar" />
</bom>
```

Another gotcha is that if the makefile includes rules with no commands, those rules will cause a break in the tree outputted by the technique in Listing 5-3. For example, if the example makefile were this:

```
all: foo bar
→ @echo Making $@

foo: baz

bar:
→ @echo Making $@

baz:
→ @echo Making $@
```

the resulting XML would not mention baz at all because the rule for foo doesn't have any commands. So SHELL is not expanded, and the hack doesn't work. Here's the XML in that case:

```
<bom>
<rule target="all">
 <prereq>
  <rule target="foo" />
  <rule target="bar" />
 </prereq>
</rule>
<rule target="foo" />
<rule target="bar" />
</bom>
```

As a workaround, we can modify foo: baz to include a useless command:

```
foo: baz ; @true
```

Now the correct results will be generated.

Advanced User-Defined Functions

In Chapter 1, we looked at creating user-defined functions in GNU make. Now we'll look inside the GNU make source code to see how we can enhance GNU make with our own built-in functions by writing some C code.

First, we get the GNU make source code from the Free Software Foundation. For this section, I'm working with GNU make 3.81. Things haven't changed much with GNU make 3.82 or 4.0.

Download make-3.81.tar.gz, and gunzip and untar, and then build GNU make using the standard configure and make:

```
$ cd make-3.81
$ ./configure
$ make
```

With that done, we are left with a working GNU make in the same directory.

Getting Started Modifying GNU make

It's handy to be able to tell which GNU make you're running, so as a first modification let's change the message printed out when we ask for the version information. Here's the default:

```
$ ./make -v
GNU Make 3.81
Copyright (C) 2006 Free Software Foundation, Inc.
This is free software; see the source for copying conditions.
```

There is NO warranty; not even for MERCHANTABILITY or FITNESS FOR A
PARTICULAR PURPOSE.

This program built for i386-apple-darwin9.2.0

As you can see, I'm working on a Mac (that final string will change depending on the machine you are working with) with GNU make version 3.81.

Let's change that message so it prints (with jgc's modifications) after
the version number. To do that, we need to open the file main.c in a text editor and find the function print_version (at line 2,922), which looks like this:

```c
/* Print version information. */

static void
print_version (void)
{
static int printed_version = 0;

char *precede = print_data_base_flag ? "# " : "";

if (printed_version)
 /* Do it only once. */
 return;

/* Print this untranslated. The coding standards recommend translating the
   (C) to the copyright symbol, but this string is going to change every
   year, and none of the rest of it should be translated (including the
   word "Copyright", so it hardly seems worth it. */

printf ("%sGNU Make %s\n\
%sCopyright (C) 2006 Free Software Foundation, Inc.\n",
    precede, version_string, precede);

printf (_("%sThis is free software; see the source for copying conditions.\n\
%sThere is NO warranty; not even for MERCHANTABILITY or FITNESS FOR A\n\
%sPARTICULAR PURPOSE.\n"),
     precede, precede, precede);

if (!remote_description || *remote_description == '\0')
 printf (_("\n%sThis program built for %s\n"), precede, make_host);
else
 printf (_("\n%sThis program built for %s (%s)\n"),
    precede, make_host, remote_description);

printed_version = 1;

/* Flush stdout so the user doesn't have to wait to see the
   version information while things are thought about. */
fflush (stdout);
}
```

The first printf in print_version is where the version number is printed. We can modify it like this:

```
printf ("%sGNU Make %s (with jgc's modifications)\n\
%sCopyright (C) 2006 Free Software Foundation, Inc.\n",
    precede, version_string, precede);
```

Save the file, and then rerun make. Now enter **make -v**:

```
$ ./make -v
GNU Make 3.81 (with jgc's modifications)
Copyright (C) 2006 Free Software Foundation, Inc.
This is free software; see the source for copying conditions.
There is NO warranty; not even for MERCHANTABILITY or FITNESS FOR A
PARTICULAR PURPOSE.

This program built for i386-apple-darwin9.2.0
```

We now know which version we're working with.

Anatomy of a Built-In Function

GNU make's built-in functions are defined in the file function.c. To begin understanding how this file works, take a look at the table of functions that GNU make knows about. It's called function_table_init[] and is on line 2,046. Because it's quite large, I've removed some lines from the middle:

```
static struct function_table_entry function_table_init[] =
{
/* Name/size */          /* MIN MAX EXP? Function */
{ STRING_SIZE_TUPLE("abspath"),    0, 1, 1, func_abspath},
{ STRING_SIZE_TUPLE("addprefix"),   2, 2, 1,
func_addsuffix_addprefix},
{ STRING_SIZE_TUPLE("addsuffix"),   2, 2, 1,
func_addsuffix_addprefix},
{ STRING_SIZE_TUPLE("basename"),   0, 1, 1, func_basename_dir},
{ STRING_SIZE_TUPLE("dir"),      0, 1, 1, func_basename_dir},
--snip--

{ STRING_SIZE_TUPLE("value"),     0, 1, 1, func_value},
{ STRING_SIZE_TUPLE("eval"),      0, 1, 1, func_eval},
#ifdef EXPERIMENTAL
{ STRING_SIZE_TUPLE("eq"),      2, 2, 1, func_eq},
{ STRING_SIZE_TUPLE("not"),      0, 1, 1, func_not},
#endif
};
```

Each line defines a single function and consists of five pieces of information: the name of the function, the minimum number of arguments that the function must have, the maximum number of arguments (specifying a maximum of zero with a non-zero minimum means that the function can have an unlimited number of arguments), whether the arguments should be expanded, and the name of the C function that actually performs the function.

For example, here's the definition of the `findstring` function:

```
{ STRING_SIZE_TUPLE("findstring"),  2, 2, 1, func_findstring},
```

`findstring` has a minimum of two arguments and a maximum of two, and the arguments should be expanded before calling the C function `func_findstring`. `func_findstring` (in `function.c` at line 819) does the work:

```
static char*
func_findstring (char *o, char **argv, const char *funcname UNUSED)
{
/* Find the first occurrence of the first string in the second. */
if (strstr (argv[1], argv[0]) != 0)
 o = variable_buffer_output (o, argv[0], strlen (argv[0]));

return o;
}
```

The C functions that implement GNU make built-in functions have three arguments: o (a pointer to a buffer into which output of the function should be written), argv (the arguments of the function as a null-terminated array of strings), and funcname (a string containing the name of the function; most functions don't need this, but it can be helpful if one C routine handles more than one GNU make function).

You can see that `func_findstring` just uses the standard C library `strstr` function to find the presence of its second argument (in `argv[1]`) in its first (in `argv[0]`).

`func_findstring` uses a handy GNU make C function called `variable_buffer_output` (defined in `expand.c` at line 57). `variable_buffer_output` copies a string into the output buffer o of a GNU make function. The first argument should be the output buffer, the second the string to copy, and the last the amount of the string to copy.

`func_findstring` either copies all of its first argument (if the `strstr` was successful) or leaves o untouched (and hence, empty, because it is initialized to an empty string before `func_findstring` is called).

With that, we have enough information to start making our own GNU make function.

Reverse a String

There's no easy way to reverse a string in GNU make, but it's easy to write a C function that does and insert it into GNU make.

First, we'll add the definition of reverse to the list of functions that GNU make knows about. reverse will have a single argument that must be expanded and will call a C function named func_reverse.

Here's the entry to add to the `function_table_init[]`:

```
{ STRING_SIZE_TUPLE("reverse"),  1, 1, 1, func_reverse},
```

Now we can define `func_reverse`, which reverses the string in `argv[0]` by swapping characters and then updates the output buffer o, as shown in Listing 5-4:

```
static char*
func_reverse(char *o, char **argv, const char *funcname UNUSED)
{
int len = strlen(argv[0]);
if (len > 0) {
 char * p = argv[0];
 int left = 0;
 int right = len - 1;
 while (left < right) {
  char temp = *(p + left);
  *(p + left) = *(p + right);
  *(p + right) = temp;
  left++;
  right--;
 }

 o = variable_buffer_output(o, p, len);
}

return o;
}
```

Listing 5-4: Defining a GNU make function using C

This function works by walking from the start and end of the string at the same time and swapping pairs of characters until left and right meet in the middle.

To test it, we can write a little makefile that tries three possibilities: an empty string, a string with even length, and a string with odd length, all calling the new built-in function reverse:

```
EMPTY :=

$(info Empty string: [$(reverse $(EMPTY))]);

EVEN := 1234
$(info Even length string: [$(reverse $(EVEN))]);

ODD := ABCDE
$(info Odd length string: [$(reverse $(ODD))]);
```

The output shows that it works correctly:

```
$ ./make
Empty string: []
Even length string: [4321]
Odd length string: [EDCBA]
```

Writing in C gives you access to the full range of C library functions; therefore, the GNU make built-in functions you can create are limited only by your imagination.

GNU make 4.0 Loadable Objects

Adding the reverse function to GNU make was fairly complex because we had to modify GNU make's source code. But using GNU make 4.0 or later, you can add C functions to GNU make without changing the source code. GNU make 4.0 added a load directive you can use to load a shared object containing GNU make functions written in C.

You can turn the reverse function from Listing 5-4 into a loadable GNU make object by saving it in a file called reverse.c with some small modifications. Here's the complete reverse.c file:

```
#include <string.h>
#include <gnumake.h>
```
❶ `int plugin_is_GPL_compatible;`
```
char* func_reverse(const char *nm, unsigned int argc, char **argv)
{
  int len = strlen(argv[0]);
  if (len > 0) {
```
❷
```
    char * p = gmk_alloc(len+1);
    *(p+len) = '\0';
    int i;
    for (i = 0; i < len; i++) {
      *(p+i) = *(argv[0]+len-i-1);
    }
    return p;
  }

  return NULL;
}

int reverse_gmk_setup()
{
```
❸
```
  gmk_add_function("reverse", func_reverse, 1, 1, 1);
  return 1;
}
```

The reverse function is added to GNU make by the call to gmk_add_function at ❸. The function reverse is then available to use just like any other GNU make built-in function. The actual reversing of a string is handled by func_reverse, which calls a GNU make API function gmk_alloc to allocate space for the new string at ❷.

At ❶ is a special, unused variable called plugin_is_GPL_compatible, which is required in any loadable module.

To use the new reverse function, you need to compile the reverse.c file into a .so file and load it into GNU make:

```
all:
--snip--

load reverse.so

❹ reverse.so: reverse.c ; @$(CC) -shared -fPIC -o $@ $<
```

The load directive loads the .so, and the rule at ❹ builds the .so from the .c file. If the .so file is missing when GNU make encounters the load directive, GNU make builds it (using the rule) and then restarts, parsing the makefile from the beginning.

Once loaded, you can use reverse as follows:

```
A_PALINDROME := $(reverse saippuakivikauppias)
```

Notice that it is not necessary to use $(call). The reverse function is just like any other built-in GNU make function.

Using Guile in GNU make

GNU make 4.0 introduced a big change with the $(guile) function. This function's argument is sent to the built-in Guile language and is executed by it. (GNU Guile is an implementation of Scheme, which itself is Lisp.) $(guile)'s return value is the return value from the Guile code that was executed after converting to a type that GNU make recognizes. Strictly speaking, GNU make doesn't have data types (everything is a string), although it sometimes treats strings as other types (for example, a string with spaces in it is treated as a list by many functions).

Here's how to reverse a list using $(guile) and the Guile function reverse:

```
NAMES := liesl friedrich louisa kurt brigitta marta gretl

❶ $(info $(guile (reverse '($(NAMES)))))
```

When run, this makefile will output:

```
$ make
gretl marta brigitta kurt louisa friedrich liesl
```

It's worth diving into ❶ to see what happens, because there are a couple of subtle points. The argument to $(guile) is first expanded by GNU make, so ❶ becomes:

```
$(info $(guile (reverse '(liesl friedrich louisa kurt brigitta marta gretl))))
```

So the Guile code to be executed is (reverse '(liesl friedrich louisa kurt brigitta marta gretl)). The GNU make variable $(NAMES) has been expanded into the list of names and is turned into a Guile list by wrapping it in '(...). Because Guile has data types, you must use the correct syntax: in this case, you need to surround a list with parentheses and quote it with a single quote to tell Guile that this is a literal list (not a function invocation).

The Guile reverse function reverses this list and returns the reversed list. GNU make then converts the Guile list into a GNU make list (a string with spaces in it). Finally, $(info) displays the list.

Because Guile is a rich language, it's possible to create more complex functions. Here, for example, is a GNU make function called file-exists that uses the Guile access? function to determine whether a file exists. It returns a Boolean value after converting the Guile #t/#f (true/false) value returned by access? to a GNU make Boolean (a non-empty string for true or an empty string for false):

```
file-exists = $(guile (access? "$1" R_OK))
```

Notice the double quotes around the parameter $1. Guile needs to know that the filename is actually a string.

You can build a more complex example by using the Guile http-get function to download data from the Web inside a makefile:

```
define setup
(use-modules (web uri))
(use-modules (web client))
(use-modules (ice-9 receive))
endef

$(guile $(setup))

UA := "Mozilla/5.0 (Macintosh; Intel Mac OS X 10_10_0)       \
AppleWebKit/537.36 (KHTML, like Gecko) Chrome/40.0.2214.115 \
Safari/537.36"

define get-url
(receive (headers body)
  (http-get
    (string->uri "$1")
    #:headers '((User-Agent . $(UA))))
  body)
endef
```

```
utc-time = $(guile $(call get-url,http://www.timeapi.org/utc/now))

$(info $(utc-time))
```

Here, http-get gets the current UTC time from a web service that returns
the time as a string in the body of the HTTP response.

The utc-time variable contains the current UTC time. It works by retriev-
ing the time from *http://www.timeapi.org/utc/now/* using the Guile code stored
in the get-url variable. The Guile code in get-url uses the http-get function
to retrieve the header and body of a web page, and returns just the body.

Notice how you can use the GNU make define directive to create large
blocks of Guile code. If the Guile code becomes unwieldy, do this:

```
$(guile (load "myfunctions.scm"))
```

This is how you can store the Guile code in a file and load it.

Self-Documenting Makefiles

Upon encountering a new makefile, many ask "What does this makefile
do?" or "What are the important targets I need to know about?" For any
sizable makefile, answering those questions can be difficult. In this section,
I present a simple GNU make trick that you can use to make a makefile self-
documenting and print out help automatically.

Before I show you how it works, here's a small example. This makefile
has three targets that the creator thinks you need to know about: all, clean,
and package. They've documented the makefile by including some extra
information with each target:

```
include help-system.mk

all: $(call print-help,all,Build all modules in Banana Wumpus system)
→ ...commands for building all ...

clean: $(call print-help,clean,Remove all object and library files)
→ ...commands for doing a clean ...

package: $(call print-help,package,Package application-must run all target first)
→ ...commands for doing package step ...
```

For each of the targets needing documentation, the makefile maintainer
has added a call to a user-defined function print-help with two arguments:
the name of the target and a brief description of that target. The call to
print-help doesn't interfere with the definition of the prerequisites of the
rule because it always returns (or is expanded to) an empty string.

Typing make with this makefile outputs:

```
$ make
Type 'make help' to get help
```

and typing make help reveals:

```
$ make help
Makefile:11: all -- Build all modules in Banana Wumpus system
Makefile:17: clean -- Remove all object and library files
Makefile:23: package -- Package application-must run all target first
```

make automatically prints the names of the interesting targets and includes an explanation of what they do, as well as the line number of the makefile where you can find more information about the commands for that target.

The interesting work is done by the included makefile help-system.mak. help-system.mak first defines the user-defined function print-help. print-help is the function called for each target that needs documenting:

```
define print-help
$(if $(need-help),$(warning $1 -- $2))
endef
```

print-help uses GNU make's $(warning) function to output the appropriate message based on the two parameters passed to it. The first parameter (stored in $1) is the name of the target, and the second (in $2) is the help text; they are separated by --. $(warning) writes a message to the console and returns an empty string; hence, you can safely use print-help in the prerequisite list of a rule.

print-help decides whether it needs to print any message by examining the need-help variable, which will be the string help if the user specified help on the make command line, or empty if they did not. In either case, the expanded value of print-help is an empty string.

need-help determines whether the user entered help on the command line by examining the built-in variable MAKECMDGOALS, which is a space-separated list of all the goals specified on the make command line. need-help filters out any goal that doesn't match the text help and, hence, is the string help if help was in MAKECMDGOALS or empty otherwise.

```
need-help := $(filter help,$(MAKECMDGOALS))
```

The definition of need-help and print-help are all we need to have make print out help on each target when run with help on the command line. The rest of help-system.mak prints the message Type 'make help' to get help when the user simply types make.

It defines a default goal for the makefile called help, which will be run if no other goal is specified on the command line:

```
help: ; @echo $(if $(need-help),,Type \'$(MAKE)$(dash-f) help\' to get help)
```

This rule will output nothing if the user has asked for help (determined by the need-help variable), but if not, it will output the message containing the name of the make program (stored in $(MAKE)) followed by the appropriate parameter to load the makefile. This last part is subtle.

If the makefile that included help-system.mak was simply called Makefile (or makefile or GNUmakefile), then GNU make would look for it automatically, and it's enough to type make help to get help. If it was not, the actual makefile name needs to be specified with the -f parameter.

This rule uses a variable called dash-f to output the correct command line. dash-f contains nothing if one of the default makefile names was used, or it contains -f followed by the correct makefile name:

```
dash-f := $(if $(filter-out Makefile makefile GNUmakefile, \
$(parent-makefile)), -f $(parent-makefile))
```

dash-f looks at the value of a variable called parent-makefile, which contains the name of the makefile that included help-system.mak. If it's not a standard name, dash-f returns the name of the parent makefile with the -f option.

parent-makefile is determined by looking at the MAKEFILE_LIST. MAKEFILE_LIST is a list of all the makefiles read so far in order. help-system.mak first determines its own name:

```
this-makefile := $(call last-element,$(MAKEFILE_LIST))
```

Then it gets the list of all the other makefiles included by removing this-makefile (that is, help-system.mak) from the MAKEFILE_LIST:

```
other-makefiles := $(filter-out $(this-makefile),$(MAKEFILE_LIST))
```

The final element of other-makefiles will be the parent of help-system.mak:

```
parent-makefile := $(call last-element,$(other-makefiles))
```

You use the last-element function to get the last element of a space-separated list:

```
define last-element
$(word $(words $1),$1)
endef
```

last-element returns the last word in a list by getting the word count using $(words) and returning the word referenced by it. Because GNU make's lists are counted from position 1, $(words LIST) is the index of the last element.

Documenting Makefiles with print-help

Documenting makefiles with print-help is easy. Just add the relevant $(call print-help,target,description) to the prerequisite list for each target you want to document. If you add the call right next to the commands that are used for the target, the help system not only prints help but also automatically points the user to the place in the makefile to look for more information.

It's also easy to keep the documentation up to date because the description of a target is actually part of the definition of the target, not in a separate help list.

The Complete help-system.mak

Finally, here's the full help_system.mak file:

```
help: ; @echo $(if $(need-help),,Type \'$(MAKE)$(dash-f) help\' to get help)

need-help := $(filter help,$(MAKECMDGOALS))

define print-help
$(if $(need-help),$(warning $1 -- $2))
endef

define last-element
$(word $(words $1),$1)
endef

this-makefile := $(call last-element,$(MAKEFILE_LIST))
other-makefiles := $(filter-out $(this-makefile),$(MAKEFILE_LIST))
parent-makefile := $(call last-element,$(other-makefiles))

dash-f := $(if $(filter-out Makefile makefile GNUmakefile, \
$(parent-makefile)), -f $(parent-makefile))
```

Just include help-system.mak to start using this system in makefiles that could use documentation.

In Chapter 6, we'll look at a helpful resource, the GMSL project. Creating GNU make built-in functions is easy, but it does cause a maintenance problem: the next time GNU make is updated, we'll need to port our changes to the new version. If we can do what we need with GNU make built-ins without modifying the source, then makefiles will be more portable. The GMSL provides lots of additional functionality without modifying the GNU make source.

6

THE GNU MAKE STANDARD LIBRARY

The *GNU Make Standard Library (GMSL)* is a SourceForge-hosted, open source project that I started to capture common functions that makefile authors end up writing over and over again. To prevent makefile writers from reinventing the wheel, the GMSL implements common functions, such as reversing lists, uppercasing a string, or mapping a function across every element of a list.

The GMSL has list and string manipulation functions, a complete integer arithmetic library, and functions for data structures. Also included are GNU make implementations of associative arrays, sets, and stacks, as well as built-in debugging facilities.

In this chapter, you'll learn how to use the functions of the GMSL in realistic makefiles. In addition, you'll see a complete reference for the different categories of GMSL functions. For the latest revision of the GMSL, visit *http://gmsl.sf.net/*.

Importing the GMSL

The GMSL is implemented as a pair of makefiles named gmsl and __gmsl. __gmsl is imported by gmsl, so to include the GMSL in your makefile, just add this:

```
include gmsl
```

You can do this in as many files as you want. To prevent multiple definitions and unintended error messages, the GMSL automatically detects if it has already been included.

Of course, GNU make must be able to find gmsl and __gmsl. To do that, GNU make looks for makefiles in a number of places by default, including /usr/local/include, /usr/gnu/include/, /usr/include, the current directory, and any directories specified by the GNU make -I (or --include-dirL) command line option.

A good place to put gmsl and __gmsl is /usr/local/include, where they'll be available to all your makefiles.

If GNU make can't find gmsl or __gmsl, you'll get the regular GNU make error message:

```
Makefile:1: gmsl: No such file or directory
```

The GMSL uses a little trick to make the location of gmsl completely flexible. Because gmsl uses include to find __gmsl, the gmsl makefile needs to know where to find __gmsl.

Let's suppose that gmsl was stored in /foo and included with include /foo/gmsl. To make this work without having to modify gmsl to hardcode the location of __gmsl, gmsl figures out where it's located using MAKEFILE_LIST and then prepends the appropriate path to the include __gmsl:

```
# Try to determine where this file is located. If the caller did
# include /foo/gmsl then extract the /foo/ so that __gmsl gets
# included transparently

__gmsl_root := $(word $(words $(MAKEFILE_LIST)),$(MAKEFILE_LIST))

# If there are any spaces in the path in __gmsl_root then give up

ifeq (1,$(words $(__gmsl_root)))
__gmsl_root := $(patsubst %gmsl,%,$(__gmsl_root))
else
__gmsl_root :=
endif

include $(__gmsl_root)__gmsl
```

That's a handy technique if you want your makefiles to be location independent.

Calling a GMSL Function

The functions in the GMSL are implemented as normal GNU make function declarations. For example, the function last (which returns the last element of a list) is declared like this:

```
last = $(if $1,$(word $(words $1),$1))
```

The function is called using GNU make's built-in $(call). For example, to return the last element of the list 1 2 3, do this:

```
$(call last,1 2 3)
```

This will return 3. $(call) expands the variable named in its first argument (in this case, last), setting special local variables ($1, $2, $3, . . .)to the arguments given to $(call) after the function name. So $1 is 1 2 3 in this case.

The GMSL defines the Boolean values true and false, which are just variables and can be accessed using $() or ${}: for example, $(true) or ${false}. false is an empty string, and true is the letter T; these definitions correspond to GNU make's notion of true (a non-empty string) and false (an empty string). You can use true and false in GNU make's $(if) function or within a preprocessor ifeq:

```
$(if $(true),It's true!,Totally false)

ifeq ($(true),$(true))
 --snip--
endif
```

These examples are contrived. You'd expect the $(true) in the $(if) and the first $(true) in the ifeq to be the return values from a function call, not a constant value.

Checking the GMSL Version

The GMSL includes a function that you can use to check that the version included is compatible with your use of the GMSL. The function gmsl_compatible checks that the version number of the included GMSL is greater than or equal to the version number passed as an argument.

At the time of this writing, the current GMSL version is v1.1.7. To check that the included GMSL is at least, say, v1.1.2, call gmsl_compatible with a list argument containing three elements: 1 1 2.

```
$(call gmsl_compatible,1 1 2)
```

This will return $(true) because the current GMSL is v1.1.7, which is greater than v1.1.2. If we asked for v2.0.0, we'd get the response $(false):

```
$(call gmsl_compatible,2 0 0)
```

A simple way to make sure that you are using the right version of GMSL is to wrap the call to gmsl_compatible in an assertion:

```
$(call assert,$(call gmsl_compatible,1 0 0),Wrong GMSL version)
```

This will stop the make process with an error if an incompatible version of GMSL is found.

Example Real-World GMSL Use

Now that you're set up with the GMSL, let's look at some examples. All of these solve problems that real-world makefiles have to deal with, like case-insensitive comparisons and searching a path for a file.

Case-Insensitive Comparison

GMSL contains two functions that let you create a simple function to do a case-insensitive comparison of two strings:

```
ifcase = $(call seq,$(call lc,$1),$(call lc,$2))
```

This works by lowercasing its two arguments (using the GMSL lc function) and then calling seq (the GMSL string equality function) to see if they are the same. Here's one way to use ifcase:

```
CPPFLAGS += $(if $(call ifcase,$(DEBUG),yes),-DDEBUG,)
```

Here it's used to see if the DEBUG variable has been set to yes; if it has, -DDEBUG is added to CPPFLAGS.

Finding a Program on the Path

Here's a function definition that will search the PATH for an executable:

```
findpath = $(call first,$(call map,wildcard,$(call addsuffix,/$1,$(call split,:,$(PATH)))))
```

For example, $(call findpath,cat) will search the PATH for the first cat program. It uses three functions from the GMSL: first, map, and split. It uses two built-in functions: wildcard and addsuffix.

The call to split breaks the PATH variable into a list, separating it at colons. Then the built-in addsuffix function is called, which adds /$1 to each element of the PATH. $1 contains the parameter to findpath, which is the name of the program we're searching for (in this case, it was cat).

Then the GMSL `map` function is called to perform a built-in `wildcard` on each possible program filename. With no wildcard characters in the filename, `wildcard` will return the name of the file if it exists or an empty string. So `map` has the effect of finding the location (or locations) of cat on the `PATH` by testing each file in turn.

Finally, a call to the GMSL function `first` returns the first element of the list that `map` returns (the list of all cat programs on the `PATH`).

A debugging feature of GMSL is the ability to trace calls to GMSL functions. By setting `GMSL_TRACE` to 1, GMSL will output each call to a GMSL function with its parameters. For example:

```
Makefile:8: split(':', '/home/jgc/bin:/usr/local/bin:/usr/bin:/usr/X11R6/bin:/
bin:/usr/games:/opt/gnome/bin:/opt/kde3/bin:/usr/lib/java/jre/bin')
Makefile:8: map('wildcard',' /home/jgc/bin/make /usr/local/bin/make /usr/bin/
make /usr/X11R6/bin/make /bin/make /usr/games/make /opt/gnome/bin/make /opt/
kde3/bin/make /usr/lib/java/jre/bin/make')
Makefile:8: first(' /usr/bin/make')
```

Here we're searching for cat using the `findpath` function with tracing turned on.

Using Assertions to Check Inputs

Typically, a makefile is executed specifying a goal for the build (or under the assumption that there's an all target or similar at the start of the makefile). In addition, there are typically environment variables (like debug options, architecture settings, and so on) that affect the build. A quick way to check that these have been set correctly is to use GMSL assertion functions.

Here's an example that checks that `DEBUG` has been set to yes or no, that `ARCH` contains the word Linux, that we've specified an output directory in the `OUTDIR` variable, and that that directory exists:

```
$(call assert,$(OUTDIR),Must set OUTDIR)
$(call assert_exists,$(OUTDIR),Must set OUTDIR)
$(call assert,$(if $(call seq,$(DEBUG),yes),$(true),$(call seq,$(DEBUG),no)),DEBUG must be yes or no)
$(call assert,$(call findstring,Linux,$(ARCH)),ARCH must be Linux)
```

The assertion functions will generate a fatal error if their first argument is $(false) (that is, an empty string).

The first assert checks that $(OUTDIR) has been set to something. If it has a non-empty value, the assertion passed; otherwise, an error is generated:

```
Makefile:3: *** GNU Make Standard Library: Assertion failure: Must set OUTDIR.
Stop.
```

The second assertion is of the form assert_exists, which checks to see whether its first argument exists in the file system. In this case, it checks to see whether the directory pointed to by $(OUTDIR) exists. It doesn't check to see whether it's a directory. We can add another assertion to do that, like this:

```
$(call assert,$(wildcard $(OUTDIR)/.),OUTDIR must be a directory)
```

This looks to see if $(OUTDIR) contains a dot (.). If not, $(OUTDIR) is not a directory, and the call to wildcard will return an empty string, causing the assertion to fail.

The third assertion checks that DEBUG is either yes or no using the GMSL seq function to check the value. Finally, we assert using findstring that $(ARCH) must contain the word Linux (with the L capitalized).

Is DEBUG Set to Y?

The GMSL has the logical operators and, or, xor, nand, nor, xnor, and not that work with GNU make's concept of truth values and the GMSL variables $(true) and $(false).

You can use GNU make's (and GMSL's) Boolean values with both GMSL functions and GNU make's built-in $(if). The GMSL logical operators were designed for use with $(if) and the GNU make preprocessor ifeq directive.

Imagine that a makefile has a debug option, enabled by setting the DEBUG environment variable to Y. Using the GMSL function seq (string equal) and the or operator, you can easily determine whether debugging is desired or not:

```
include gmsl

debug_needed := $(call or,$(call seq,$(DEBUG),Y),$(call seq,$(DEBUG),y))
```

Because the GMSL has a lowercase function (lc), you can write this example without the or:

```
include gmsl

debug_needed := $(call seq,$(call lc,$(DEBUG)),y)
```

But the logical operator or lets us be even more generous and accept YES as well as Y for the debug option:

```
include gmsl

debug_needed := $(call or,$(call seq,$(call lc,$(DEBUG)),y),$(call seq,$(call lc,$(DEBUG)),yes))
```

The function debug_needed is case insensitive too.

Is DEBUG Set to Y or N?

Another possible use of the logical operators is to force the user of the makefile to set DEBUG to either Y or N, thus avoiding problems if they forget about the debug option. The GMSL assertion function assert will output a fatal error if its argument is not true. So we can use it to assert that DEBUG must be Y or N:

```
include gmsl

$(call assert,$(call or,$(call seq,$(DEBUG),Y),$(call seq,$(DEBUG),N)),DEBUG must be Y or N)
```

Here's an example:

```
$ make DEBUG=Oui
Makefile:1: *** GNU Make Standard Library: Assertion failure: DEBUG must be Y
or N. Stop.
```

The assertion generates this error if the user makes the mistake of setting DEBUG to Oui.

Using Logical Operators in the Preprocessor

Because GNU make's preprocessor (which has ifeq, ifneq, and ifdef directives) doesn't have any logical operations, it's difficult to write a complex statement. For example, to define a section of a makefile if DEBUG is set to Y or Yes in GNU make, you must either duplicate a section of code (yuck!) or write a statement that's hard to understand:

```
ifeq ($(DEBUG),$(filter $(DEBUG),Y Yes))
--snip--
endif
```

This works by filtering the list Y Yes with the value of $(DEBUG), which returns an empty list if $(DEBUG) is not Y or Yes, or returns the value of $(DEBUG) if it is. The ifeq then compares the resulting value with $(DEBUG). That's pretty ugly, hard to maintain, and contains a subtle bug. (What happens if $(DEBUG) is empty? Hint: empty is the same as Y or Yes.) Fixing the bug means doing something like this:

```
ifeq (x$(DEBUG)x,$(filter x$(DEBUG)x,xYx xYesx))
--snip--
endif
```

The GMSL or operator makes this much clearer:

```
include gmsl

ifeq ($(true),$(call or,$(call seq,$(DEBUG),Y),$(call seq,$(DEBUG),Yes)))
--snip--
endif
```

This is much more maintainable. It works by oring two calls to seq and comparing the result with $(true).

Removing Duplicates from a List

The GMSL function uniq removes duplicates from a list. GNU make has a built-in sort function that sorts a list and removes duplicates; uniq removes duplicates without sorting the list (which can be handy if list order is important).

For example, $(sort c b a a c) will return a b c, whereas $(call uniq,c b a a c) returns c b a.

Say you need to simplify the PATH variable by removing duplicate entries while preserving the order. The PATH is typically a colon-separated list of paths (like /usr/bin:/bin:/usr/local/bin:/bin). Here simple-path is the PATH with duplicates removed and order preserved:

```
include gmsl

simple-path := $(call merge,:,$(call uniq,$(call split,:,$(PATH))))
```

This uses three GMSL functions: uniq, split (which splits a string into a list at a certain separator character; in this case, a colon), and merge (which merges a list into a string separating list entries with a character; in this case, a colon).

Automatically Incrementing a Version Number

When it's release time for a piece of software, it's handy to have a way to increment the version number automatically. Suppose that a project contains a file called version.c that contains the current version number as a string:

```
char * ver = "1.0.0";
```

It would be ideal to just type make major-release, make minor-release, or make dot-release and have one of the three parts of the version number automatically update and the version.c file change.

Here's how to do that:

```
VERSION_C := version.c
VERSION := $(shell cat $(VERSION_C))

space :=
space +=

PARTS := $(call split,",$(subst $(space),,$(VERSION)))

VERSION_NUMBER := $(call split,.,$(word 2,$(PARTS)))
MAJOR := $(word 1,$(VERSION_NUMBER))
MINOR := $(word 2,$(VERSION_NUMBER))
DOT := $(word 3,$(VERSION_NUMBER))
```

```
      major-release minor-release dot-release:
❶ →  @$(eval increment_name := $(call uc,$(subst -release,,$@)))
❷ →  @$(eval $(increment_name) := $(call inc,$($(increment_name))))
❸ →  @echo 'char * ver = "$(MAJOR).$(MINOR).$(DOT)";' > $(VERSION_C)
```

The VERSION variable contains the contents of the version.c file, which will be something like char * ver = "1.0.0";. The PARTS variable is a list created by first removing all the whitespace from VERSION and then splitting on the double quotes. That splits VERSION into the list char*ver= 1.0.0 ;.

So PARTS is a list with three elements, and the second element is the current version number, which is extracted into VERSION_NUMBER and turned into a list of three elements: 1 0 0.

Next, variables called MAJOR, MINOR, and DOT are extracted from VERSION_NUMBER. If the version number in version.c was 1.2.3, then MAJOR will be 1, MINOR will be 2, and DOT will be 3.

Finally, three rules are defined for major, minor, and dot releases. These use some $(eval) trickery to use the same rule body to update the major, minor, or dot release number depending on which of major-release, minor-release, or dot-release was specified on the command line.

To understand how it works, follow what happens when you do make minor-release with an existing version number of 1.0.0.

The $(eval increment_name := $(call uc,$(subst -release,,$@))) ❶ first uses $(subst) to remove -release from the target name (so minor-release becomes simply minor).

Then it calls the GMSL uc function (which uppercases a string) to turn minor into MINOR. It stores that in a variable called increment-name. Here's the tricky part: increment-name will be used as the name of a variable to increment (one of MAJOR, MINOR, or DOT).

At ❷, $(eval $(increment_name) := $(call inc,$($(increment_name)))) actually does that work. It uses the GMSL inc function to increment the value stored in the variable whose name is in increment-name (notice the $($(increment-name)), which finds the value of a variable whose name is in another variable) and then sets that value to the incremented value.

Finally, it just creates a new version.c containing the new version number ❸. For example:

```
$ make -n major-release
echo 'char * ver = "2.0.0";' > version.c
$ make -n minor-release
echo 'char * ver = "1.1.0";' > version.c
$ make n dot-release
echo 'char * ver = "1.0.1";' > version.c
```

This is the result of using the -n option when starting from version 1.0.0 and asking for the different possible releases.

GMSL Reference

This section is a complete reference for the GNU Make Standard Library version 1.1.7 and covers GMSL logical operators; integer functions; list, string, and set manipulation functions; associative arrays; and named stacks. For each category of GMSL functions, you'll see an introduction to the functions, followed by a quick reference section that lists arguments and returns. For the latest version of the complete reference, check the GMSL website at *http://gmsl.sf.net/*.

If you're interested in advanced GNU make programming, it's worth studying the source code of the GMSL (especially the file __gmsl). The techniques used to create individual GMSL functions are often useful in other situations.

Logical Operators

GMSL has Booleans $(true), a non-empty string actually set to the single character T, and $(false), an empty string. You can use the following operators with those variables or with functions that return those values.

Although these functions are consistent in that they always return $(true) or $(false), they are lenient about accepting any non-empty string that indicates *true*. For example:

```
$(call or,$(wildcard /tmp/foo),$(wildcard /tmp/bar))
```

This tests for the existence of either of two files, /tmp/foo and /tmp/bar, using $(wildcard) and the GMSL or function. Doing $(wildcard /tmp/foo) will return /tmp/foo if the file exists or an empty string if not. So the output of the $(wildcard /tmp/foo) can be fed directly into or, where /tmp/foo will be interpreted as *true* and an empty string as *false*.

If you feel more comfortable working exclusively with values like $(true) and $(false), define a make-bool function like this:

```
make-bool = $(if $(strip $1),$(true),$(false))
```

This will turn any non-empty string (after stripping off whitespace) into $(true) and leave a blank string (or one that had only whitespace in it) as $(false). make-bool can be handy when whitespace might slip into values returned by functions.

For example, here's a small GNU make variable that is $(true) if the current month is January:

```
january-now := $(call make-bool,$(filter Jan,$(shell date)))
```

This runs the date shell command, extracts the word Jan, and turns it into a truth value using make-bool. Using $(filter) like this treats the result of date as a list and then filters out any word in the list that is not Jan. This technique can be handy in other situations for extracting parts of a string.

You can make a generic function to discover if a list contains a word:

```
contains-word = $(call make-bool,$(filter $1,$2))
january-now := $(call contains-word,Jan,$(shell date))
```

Using contains-word, you can redefine january-now.

not

The GMSL includes all the common logical operators. The simplest is the not function, which logically negates its argument:

---
not

Argument: A single boolean value
Returns: $(true) if the boolean is $(false) and vice versa

For example, $(call not,$(true)) returns $(false).

and

The and function returns $(true) if (and only if) both its arguments are true:

---
and

Arguments: Two boolean values
Returns: $(true) if both of the arguments are $(true)

For example, $(call and,$(true),$(false)) returns $(false).

or

The or function returns $(true) if either of its arguments is true:

---
or

Arguments: Two boolean values
Returns: $(true) if either of the arguments is $(true)

For example, $(call or,$(true),$(false)) returns $(true).

xor

The xor function is *exclusive or:*

---
xor

Arguments: Two boolean values
Returns: $(true) if exactly one of the booleans is true

For example, $(call xor,$(true),$(false)) returns $(true).

nand

nand is simply *not and*:

---

nand

```
Arguments: Two boolean values
Returns:   Value of 'not and'
```

For example, $(call nand,$(true),$(false)) returns $(true) where $(call and,$(true),$(false)) returns $(false).

nor

nor is simply *not or*:

---

nor

```
Arguments: Two boolean values
Returns:   Value of 'not or'
```

For example, $(call nor,$(true),$(false)) returns $(false) where $(call or,$(true),$(false)) returns $(true).

xnor

The rarely used xnor is *not xor*:

---

xnor

```
Arguments: Two boolean values
Returns:   Value of 'not xor'
```

Note that the GMSL logical functions and and or are not *short circuiting*; both of the arguments to those functions are expanded before performing the logical and or or. GNU make 3.81 introduced built-in and and or functions that are short circuiting: they evaluate their first argument and then decide whether it's necessary to evaluate their second.

Integer Arithmetic Functions

In Chapter 5, you saw how to perform arithmetic inside GNU make by representing non-negative integers as lists of xs. For example, 4 is x x x x. GMSL uses the same representation for integers and provides a wide range of functions for integer calculations.

The arithmetic library functions come in two forms: one form of each function takes integers as arguments, and the other form takes encoded arguments (xs created by a call to int_encode). For example, there are two plus functions: plus (called with integer arguments, returns an integer) and int_plus (called with encoded arguments, returns an encoded result).

plus will be slower than int_plus because its arguments and result must be translated between the x format and integers. If you're doing a complex calculation, use the int_* forms with a single encoding of inputs and single decoding of the output. For simple calculations, you can use the direct forms.

int_decode

The int_decode function takes a number in x-representation and returns the decimal integer that it represents:

---

int_decode

```
Arguments: 1: A number in x-representation
Returns:   The integer for human consumption that is represented
           by the string of x's
```

---

int_encode

int_encode is the opposite of int_decode: it takes a decimal integer and returns the x-representation:

---

int_encode

```
Arguments: 1: A number in human-readable integer form
Returns:   The integer encoded as a string of x's
```

---

int_plus

int_plus adds two numbers in x-representation together and returns their sum in x-representation:

---

int_plus

```
Arguments: 1: A number in x-representation
           2: Another number in x-representation
Returns:   The sum of the two numbers in x-representation
```

---

plus

To add decimal integers, use the plus function, which converts to and from x-representation and calls int_plus:

---

plus (wrapped version of int_plus)

```
Arguments: 1: An integer
           2: Another integer
Returns:   The sum of the two integers
```

---

int_subtract

int_subtract subtracts two numbers in x-representation and returns the difference in x-representation:

---

int_subtract

Arguments: 1: A number in x-representation
          2: Another number in x-representation
Returns: The difference of the two numbers in x-representation,
          or outputs an error on a numeric underflow

If the difference will be less than 0 (which can't be represented), an error occurs.

subtract

To subtract decimal integers, use the subtract function, which converts to and from x-representation and calls int_subtract:

---

subtract (wrapped version of int_subtract)

Arguments: 1: An integer
          2: Another integer
Returns: The difference of the two integers, or outputs an error on a
          numeric underflow

If the difference will be less than 0 (which can't be represented), an error occurs.

int_multiply

int_multiply multiplies two numbers that are in x-representation:

---

int_multiply

Arguments: 1: A number in x-representation
          2: Another number in x-representation
Returns: The product of the two numbers in x-representation

---

multiply

multiply will multiply two decimal integers and return their product. It automatically converts to and from x-representation and calls int_multiply:

---

multiply (wrapped version of int_multiply)

Arguments: 1: An integer
          2: Another integer
Returns: The product of the two integers

---

int_divide

int_divide divides one number by another; both are in x-representation, as is the result:

---

int_divide

Arguments: 1: A number in x-representation
           2: Another number in x-representation
Returns: The result of integer division of argument 1 divided
           by argument 2 in x-representation

---

divide

The divide function calls int_divide to divide two decimal integers, automatically converting to and from x-representation:

---

divide (wrapped version of int_divide)

Arguments: 1: An integer
           2: Another integer
Returns: The integer division of the first argument by the second

---

int_max and int_min

int_max and int_min return the maximum and minimum, respectively, of two numbers in x-representation:

---

int_max, int_min

Arguments: 1: A number in x-representation
           2: Another number in x-representation
Returns: The maximum or minimum of its arguments in x-representation

---

max and min

The decimal integer equivalents of int_max and int_min are max and min; they automatically convert to and from x-representation:

---

max, min

Arguments: 1: An integer
           2: Another integer
Returns: The maximum or minimum of its integer arguments

---

int_inc

int_inc is a small helper function that just adds one to an x-representation number:

---

int_inc

Arguments: 1: A number in x-representation
Returns: The number incremented by 1 in x-representation

---

inc

The inc function adds one to a decimal integer:

---

inc

Arguments: 1: An integer
Returns: The argument incremented by 1

---

int_dec

The opposite of int_inc is int_dec: it decreases a number by one:

---

int_dec

Arguments: 1: A number in x-representation
Returns: The number decremented by 1 in x-representation

---

dec

The dec function decrements a decimal integer by one:

---

dec

Arguments: 1: An integer
Returns: The argument decremented by 1

---

int_double

The double and halve functions (and their int_double and int_halve equivalents) are provided for performance reasons. If you're multiplying by two or dividing by two, these functions will be faster than multiplication and division.

int_double will double an integer:

---

int_double

Arguments: 1: A number in x-representation
Returns: The number doubled (* 2) and returned in x-representation

---

double

double will double a decimal integer:

---

double

Arguments: 1: An integer
Returns: The integer times 2

Internally, it converts to x-representation and calls int_double.

int_halve

You can perform an integer division by two by calling int_halve on an
x-representation number:

---

int_halve

Arguments: 1: A number in x-representation
Returns: The number halved (/ 2) and returned in x-representation

---

halve

Finally, there's halve:

---

halve

Arguments: 1: An integer
Returns: The integer divided by 2

This is the decimal integer equivalent of int_halve.

Integer Comparison Functions

All the integer comparison functions return $(true) or $(false):

---

int_gt, int_gte, int_lt, int_lte, int_eq, int_ne

Arguments: Two x-representation numbers to be compared
Returns: $(true) or $(false)

int_gt   First argument is greater than second argument
int_gte First argument is greater than or equal to second argument
int_lt   First argument is less than second argument
int_lte First argument is less than or equal to second argument
int_eq   First argument is numerically equal to the second argument
int_ne   First argument is not numerically equal to the second argument

---

These can be used with GNU make and GMSL functions as well as with
directives that expect Boolean values (such as the GMSL logical operators).

But you are more likely to use these versions of the comparison functions:

`gt, gte, lt, lte, eq, ne`

Arguments: Two integers to be compared
Returns: $(true) or $(false)

gt First argument is greater than second argument
gte First argument is greater than or equal to second argument
lt First argument is less than second argument
lte First argument is less than or equal to second argument
eq First argument is numerically equal to the second argument
ne First argument is not numerically equal to the second argument

---

These operate on decimal integers, not the internal x-representation that GMSL uses.

Miscellaneous Integer Functions

Most likely, you're not going to need to do anything advanced with GNU make arithmetic, but the miscellaneous functions detailed here do base conversions and generation of numeric sequences. They can, on occasion, be useful.

sequence

You use the sequence function to generate a sequence of numbers:

---

sequence

Arguments: 1: An integer
           2: An integer
Returns: The sequence [arg1 arg2] if arg1 >= arg2 or [arg2 arg1] if arg2 > arg1

For example, $(call sequence,10,15) will be the list 10 11 12 13 14 15. To create a decreasing sequence, you invert the parameters to sequence. For example, $(call sequence,15,10) will be the list 15 14 13 12 11 10.

dec2hex, dec2bin, and dec2oct

The dec2hex, dec2bin, and dec2oct functions perform conversion between decimal numbers and hexadecimal, binary, and octal forms:

---

dec2hex, dec2bin, dec2oct

Arguments: 1: An integer
Returns: The decimal argument converted to hexadecimal, binary or octal

---

For example, $(call dec2hex,42) will be 2a.

No options are available for padding with leading zeroes. If that's necessary, you can use GMSL string functions. For example, here's a padded version of dec2hex that takes two parameters: a decimal number to be converted to hexadecimal and the number of digits to output:

```
__repeat = $(if $2,$(call $0,$1,$(call rest,$2)),$1$3),$3)

repeat = $(call __repeat,$1,$(call int_encode,$2),)
```

This works by defining some helper functions. First, repeat creates a string consisting of a number of copies of another string. For example, $(call repeat,10,A) will be AAAAAAAAAA.

Some subtle things are happening in this definition. The repeat function calls __repeat with three parameters: $1 is the string to be repeated, $2 is the number of times to repeat $1, and $3 has been set to a blank string by the trailing comma in the $(call) to __repeat. The $0 variable contains the name of the current function; in __repeat it will be __repeat.

The __repeat function is recursive and uses the $2 as the recursion guard. The repeat function converts the number of desired repeats into the x-representation used by GMSL arithmetic functions and passes it to __repeat. For example, $(call repeat,Hello,5) turns into $(call __repeat,Hello,x x x x,), and __repeat chops an x off $2 each time around until $2 is empty.

With repeat written, we just need a way to pad a string to some number of characters with a padding character. The function pad achieves that:

```
pad = $(call repeat,$1,$(call subtract,$2,$(call strlen,$3)))$3

paddeddec2hex = $(call pad,0,$2,$(call dec2hex,$1))
```

Its three arguments are the character to pad with, the total width of the padded output in character, and the string to pad. For example, $(call pad,0,4,2a) would return 002a. From that, a padded dec2hex can easily be defined. It takes two parameters: the first is the decimal number to convert to hexadecimal, and the second is the number of characters to pad to.

As you'd expect, $(call paddeddec2hex,42,8) returns 0000002a.

List Manipulation Functions

In GNU make and GMSL terms, a list is a string of characters that has whitespace as separators. Both the GNU make built-in functions that work on lists and the GMSL functions treat multiple whitespaces as a single space. So the lists 1 2 3 and 1   2   3 are the same.

I'll explain a few of the list manipulation functions in detail in the following sections. These functions are more complicated than the others in their use, and they're typically available in functional languages.

Applying a Function to a List with map

When you're working with GNU make functions (either built-ins or your own), you're actually programming in a simple functional language. In functional programming, it's common to have a map function that applies a function to every element of a list. GMSL defines map to do exactly that. For example:

```
SRCS := src/FOO.c src/SUBMODULE/bar.c src/foo.c
NORMALIZED := $(call uniq,$(call map,lc,$(SRCS)))
```

Given a list of filenames (perhaps with paths specified) in SRCS, this will ensure that all the filenames are lowercased and then apply the uniq function to get a unique list of source files.

This uses the GMSL function lc to lowercase each filename in SRCS. You can use the map function with both built-in and user-defined functions. Here, NORMALIZED would be src/foo.c src/submodule/bar.c.

Another use of map might be to get the size of every source file:

```
size = $(firstword $(shell wc -c $1))

SOURCE_SIZES := $(call map,size,$(SRCS))
```

Here we define a size function that uses $(shell) to call wc, and then we apply it to every file in SRCS.

Here SOURCE_SIZES might be something like 1538 1481 with one element for each source file.

Making a reduce Function

Another common function in functional languages is reduce. reduce applies a function that takes two parameters to successive elements of a list, feeding the return value from the function into the next call to it. The GMSL doesn't have a built-in reduce function, but you can easily define it:

```
reduce = $(if $2,$(call $0,$1,$(call rest,$2),$(call $1,$3,$(firstword $2))),$3)
```

Summing a List of Numbers Using reduce

Combining reduce with the plus function, you can easily make a GNU make function that sums a list of numbers:

```
sum-list = $(call reduce,plus,$1,0)
```

The sum-list function takes a single parameter, a list of numbers, and returns the sum of those numbers. It passes three things to reduce: the name of the function to call for each element of the list (in this case, plus), the list of numbers, and a starting number (in this case, 0).

Here's how it works. Suppose $(call sum-list,1 2 3 4 5) is called. The following sequence of calls to plus will be performed:

```
$(call plus,1,0) which returns 1
$(call plus,1,2) which returns 3
$(call plus,3,3) which returns 6
$(call plus,6,4) which returns 10
$(call plus,10,5) which returns 15
```

The first call uses the first element of the list and the starting number 0. Each subsequent call uses the next element from the list and the last result of calling plus.

You could combine sum-list with the SOURCE_SIZES variable to get the total size of the source code:

```
TOTAL_SIZE := $(call sum-list,$(SOURCE_SIZES))
```

In this case, TOTAL_SIZE would be 3019.

Mapping a Function Across a Pair of Lists

The other interesting function that GMSL defines for lists is pairmap. It takes three arguments: two lists (which should be the same length) and a function. The function is applied to the first element of each list, the second element, the third element, and so on.

Suppose SRCS contains a list of source files. Using the size function we defined, combined with map, we defined SOURCE_SIZES, which contains a list of the sizes of each source file. Using pairmap, we can zip the two lists together to output the name of each file and its size:

```
zip = $1:$2

SOURCES_WITH_SIZES := $(call pairmap,zip,$(SRCS),$(SOURCE_SIZES))
```

The zip function is applied to each source filename and size in turn, and makes a string separating the filename and its size with a colon. Using our example files and sizes from this section, SOURCES_WITH_SIZES would be src/foo.c:1538 src/submodule/bar.c:1481.

first

first takes in a list and returns its first element:

```
first
```

```
Arguments: 1: A list
Returns:   Returns the first element of a list
```

Note that first is identical to the GNU make function $(firstword).

last

The last function returns the final element of a list:

---

last

Arguments: 1: A list
Returns: The last element of a list

GNU make 3.81 introduced $(lastword), which works the same way last does.

rest

The rest function is almost the opposite of first. It returns everything but the first element of a list:

---

rest

Arguments: 1: A list
Returns: The list with the first element removed

---

chop

To remove the last element of a list, use the chop function:

---

chop

Arguments: 1: A list
Returns: The list with the last element removed

---

map

The map function iterates over a list (its second argument) and calls a function (named in its first argument) on each list element. The list of values returned by each call to the named function is returned:

---

map

Arguments: 1: Name of function to $(call) for each element of list
           2: List to iterate over calling the function in 1
Returns: The list after calling the function on each element

---

pairmap

pairmap is similar to map but iterates over a pair of lists:

---

pairmap

Arguments: 1: Name of function to $(call) for each pair of elements
           2: List to iterate over calling the function in 1
           3: Second list to iterate over calling the function in 1
Returns: The list after calling the function on each pair of elements

---

The function in the first argument is called with two arguments: one element from each of the lists being iterated over.

leq

The leq list equality testing function will correctly return $(true) for lists that are identical other than having different whitespace:

---

leq

```
Arguments: 1: A list to compare against...
           2: ...this list
Returns:   $(true) if the two lists are identical
```

For example, leq considers 1 2 3 and 1   2   3 to be the same list.

lne

lne is the opposite of leq: it returns $(true) when two lists are not equal:

---

lne

```
Arguments: 1: A list to compare against...
           2: ...this list
Returns:   $(true) if the two lists are different
```

---

reverse

To reverse a list can be useful (particularly because it can then be fed into $(foreach) and iterated backward).

---

reverse

```
Arguments: 1: A list to reverse
Returns:   The list with its elements in reverse order
```

---

uniq

The built-in $(sort) function will deduplicate a list, but it does so at the same time as sorting it. The GMSL uniq function deduplicates a list while preserving the order in which elements are first found:

---

uniq

```
Arguments: 1: A list to deduplicate
Returns:   The list with elements in the original order but without duplicates
```

For example, $(call uniq,a c b a c b) will return a c b.

length

To find out the number of elements in a list, call `length`:

```
length

Arguments: 1: A list
Returns:   The number of elements in the list
```

The length function is the same as the GNU make $(words) function.

String Manipulation Functions

A string is a sequence of any characters, including whitespace. The string equality (and string inequality) function seq works even with strings that contain whitespace or consist only of whitespace. For example:

```
# space contains the space character

space :=
space +=

# tab contains a tab

tab :=→  # needed to protect the tab character

$(info $(call seq,White Space,White Space))
$(info $(call seq,White$(space)Space,White Space))
$(info $(call sne,White$(space)Space,White$(tab)Space))
$(info $(call seq,$(tab),$(tab)))
$(info $(call sne,$(tab),$(space)))
```

This outputs T five times, indicating that each call to seq or sne returned $(true).

As with the list manipulation functions, I'll cover a few of the more complicated functions in detail in the following sections.

Splitting CSV Data into a GNU make List

You can use the `split` function to turn a value in CSV format into a GNU make list. For example, splitting on a comma turns a CSV line into a list from which individual items can be extracted:

```
CSV_LINE := src/foo.c,gcc,-Wall

comma := ,
FIELDS := $(call split,$(comma),$(CSV_LINE))

$(info Compile '$(word 1,$(FIELDS))' using compiler '$(word 2,$(FIELDS))' with \
options '$(word 3,$(FIELDS))')
```

Notice how the variable comma is defined to contain a comma character so it can be used in the $(call) to the split function. This trick was discussed in Chapter 1.

Making a PATH from a List of Directories

The merge function does the opposite of split: it makes a string from a list by separating the list items by some character. For example, to turn a list of directories into a form suitable for the PATH (which is usually separated by colons), define list-to-path as follows:

```
DIRS := /usr/bin /usr/sbin /usr/local/bin /home/me/bin

list-to-path = $(call merge,:,$1)

$(info $(call list-to-path,$(DIRS)))
```

This outputs /usr/bin:/usr/sbin:/usr/local/bin:/home/me/bin.

Translating Characters Using tr

The most complicated string function is tr, which operates like the tr shell program. It transforms each character from a collection of characters into a corresponding character in a second list. The GMSL defines some common character classes for use with tr. For example, it defines variables called [A-Z] and [a-z] (yes, those are really the names) that contain the uppercase and lowercase characters.

We can use tr to make a function that translates to leet-speak:

```
leet = $(call tr,A E I O L T,4 3 1 0 1 7,$1)

$(info $(call leet,I AM AN ELITE GNU MAKE HAXOR))
```

This outputs 1 4M 4N 31173 GNU M4K3 H4XOR.

seq

The slightly confusingly named seq function tests whether two strings are equal:

seq

```
Arguments: 1: A string to compare against...
           2: ...this string
Returns:   $(true) if the two strings are identical
```

sne

The opposite, string inequality, is tested with sne:

---

sne

```
Arguments: 1: A string to compare against...
           2: ...this string
Returns:   $(true) if the two strings are not the same
```

---

streln

The length function gets the length of a list; the equivalent for strings is strlen:

---

strlen

```
Arguments: 1: A string
Returns:   The length of the string
```

---

substr

It's possible to extract a substring using the substr function:

---

substr

```
Arguments: 1: A string
           2: Starting offset (first character is 1)
           3: Ending offset (inclusive)
Returns:   A substring
```

Note that in GMSL, strings start from position 1, not 0.

split

To split a string into a list, you use the split function:

---

split

```
Arguments: 1: The character to split on
           2: A string to split
Returns:   A list separated by spaces at the split character in the
           first argument
```

Note that if the string contains spaces, the result may not be as expected. GNU make's use of spaces as the list delimiter makes working with spaces and lists together very difficult. See Chapter 4 for more on GNU make's handling of spaces.

merge

merge is the opposite of split. It takes a list and outputs a string with a character between each list element:

---

merge

Arguments: 1: The character to put between fields
          2: A list to merge into a string
Returns: A single string, list elements are separated by the character in
          the first argument

---

tr

You use the tr function to translate individual characters, and it's a building block for creating the uc and lc functions:

---

tr

Arguments: 1: The list of characters to translate from
          2: The list of characters to translate to
          3: The text to translate
Returns: The text after translating characters

---

uc

uc performs simple uppercasing of the alphabet a-z:

---

uc

Arguments: 1: Text to uppercase
Returns: The text in uppercase

---

lc

Finally, we have lc:

---

lc

Arguments: 1: Text to lowercase
Returns: The text in lowercase

This performs simple lowercasing of the alphabet A-Z.

Set Manipulation Functions

Sets are represented by sorted, deduplicated lists. To create a set from a list, use set_create or start with the empty_set and set_insert individual elements. The empty set is defined by the variable empty_set.

For example, a makefile could keep track of all the directories that it made using the marker technique discussed in "Making Directories" on page 131:

```
MADE_DIRS := $(empty_set)

marker = $1.f
make_dir = $(eval $1.f: ; @$$(eval MADE_DIRS := $$(call        \
set_insert,$$(dir $$@),$$(MADE_DIRS))) mkdir -p $$(dir $$@); \
touch $$@)

all: $(call marker,/tmp/foo/) $(call marker,/tmp/bar/)
→   @echo Directories made: $(MADE_DIRS)

$(call make_dir,/tmp/foo/)
$(call make_dir,/tmp/bar/)
```

Updating the make_dir function (which creates rules to make directories) with a call to set_insert means that the variable MADE_DIRS will keep track of the set of directories created.

In a real makefile, many directories would likely be built, and using a set would be an easy way to discover which had been built at any point.

Note that because a set is implemented as a GNU make list, you can't insert an item that contains a space.

set_create

You create a set by using the set_create function:

set_create

```
Arguments: 1: A list of set elements
Returns:   The newly created set
```

It takes a list of elements and adds them to a set. The set itself is returned. Note that set elements may not contain spaces.

set_insert

Once a set has been created using set_create, you can add an element to it using set_insert:

set_insert

```
Arguments: 1: A single element to add to a set
           2: A set
Returns:   The set with the element added
```

set_remove

To remove an element from a set, call set_remove:

---

set_remove

```
Arguments: 1: A single element to remove from a set
           2: A set
Returns:   The set with the element removed
```

It is not an error to remove an element from a set when that element was not present.

set_is_member

To test whether an element is a member of a set, call set_is_member. It returns a Boolean value indicating whether the element was present:

---

set_is_member

```
Arguments: 1: A single element
           2: A set
Returns:   $(true) if the element is in the set
```

---

set_union

You merge two sets together by calling the set_union function on the two sets. The merged set is returned:

---

set_union

```
Arguments: 1: A set
           2: Another set
Returns:   The union of the two sets
```

---

set_intersection

To determine the elements common to two sets, use set_intersection. It returns the set of elements that were present in both sets passed in as arguments:

---

sct_intersection

```
Arguments: 1: A set
           2: Another set
Returns:   The intersection of the two sets
```

---

set_is_subset

It is sometimes useful to know if one set is a subset of another, which you can test by calling set_is_subset:

---

set_is_subset

```
Arguments: 1: A set
           2: Another set
Returns:   $(true) if the first set is a subset of the second
```

---

set_is_subset returns a Boolean value indicating whether the first set is a subset of the second.

set_equal

To determine if two sets are equal, call set_equal:

---

set_equal

```
Arguments: 1: A set
           2: Another set
Returns:   $(true) if the two sets are identical
```

---

set_equal returns $(true) if the two sets have exactly the same elements.

Associative Arrays

An *associative array* maps a key value (a string with no spaces in it) to a single value (any string). Associative arrays are sometimes referred to as maps or even hash tables (although that's an implementation detail, and the GMSL associative arrays do not use hashing).

You can use associative arrays as *lookup tables*. For example:

```
C_FILES := $(wildcard *.c)

get-size = $(call first,$(shell wc -c $1))
$(foreach c,$(C_FILES),$(call set,c_files,$c,$(call get-size,$c)))

$(info All the C files: $(call keys,c_files))
$(info foo.c has size $(call get,c_files,foo.c))
```

This small makefile gets a list of all the .c files in the current directory and their sizes, and then it makes an associative array mapping from a filename to its size.

The get-size function uses wc to get the number of bytes in a file. The C_FILES variable contains all the .c files in the current directory. The $(foreach) uses the GMSL set function to set a mapping in an associative array called c_files between each .c file and its size.

Here's an example run:

```
$ make
All the C files: bar.c foo.c
foo.c has size 551
```

The first line is a list of all the .c files found; it's printed using the keys function to get all the keys in the associative array. The second line comes from looking up the length of foo.c using get.

set

The GMSL keeps internal track of named associative arrays, but it is not necessary to explicitly create them. Simply call set to add elements to the array, and the array will be created if it does not exist. Note that array keys cannot contain spaces.

```
set

Arguments: 1: Name of associative array
           2: The key value to associate
           3: The value associated with the key
Returns:   Nothing
```

get

To retrieve an item from an associate array, call get. If the key is not present, get will return an empty string.

```
get

Arguments: 1: Name of associative array
           2: The key to retrieve
Returns:   The value stored in the array for that key
```

keys

The keys function returns a list of all the keys present in an associative array. You can use this with $(foreach) to iterate an associative array:

```
keys

Arguments: 1: Name of associative array
Returns:   A list of all defined keys in the array
```

defined

To test whether a key is present in an associated array, call `defined`:

---

defined

```
Arguments: 1: Name of associative array
           2: The key to test
Returns:   $(true) if the key is defined (i.e., not empty)
```

`defined` returns a Boolean indicating whether the key was defined or not.

Named Stacks

A *stack* is an ordered list of strings (with no spaces in them). In GMSL, stacks are stored internally, and they have names, like associative arrays do. For example:

```
traverse-tree = $(foreach d,$(patsubst %/.,%,$(wildcard $1/*/.)),  \
$(call push,dirs,$d)$(call traverse-tree,$d))

$(call traverse-tree,sources)

dump-tree = $(if $(call sne,$(call depth,dirs),0),$(call pop,dirs) \
$(call dump-tree))

$(info $(call dump-tree))
```

This small makefile uses a stack to follow a tree of directories.

traverse-tree

The traverse-tree function finds all the subdirectories of its argument (stored in $1) using the $(wildcard) function to find the . file that is always present in a directory. It uses the $(patsubst) function to strip off the trailing /. from each value returned by $(wildcard) to get the full directory name.

Before it traverses down into that directory, it pushes the directory found onto a stack called dirs.

dump-tree

The dump-tree function pops items off the dirs tree until there are none left (until the depth becomes 0).

Listing 6-1 shows a directory structure.

```
$ ls -R sources
sources:
bar  foo

sources/bar:
barsub
```

```
sources/bar/barsub:

sources/foo:
subdir   subdir2

sources/foo/subdir:
subsubdir

sources/foo/subdir/subsubdir:

sources/foo/subdir2:
```

Listing 6-1: A directory structure

If this directory structure exists under sources, the makefile will output:

```
sources/foo sources/foo/subdir2 sources/foo/subdir sources/foo/subdir/
subsubdir sources/bar sources/bar/barsub
```

If it's desirable to traverse the directory tree in a depth-first fashion, you can use the stack functions to define dfs, which searches a directory tree and builds the dirs stack containing the directories in depth-first order:

```
__dfs = $(if $(call sne,$(call depth,work),0),$(call push,dirs,$(call     \
peek,work)$(foreach d,$(patsubst %/.,%,$(wildcard $(call                   \
pop,work)/*/.)),$(call push,work,$d)))$(call __dfs))

dfs = $(call push,work,$1)$(call __dfs)

$(call dfs,sources)

dump-tree = $(if $(call sne,$(call depth,dirs),0),$(call pop,dirs) $(call \
dump-tree))

$(info $(call dump-tree,dirs))
```

The dump-tree function hasn't changed (it just outputs everything in the stack by successive calls to pop). But the dfs function is new. It uses a working stack called work to keep track of directories to visit. It first pushes the starting directory onto the work stack and then calls the __dfs helper.

The real work is done by __dfs. It pushes the current directory onto the dirs stack, pushes all the children of that directory onto the work stack, and then it recurses. Recursion stops when the work stack is empty.

The output for the directory structure in Listing 6-1 is now:

```
sources/bar/barsub sources/bar sources/foo/subdir/subsubdir sources/foo/subdir
sources/foo/subdir2 sources/foo sources.
```

push

Anyone who has used a stack will be familiar with pushing and popping elements. The GMSL stack functions are very similar. To add an element to the top of the stack, call push:

---

push

```
Arguments: 1: Name of stack
           2: Value to push onto the top of the stack (must not contain
           a space)
Returns:   None
```

---

pop

To retrieve the top element, call pop:

---

pop

```
Arguments: 1: Name of stack
Returns:   Top element from the stack after removing it
```

---

peek

The peek function operates like pop but doesn't remove the top stack element; it just returns its value:

---

peek

```
Arguments: 1: Name of stack
Returns:   Top element from the stack without removing it
```

---

depth

Finally, you can call depth:

---

depth

```
Arguments: 1: Name of stack
Returns:   Number of items on the stack
```

---

depth determines how many elements are present on the stack.

Function Memoization

To reduce the number of calls to slow functions, such as $(shell), a single memoization function is provided. For example, suppose a makefile needs to know the MD5 values of various files and defines a function md5.

```
md5 = $(shell md5sum $1)
```

That's a pretty expensive function to call (because of the time md5sum would take to execute), so it would be desirable to call it only once for each file. A memoized version of the md5 function looks like this:

```
md5once = $(call memoize,md5,$1)
```

It will call the md5sum function just once for each inputted filename and record the returned value internally so that a subsequent call to md5once with the same filename returns the MD5 value without having to run md5sum. For example:

```
$(info $(call md5once,/etc/passwd))
$(info $(call md5once,/etc/passwd))
```

This prints out the MD5 value of /etc/passwd twice but executes md5sum only once.

The actual memoize function is defined using the GMSL associative array functions:

```
memoize

Arguments: 1: Name of function to memoize
           2: String argument for the function
Returns:   Result of $1 applied to $2 but only calls $1 once for each unique $2
```

Miscellaneous and Debugging Facilities

Table 6-1 shows constants that GMSL defines.

Table 6-1: GMSL Constants

Constant	Value	Purpose
true	T	The Boolean value true
false	(an empty string)	The Boolean value false
gmsl_version	1 1 7	Current GMSL version number (major minor revision)

You access these constants as normal GNU make variables by wrapping them in $() or ${}.

gmsl_compatible

You know the gmsl_compatible function from "Checking the GMSL Version" on page 189:

```
gmsl_compatible

Arguments: List containing the desired library version number (major minor
           revision)
```

Returns: $(true) if the current version of the library is compatible
           with the requested version number, otherwise $(false)

In Chapter 1, you saw a recipe for outputting variable values using a
pattern rule with target print-%. Because this is such a useful rule, GMSL
defines its own gmsl-print-% target that you can use to print the value of any
variable defined in a makefile that includes GMSL.

For example:

```
include gmsl

FOO := foo bar baz
all:
```

gmsl-print-%

gmsl-print-% can be used to print any makefile variable, including variables
inside GMSL. For example, make gmsl-print-gmsl_version would print the current GMSL version.

gmsl-print-% (target not a function)

Arguments: The % should be replaced by the name of a variable that you
           wish to print
Action: Echoes the name of the variable that matches the % and its value

assert

As discussed in "Makefile Assertions" on page 55, it can be useful to have
assertions in a makefile. GMSL provides two assertion functions: assert and
assert_exists.

assert

Arguments: 1: A boolean that must be true or the assertion will fail
           2: The message to print with the assertion
Returns: None

assert_exists

To assert that an individual file or directory exists, GMSL provides the
assert_exists function:

assert_exists

Arguments: 1: Name of file that must exist, if it is missing an assertion
           will be generated
Returns: None

Environment Variables

Table 6-2 shows GMSL environment variables (or command line overrides), which control various bits of functionality.

Table 6-2: GMSL Environment Variables

Variable	Purpose
GMSL_NO_WARNINGS	If set, prevents GMSL from outputting warning messages. For example, arithmetic functions can generate underflow warnings.
GMSL_NO_ERRORS	If set, prevents GMSL from generating fatal errors: division by zero or failed assertions are fatal.
GMSL_TRACE	Enables function tracing. Calls to GMSL functions will result in name and arguments being traced. See "Tracing Variable Values" on page 47 for a discussion of makefile tracing.

These environment variables can all be set in the environment or on the command line.

For example, this makefile contains an assertion that will always fail, stopping the make process:

```
include gmsl

$(call assert,$(false),Always fail)

all:
```

Setting GMSL_NO_ERRORS prevents the assertion from stopping the make process. In that case the output of the assert is hidden and make continues normally:

```
$ make
Makefile:5: *** GNU Make Standard Library: Assertion failure: Always fail.
Stop.
$ make GMSL_NO_ERRORS=1
make: Nothing to be done for `all'.
```

A few well-placed GMSL assertions in a makefile can make a big difference. By checking for makefile prerequisites (such as the presence of a specific file or that a compiler has a certain version number), a conscientious makefile writer can alert a user to a problem without forcing them to debug the often arcane output from make.

INDEX

GNU make
    version 3.81
        abspath and realpath, 146
        features, 14–15, 29–33
    version 3.82 features, 15, 34–38
    version 4.0
        features, 15, 38–41
        loadable objects, 179–180
        --trace command line option,
            54–55
    version 4.1, features, 42
    version checking, 13–16
GNU make debugger, 58–64
    adding breakpoint functions, 67
    breakpoints in patterns, 60–61
    code, 64–65
    dynamic breakpoints, 65–69
    help for, 59
    information output from, 59
    internals, 62–65
    stopping, 59
    use of, 58–60
GNU Make Standard Library
        (GMSL), 187
    assertion functions, 55
    associative arrays, 216–218
    calling functions, 189
    checking version, 189–190
    environment variables, 223
    debugging facilities, 221–223
    function memoization, 220–221
    importing, 188
    integer arithmetic functions,
        198–203
    integer comparison functions,
        203–204
    importing, 188
    list manipulation functions,
        205–210
    logical operators, 196–198
    miscellaneous integer functions,
        204–205
    named stacks, 218–220
    real-world example, 190–195
    reference. See GMSL reference
    set manipulation functions,
        213–216
    string manipulation functions,
        210–213
goals, of make command, 183
greater than (gt) operator, 164, 165, 168
gte function, 164, 166, 168

gt function, 164, 165, 168
Guile. See GNU Guile language
$(guile) function, 15, 38, 180–182

H

halve function, 202, 203
hash mark (#), for starting
        comment, 124
help, for debugger, 59, 66
help_system.mak file, 185
hexadecimal numbers, converting
        decimal to, 204–205
hidden targets, 120–122
hidden temporary file, 151–153
http-get function, 181–182

I

ifcase function, 190
ifdef directive, 16–17, 193–194
ifeq directive, 193–194 if-exists
        function, 127–128
$(if) function, 16–17
    nested in _DEBUG, 63
ifndef directive, 5
    problem from, 110–111
ifneq directive, 20–21, 193–194
importing, GNU Make Standard
        Library (GMSL), 188
inc function, 202
include statement, 96
#include statements in .c files, 88
increment function, 169
incrementing, 162
information, output from debugger, 59
$(info text) function, 32
inline directory making, 137
input, assertions to check, 191–192
int_dec function, 202
int_decode function, 199
int_divide function, 201
int_double function, 202
integer arithmetic functions, in GMSL,
        198–203
integer comparison functions,
        in GMSL, 203–204
int_encode function, 199
int_halve function, 203
int_inc function, 202
int_max function, 201
int_min function, 201

N

name
> of current makefile, finding, 158
> of variable, whitespace in, 35

named stacks, in GMSL, 218–220

nand function, 20, 198

ndef (not defined) directive, 5

ne (not-equal) operator, 165, 168

need-help variable, 183–184

newline character, 124

NEWS file, 29

non-blank string, function to
> return, 33

non-empty string, as true, 18

non-recursive make command, 96–107

nor function, 20, 198

No rule to make error, 145

not defined (ndef) directive, 5

notdir function, 145–146

not-equal (ne) operator, 165

not function, 19, 197

.NOTPARALLEL, 153

O

.o (object) files
> for corresponding .sig files, 79
> hack updates to, 85–86
> pattern rule to make, 137
> unnecessary rebuild, 133

octal numbers, converting decimal to,
> 204–205

oneshell feature, 15

.ONESHELL target, 36

or function, 19, 20–21, 197
> for debugging setting, 192

$(or) function, 33

order-only feature, in GNU make 3.81, 14

order-only prerequisite, to build
> directories, 135–136

$(origin) function, 1–3, 26, 45

--output-sync option, 15, 38

override directive, 2–3

P

padding numbers, string
> functions for, 205

pairmap function, 207, 208–209

parallel build, 93
> hidden targets and, 121–122

parallel execution, 148–157
> Amdahl's law and limits, 154–157
> -j or --jobs option, 149–150

parent-makefile variable, 184

PARTS variable, 194

PATH, from document list, 211

paths, 141–146
> built-in functions, 145–146
> of current makefile, 158
> finding program on, 190–191
> functions for splitting, 145–146
> list of, 142–143
> variables to build, 100
> and wildcards, 123

$(patsubst) function, 218

pattern rules, 93–94
> to build targets, 136–137
> %.o: %.c, 12

patterns, breakpoints in, 60–61

pattern-specific variables, 9–13

peek function, 220

percent sign (%)
> escaping, 123
> as wildcard, 44

plugin_is_GPL_compatible variable, 180

plus function, 162–163, 168, 198–199

plus sign (+), for escaped spaces, 141

pop function, 169, 219, 220

POSIX systems
> / for path separator, 143
> case sensitive files in, 144–145
> and make, 34

precious files, 137

preprocessor, logical operators in,
> 193–194

prerequisite list
> automatic variables in, 136
> of rules, 29

prerequisites, = sign not permitted,
> 34–35

print command, 76

print-help function, 182–183, 185

printing
> commands, 52
> every defined variable in makefile,
> 45–46
> makefile variable value, 43–45

print_variable function, 27–28

print_variables function, 28

print_version function, 175

private keyword, 37–38

problem solving, splitting argument
list, 26–27
processors, maximum speed based on
number of, 156–157
program, finding on path, 190–191
pushd function, 169
push function, 169, 220
pwd command, 112
PWD environment variable, 145

Q

q command, 63
qs function, 140
question mark (?)
    converting space to, 140
    in filename, 123
quotation marks, adding to target
names, 67

R

r command (remove breakpoint), 66
realpath function, 33, 146
rebuild
    after CPPFLAGS changes, 77–82
    example makefile, 78–79
    when file's checksum changes,
        82–86
.RECIPEPREFIX variable, 36
recursion
    with clean, 148
    in dfs function, 219
    as error, 69
    functions for, 28
    with make, 96, 97–98, 153–154
recursively expanded variables, 112
    long evaluation time for, 117
recursive variable, = to define, 23
reduce function, 206
    recursive implementation, 28
remake project, 69–76
    interactive debugger in, 72–74
repeat function, 205
rest function, 208
reverse.c file, 179–180
reverse function, 209
    in Guile, 181
Reverse Polish Notation calculator,
    167–170
reversing
    lists, 180–181
    strings, 177–179

rules
    definition and variable value, 112
    escaping, 122–127
    with no commands, 173
    order to apply, 35
    prerequisite list of, 29
    tracing execution, 40
    wrapping commands in, 82
running GNU make without command
line options, 78–79
runtime debugging aid, 55

S

second-expansion feature, 136
    in GNU make 3.81, 14
.SECONDEXPANSION target, 29, 136
self-documenting makefiles, 182
semicolon (;), for commands on
one line, 4
sentinel file, 94–96
    deleting, 96
seq (string equal) function, 169,
    192, 211
    for debugging setting, 192
sequence function, 204
set_create function, 213, 214
set_equal function, 216
set function, 76, 217
set_insert function, 213, 214
set_intersection function, 215
set_is_member function, 67, 68, 215
set_is_subset function, 216
set manipulation functions, in GMSL,
    213–216
setq command, 76
set_remove function, 215
set_union function, 215
s+ function, 141
shared file, problem from, 152
$(shell) call, 49
    and :=, 111–115
    to create directory, 133
    environment, 7
    recursively expanded
        variables and, 114
    which command in, 21
shell command, != operator for
execution, 41
.SHELLFLAGS variable, 36, 52
SHELL hack, 172
shell invocation, single vs. multiple, 36

Windows
    \ as path separator, 143
    8.3 filenames for, 140
    case insensitivity, 144–145
$(word) function, 24
$(wordlist) function, 24, 25
$(words) function, 24, 162
working directory, call to get, 114–115
work stack, 219

X

XML document
    bill of materials, 170–174
    with example makefile
        structure, 171
-x option, for shell, 52
xor function, 197
xor operator, 20

Z

zip function, 207

The Electronic Frontier Foundation (EFF) is the leading organization defending civil liberties in the digital world. We defend free speech on the Internet, fight illegal surveillance, promote the rights of innovators to develop new digital technologies, and work to ensure that the rights and freedoms we enjoy are enhanced — rather than eroded — as our use of technology grows.

EFF.ORG
ELECTRONIC FRONTIER FOUNDATION
Protecting Rights and Promoting Freedom on the Electronic Frontier

CPSIA information can be obtained at www.ICGtesting.com
Printed in the USA
BVOW09s1229181115

427624BV00012B/102/P